OCCULT POWERS AND HYPOTHESES

Occult Powers and Hypotheses

Cartesian Natural Philosophy under Louis XIV

DESMOND M. CLARKE

CLARENDON PRESS · OXFORD
1989

Oxford University Press, Walton Street, Oxford OX2 6DP
Oxford New York Toronto
Delhi Bombay Calcutta Madras Karachi
Petaling Jaya Singapore Hong Kong Tokyo
Nairobi Dar es Salaam Cape Town
Melbourne Auckland
and associated companies in
Berlin Ibadan

Oxford is a trade mark of Oxford University Press

Published in the United States
by Oxford University Press, New York

British Library Cataloguing in Publication Data
Clarke, Desmond M.
Occult powers and hypotheses: Cartesian natural
philosophy under Louis XIV.
1. Nature. Philosophical perspectives, Philosophy
of nature. French theories. Cartesianism, history
I. Title
113'.0944
ISBN 0–19–824812–1

Library of Congress Cataloging in Publication Data
Clarke, Desmond M.
Occult powers and hypotheses.
Bibliography: p. Includes index.
1. Science, Medieval—Philosophy.   2. Explanation (Philosophy)
3. Descartes, René, 1596–1650—Influence.
I. Title.
Q174.8.C57 1989   501   88–31260
ISBN 0–19–824812–1

Set by Hope Services, Abingdon
Printed and bound in
Great Britain by Biddles Ltd
Guildford and King's Lynn

To Ernan McMullin

ACKNOWLEDGEMENTS

THIS work was begun while I was visiting the Philosophy Department at the University of Notre Dame during the academic year 1982–3. I am grateful to the members of the Department for their hospitality and to the Council for International Exchange of Scholars for a grant towards the cost of relocating for the year. I have read early versions of various sections of the book to meetings of the following: Philosophy Department seminar, Notre Dame; Philosophy Department, Trinity College Dublin; Royal Institute of Philosophy; Irish Philosophical Society; Royal Irish Academy; joint meeting of the British Society for History of Philosophy and the British Society for History of Science, Cambridge; British Society for the Philosophy of Science. A shorter version of part of the discussion in Chapter 5 was presented at the conference on 'Descartes: il discorso sul metodo e i saggi di questo metodo, 1637–1987' in Lecce, Italy. I am grateful to participants at these gatherings for their comments.

I also wish to acknowledge financial assistance from the Arts Faculty, University College, Cork, for research at the Bibliothèque Nationale, Paris; and a study-visit grant from the British Academy for Research at the University Library, Cambridge.

Finally, I exploited the patience and generosity of Dr Colm O'Sullivan, Department of Experimental Physics, University College, Cork, in discussing the contribution of Leibniz and the Cartesians to the debate about forces. I am grateful to him for his assistance.

D. M. C.

CONTENTS

NOTE ON TEXTS

I HAVE quoted from English translations of primary texts, wherever they were available. In a few cases, for example in the John Clarke translation of Rohault's *Traité de physique* or Taylor's translation of Père Daniel's *Voyage du monde de Descartes*, the English versions are somewhat archaic; however, I have still kept them on the assumption that early translators may have had a better insight than I about the most appropriate English equivalent for the original French or Latin. In all other cases, I have translated the original texts myself.

The spelling of French words and the use of accents were not standardized in the seventeenth century; as a result, there is considerable variation in spelling in the names of primary texts. In the case of a few texts which are most often cited, I have adopted the following short titles in footnotes: Jacques Rohault, *A System of Natural Philosophy*, is identified as *Traité de physique*; and P.-S. Régis, *Système de philosophie, contenant la logique, la metaphysique, la physique et la morale*, is cited as *Système*.

Introduction

THIS is an essay in the history of philosophy; in particular, it is an essay in the history of philosophies of science. The histories of medicine or of science, just like economic or political history, are usually written by historians in a style which is recognizably historical. In contrast, the history of philosophy in the English-speaking world tends to be written by philosophers; the result of their efforts, in many cases, would hardly be recognized as history by genuine practitioners of the historian's art. The apparently anomalous character of the history of philosophy coincides with an intradisciplinary debate about the role of history in relation to philosophy. Philosophers do not agree about the significance of historical work for their own discipline, nor do they agree about how history of philosophy should be written even when it is done by philosophers. Indeed, the available evidence suggests that there are national and historical variations in identifying what might be called the canon of philosophers in the modern period who are worth discussing for philosophical edification. Philosophers do not even agree about which authors of an earlier era are worth reading.[1]

Bernard Williams, in his Preface to *Descartes: The Project of Pure Enquiry*,[2] tried to throw some light on this cluster of issues by drawing a distinction between what he called 'history of philosophy' and 'history of ideas'. In 'history of ideas', one attempts to identify the meaning of a given work for those for whom it was originally written, in most cases contemporaries of the author. The result of such an undertaking should preserve all the ambiguity and philosophical tentativeness which characterized the insights of the original author; in a sense, this is an effort in helping us as modern readers to understand a work which might otherwise appear to be

[1] See the contributions of B. Kuklick and W. Lepenies to Rorty *et al.* (1984), 125, 143–4.

[2] Williams (1978), 9–10.

more or less unintelligible. Thus history of ideas unmasks the meaning of an old text. History of philosophy, however, is—for Williams—the attempt by a contemporary to disambiguate the original work by the application of modern philosophical insights or analyses. Here the objective is rational reconstruction, in which we treat the original text in much the same way as we would treat the work of our contemporaries. We question them, challenge their arguments, and force them to clarify what we do not understand; in this interaction we accept no sociological, psychological, or religious explanations of why they apparently hold certain beliefs. Although we would welcome historical comments which might explain what an author may have meant by his work, we would not be satisfied until we had also assessed the validity of the author's claims. Our objective is to reach a conclusion which involves accepting or rejecting the author's claims as sound, and giving our reasons for acceptance or rejection, in whole or in part.

There can be little doubt that something like Williams's distinction is implicit in much recent work in the history of philosophy. Unfortunately, what he calls history of philosophy is not history at all, but rather a philosophical inquiry which focuses on old texts rather than on recently published texts. This suggests that there are two types of enterprise, a genuinely historical one which is called history of ideas (embracing much more than philosophy) and a strictly philosophical one which may choose to philosophize about dead philosophers rather than living ones. In such a division of labour, there is no enterprise which is specifically a history of philosophy.

Recent discussions of this issue have not resulted in anything that might be accepted by philosophers as a standard account of the relationship between philosophy and its history, or in an agreed model of how the history of philosophy should be written.[3] As soon as we acknowledge that we are not evaluating the philosophers of the past from some transcendental perspective from which we can distinguish truth and falsehood, it must be obvious that our own philosophical efforts are historically conditioned. If our reflections on earlier generations are qualified by the same historicity which is

---

[3] See the divergent views of C. Taylor, A. MacIntyre, R. Rorty, L. Kruger, and I. Hacking in Rorty *et al.* (1984); also Holland (1985). For a summary of similar issues concerning the relationship between history of science and philosophy of science, see McMullin (1970) and Garber (1986).

most obvious, to us, in those philosophical opinions which we no longer share, then we have no secure foothold from which we can distinguish history of ideas and philosophical reconstruction. We can only hope to engage in a conversation across space–time distances with others who were apparently concerned with issues which still bother us. In this conversation, we have a privileged status only because our interlocuters are silent. Therefore we must approach our philosophical ancestors as we approach the apparently inexplicable behaviour of our contemporaries. We can make sense of our contemporaries' behaviour if we are willing to attribute to them an appropriately rational combination of beliefs and desires.[4] In a similar way, interpreting old texts and rationally reconstructing them are complementary features of any dialogue with our philosophical ancestors; as soon as we find ourselves attributing to others a position which strikes us as absurd, it is time to apply a principle of charity in reinterpreting what we thought they meant. In this sense, we cannot separate history of ideas and rational reconstruction. History of philosophy, therefore, must involve both elements as complementary features of any attempt to interpret the written work of an earlier era.

This implies that philosophers who are interested in reading old texts should be willing to learn from historians. One of the features which characterizes the work of genuine historians is the extent to which temporal and geographical parameters, rather than logical relations, control the scope of a particular study. For example, if one looks at the history of what is now called science, especially the history of its development from about 1600, it is accepted current practice to write a history of science in England in the Interregnum, or the history of one of the sciences in England during the Restoration, and in each case to provide only necessary references to what might have been happening at the other end of the island in Scotland or across the English Channel in France.[5] In fact, recent trends in history would commend the kind of concentration on a limited geographical and temporal period which might best be exemplified in the history of a hamlet in a five-year slice of its past.

---

[4] D. Davidson has developed this feature of interpretation in a number of works, e.g. Davidson (1980).
[5] The historian's focus on a limited geographical and chronological period is illustrated, for instance, by the exemplary works of Webster (1975) and Hunter (1981).

In contrast, philosophers have tended to expand the scope of their historical studies in a way which requires Leibniz or Descartes to answer the kind of objections which we make in the twentieth century. If we are bold enough to bridge that chronological gap, we may also be tempted to interrogate them about their likely responses to their contemporaries whom they should have thought about and did not! When this strategy is followed to its logical conclusion, no one in the history of seventeenth-century natural philosophy is allowed to avoid confrontation, in a rational reconstruction, with Newton, even if the authors in question were oblivious to the merits of the *Principia*.

The present work is written with a respectful deference towards the art of the historian. I have assumed the privileges of the historian in deciding on a non-arbitrary slice of the past, and in setting both the temporal and geographical limits of the project. On the other hand, one must recognize that any attempt to understand our past will be influenced by our current interests and our present assumptions about what is worth re-examining. One of the concerns which has been prominent in recent philosophy of science is the historical character of our concept of science; hence the recent interest in the history of philosophies of science, in the changing concepts of science which were peculiar to different eras and different religious or social contexts.

This is a study of one strand in the history of philosophies of science, namely, the Cartesian concept of science in the period in which it became established in France between approximately 1660 and 1700. Descartes's major works in natural philosophy were published in 1637 and 1644,[6] and were immediately recognized in France and Holland, and subsequently in England, as important and influential works. The ways in which Descartes's contribution to natural philosophy was assessed in various countries depended essentially on local conditions. It would be patently ahistorical to attempt to tell this story as if Cartesians in England faced exactly the same objections and difficulties as Cartesians in Holland, France, Germany, or later in Geneva. It would be equally ahistorical to assume that Cartesians in various countries were abstractly considering the merits of their preferred theories in contrast with what

---

[6] The *Discours de la methode . . . plus la dioptrique, les météores et la géometrie qui sont des essais de cete méthode* was published in Leiden in 1637; the *Principia Philosophiae* was published in Amsterdam in 1644.

was available from Huygens, Newton, or Leibniz. The methodology of the historian requires that we be as faithful as possible to the facts which can be established, and that we should interpret the development of Cartesianism in any region only in the light of the local factors which actually influenced it.

Secondly, any abstraction of one slice of the past from the continuity which we require to make sense of it is to some extent arbitrary. We have come to accept this degree of arbitrariness in philosophy as long as the time-slice chosen coincides with the lifespan of one individual, on the assumption that there is a unity in one person's thought which is unlikely to be found in the ideas of a group. There is no a priori reason why we should assume this; it seems to be a kind of biographical convention which is often successful in reconstructing a coherent account of the thought of one individual. However, there may be as much coherence in the thought of a group as in the beliefs of an individual author. From our retrospective point of view on the past, therefore, it is the coherence of our interpretative reconstruction rather than any intrinsic features of the original history which determines the relative arbitrariness of the temporal limits adopted for a given historical account.

The dissemination of Cartesianism both during Descartes's life and after his death in 1650 was significantly influenced by local factors in the various regions in which it took root. In the Netherlands Descartes won the early support of his contemporary Henri de Roy (Regius) at Utrecht, even though subsequently he had cause to regret de Roy's allegiance; he also gained a series of faithful supporters at Leiden, including Adriaan Heereboord, Joannes de Raey, Arnold Geulinex, and Burchardus de Volder.[7] In England, Henry More was initially impressed by Cartesian philosophy; later he became an implacable opponent because of his concerns with the implicit 'atheism' of the Cartesian enterprise.[8] And, in Geneva, the introduction of Cartesian ideas was almost exclusively due to the influence of Jean-Robert Chouet.[9]

Cartesian natural philosophy began to have an impact in France

[7] Cf. Struik (1981), Ruestow (1973), Dijksterhuis et al. (1950), and, for a general discussion of the dissemination of Cartesian physics, the standard work by Mouy (1934), esp. pp. 8–17.

[8] The change of heart by More is discussed by Gabbey (1982); see also Webster (1975) and Laudan (1966).

[9] Heyd (1982) provides a detailed examination of Chouet's influence in Geneva.

during Descartes's own lifetime. The process of accommodating the new philosophy was initiated by the publication of the *Principia Philosophiae* in 1644, and was facilitated by the posthumous editions of three volumes of letters which were edited by Claude Clerselier in 1657, 1659, and 1666. There had already been some supporters in France who were willing to defend Cartesian ideas publicly at a time when they had not yet had any significant impact on the schools. Among those who favoured elements of the Cartesian system, the Jesuit Père Mesland (d. 1672) engaged in discussion with Descartes concerning the implications of the Cartesian theory of matter for the theology of the Eucharist. Unfortunately, Mesland's interest in such revisionary views led to his being sent to Martinique as a missionary in 1646, and he stayed there until his death twenty-six years later.[10] Mesland's missionary reward for his support of Cartesianism was not an isolated incident; it was one of the first signs that those who dominated the system of education in colleges in France planned to resist the new philosophy and to defend their traditional offering of scholasticism. Thus, although there were some individuals who were publicly favourable to Cartesianism and quite a number who attended at informal Cartesian conferences, especially in Paris, it remained true prior to the 1660s that those who were potentially key figures in the dissemination of Cartesianism were unimpressed by the new system of philosophy and opposed to its introduction in the schools.

The initial failure of Descartes to have any impact on the standard texts in natural philosophy is evident if one consults, for example, the work of another Jesuit, Honoré Fabri (1607–88), who taught philosophy at Lyons before going to Rome as theologian to the Sacred Penitentiary.[11] Fabri's lectures were edited by Pierre Mousnier (Mosner) as *Philosophiae Tomus Primus* and were published in Lyons in 1646. His *Tractatus Physicus de Motu Locali* found its way into print in the same way in 1666, and a five-volume compendium of his work was published in 1669 as *Physica, Id Est, Scientia Rerum Corporearum*. The most obvious feature of all three books is that they provide a standard exposition of scholastic

[10] Père Mesland's support for Descartes and his missionary exile are discussed in Sortais (1929), 14–19.

[11] Cf. Sortais (1929), 47–52. Baillet suggests that Fabri was responsible for having a number of Descartes's works put on the Index of forbidden books in 1663. This episode is discussed further in Chapter 1 below.

philosophy in the canonical four parts, logic, metaphysics, physics, and morals, which could have been written in the same way a half-century earlier, and they make no effort to teach students the new approaches to natural philosophy which had been suggested by Descartes, Gassendi, or others. Thus despite the posthumous publication of Descartes's works and correspondence, there are few signs of a Cartesian influence on the teaching of natural philosophy in France prior to the publications of the Saumur physician, Louis de la Forge, in 1664 and 1666.

By the end of the century, the fortunes of Cartesianism as an innovative concept of science had improved significantly, and the merits of a hypothetical method were widely respected and generally applauded. However, a new challenge was developing with the delayed introduction of Newtonianism into France.[12] The first edition of Newton's *Philosophiae Naturalis Principia Mathematica* was published in 1687; it was published in Latin and therefore should have been accessible to a wide readership in France. Despite that, and despite the fact that Newton was elected as an *associé étranger* of·the Académie royale des sciences in 1699, there is little evidence that the *Principia* had any impact on French science before the 1720s.[13] The fate of the *Opticks* was very different. Originally published in English in 1704, it was translated and published in a Latin edition as the *Optice* in 1706. The first translation into a modern European language was the French edition of Pierre Coste, which was published in Amsterdam in 1720; a revised French edition appeared in Paris in 1722. Etienne-François Geoffroy, one of the French correspondents of Hans Sloane who was secretary of the Royal Society at that time, prepared summaries of Newton's optical theories and read them to the Académie royale des sciences during 1706–7; Malebranche also became acquainted with the *Opticks* at about the same time.[14] In a word, the historical evidence suggests that Newton was acknowledged initially in France, after the publication of the *Principia*, as a creative mathematician or as merely another contributor to the typically 'English' tradition of empirical science which was associated with the names of Boyle or Wallis. The *Opticks*, however, included

[12] There are extensive historical studies of the introduction of Newtonianism into France. See e.g. the standard early work of Brunet (1931) and the more recent contributions of Cohen (1964b), Hall (1975), Guerlac (1981), and Greenberg (1986).
[13] See Hall (1975), 247.   [14] See Guerlac (1981), 63.

much more than a mathematical theory of optical phenomena; the supplementary 'Queries' raised fundamental issues about gravity and the role of hypotheses in framing the fundamental laws of nature. Consequently French savants in the early decades of the eighteenth century began to understand the implications of the Newtonian system for the whole of natural philosophy, and they first learned the significance of this challenge by reading translations of the *Opticks*.

Thus, the period between approximately 1660 and 1700 in France represents a period of reluctant acceptance, followed by widespread but still grudging support for Cartesian natural philosophy. It is the period between the publication and gradual dissemination of Cartesian ideas, occasioned by the publication of posthumous works by Clerselier and La Forge, and the new crisis which was provoked by the migration of Newtonianism across the English Channel some twenty years or more after the significance and novelty of Newtonianism had been acknowledged in England. In this period, Descartes found a group of very committed followers who were primarily concerned to explain, defend, and disseminate the Cartesian system in France. In doing so, they helped to articulate a distinctive concept of science which significantly affected the subsequent development of the various sciences in France and, more generally, in Europe.

This period of burgeoning Cartesianism in France also coincided with the most active years of the reign of Louis XIV. Louis reached the age at which he could assume his full regal duties in 1651, but he continued to rely on the advice of Mazarin for another ten years until the latter's death in 1661. Thereafter, the *roi soleil* took full charge of the affairs of state until the end of his lengthy reign in 1715.[15] The coincidence between the early history of Cartesianism in France and the absolutism of Louis XIV is not irrelevant for this study; the discussion in Chapter 1 of the religious and historical context of the French Cartesians' campaign on behalf of the new philosophy underlines the extent to which the fortunes of Descartes's followers in France were significantly influenced by the religious and political policies of the monarch. The consolidation of a policy

[15] Louis was proclaimed king on 14 May 1643 and was legally entitled to assume his regal duties in 1651; however, he took full control of the affairs of state only on 9 Mar. 1661, at the age of 22, on the death of his first minister, Mazarin. See Méthivier (1983).

of religious intolerance and the death of the academy's patron, Colbert, in 1683 made it difficult for French savants to maintain international scientific contacts with renowned contemporaries such as Huygens and Leibniz. Indeed, the difficulties experienced during the war of the League of Augsburg (1689–97) in the international exchange of journals and records of scientific meetings helped to cultivate a new kind of insularity in French science in the final decades of the seventeenth century which had been repudiated in the first years of the academy's life. The return to normalcy came gradually in the first two decades of the eighteenth century, with a very significant development of mathematics in France and a consequent interest in the merits of Newtonianism which had otherwise remained inaccessible to both the school philosophers and most members of the academy.[16]

It was during this period, in the central years of the reign of Louis XIV, that Cartesian natural philosophy was articulated and defended by a closely knit group of supporters in France; by the end of the century the transition had effectively been made from scholastic natural philosophy to Cartesian mechanism.

In discussing the impact of Cartesians on the development of natural philosophy in France, I have tried to avoid the anachronistic connotations of the word 'science'. However, Descartes and his contemporaries were all concerned with what they called, in the vernacular, *science*. The *Discourse on Method* (1637), for example, was designed to provide a method for discovering *la vérité dans les sciences*. While accepting that the French word *science* in Descartes's time did not share all the connotations of the nineteenth-century English word 'science', it is difficult to avoid using the English equivalent in some contexts without unnecessary circumlocution. Besides, we have learned to cope with this problem in translating many of the central theoretical concepts of the seventeenth century, including the word 'force'. For this reason, while preferring the term 'natural philosophy' to describe the foundational enterprise to which Cartesians devoted their energies between 1660 and 1700, I have also lapsed into using the more modern term 'science' in recognition of the transition in which the Cartesians were centrally involved, from scholastic natural philosophy to modern science.

The specific Cartesian contribution to this transition during the

---

[16] For the development of mathematics in France in the early 18th cent. see Greenberg (1986), 62–72, and Robinet (1960).

seventeenth century was primarily philosophical; it amounted to a fundamental change in the concept of scientific explanation. The central theme of the Cartesians' system, which they stubbornly defended even in the face of very plausible counter-evidence, was a rejection of the forms or qualities of scholastic philosophy as pseudo-explanations and the substitution in their place of mechanical explanations which were unavoidably hypothetical. It was a radical rejection of what they considered to be occult powers in favour of mechanical hypotheses.

I

The Religious and Political Context

ON 20 November 1663 the Sacred Congregation of the Index in Rome condemned the philosophical works of Descartes and prohibited printing, reading, or even possessing copies of named works until such time as they were corrected.[1] This intervention by Rome, following a similar condemnation of Cartesianism by the Theology Faculty at Louvain in 1662, was an omen of the fortunes of Descartes's followers for the subsequent forty years. The philosophy of Descartes was censored, condemned, or proscribed by the churches, by the universities in France, and by the king or his representatives, as heretical, false, and even dangerous for the peace of the realm. Yet, despite the near unanimity of official disapproval, Cartesianism prospered during Louis XIV's reign and helped significantly in the development of an alternative philosophy to the officially established scholasticism of the schools.

The earliest signs of the persistent opposition to Cartesianism were evident even before the publication of the *Discourse on Method* and scientific essays in 1637. On 4 September 1624 the *parlement* of Paris had accepted the advice of the Theology Faculty and prohibited 'all persons on pain of their lives, from either holding or teaching any theses contrary to the ancient and approved authors, and from holding any public debates apart from those which are approved by the doctors of the Theology Faculty'.[2] This alliance between the Theology Faculty of Paris and the *parlement* as protectors of religious and philosophical orthodoxy continued for the rest of the century. The theologians of the Sorbonne were

---

[1] The most recent edition of the *Index Librorum Prohibitorum* (Rome, 1948) continues to list Descartes among proscribed authors on pp. 129–30. The *donec corrigantur* which was originally included in the official sanction and which qualified the prohibition on reading Descartes was understood to imply that the works had some redeeming features and could possibly be amended to the satisfaction of the censors in Rome.

[2] Jourdain (1888), i. 195.

equally disturbed by the 'heretical' beliefs of Protestants (especially Huguenots) and by the unorthodoxy of dissident Catholics. As a result, the history of religious disputes during this period in France reveals a very insecure theological counter-reformation which was committed to Aristotelian categories and principles, and which felt threatened on two fronts: the influence of Calvinism in winning converts from the Catholic faith, and the challenge from within the Roman Church by those who rejected scholasticism. Cartesianism and, in general, the new sciences became suspect under the second rubric to the extent to which they provided philosophical support for alternative theologies.

Descartes was sensitive enough to the power and insecurity of the theologians to defer officially to their expertise on a number of occasions. He explicitly acknowledged the threat of condemnation when he suppressed publication of *Le Monde* in 1633. When venturing into print with the *Meditations* in 1641, he dedicated the work to the Paris theologians in an effort publicly to associate his philosophy with their implicit approval. Likewise, although Descartes claimed to have provided philosophy and physics with new, indubitable foundations in the *Principles of Philosophy* (1644), he concluded the work with a comprehensive waiver to the effect that—despite all the claims about certainty and demonstration—anything in his work which conflicted with the faith should be rejected as false. 'Nevertheless, mindful of my significance, I affirm nothing: but submit all these things both to the authority of the Catholic Church and to the judgment of men wiser than I [i.e. theologians]; nor would I wish anyone to believe anything except what he is convinced of by clear and irrefutable reason.'[3]

This irenic attitude failed to avoid the inevitable confrontation with theology faculties, because Cartesian philosophy challenged many of the fundamental principles on which the philosophy and theology of the schools was built. If Catholic theology were to develop in seventeenth-century France, it could do so only by modifying its exclusive allegiance to scholastic philosophy. To some extent, therefore, the reluctant emancipation of theology from its scholastic heritage coincides with the emerging confidence of Cartesians in the validity of their new system of thought. Many of the battles in which Cartesians became embroiled in the second half

---

[3] *Principles of Philosophy*, p. 288.

of the century were precipitated by attempts on the part of theologians to extricate their religious beliefs from entanglement with moribund philosophical theories. In this process, Cartesianism was frequently identified as the most obvious and powerful critic of established Catholic theology within the ranks of the faithful.

The complexity of Cartesian debates in France is not uniquely explained by theological controversies. Descartes's philosophical bequest to his followers was not a neat, consistent theory which could claim to resolve all the issues raised by the advent of the new sciences.[4] Of course there were reasonably clear indications of what problems were regarded as important, and what general strategies were favoured for resolving them. However, the language of clear and distinct ideas only masked the variety of intractable questions which continued to challenge natural philosophers during the subsequent centuries. Among the issues which gained prominence during the seventeenth century were the following:

1. The significance to be accorded to experimental work in a science of nature: there are ambiguous signals in Descartes's work in favour of experimental evidence as a decisive factor in both the construction and testing of scientific theories. The ambiguity of these signals compounded the flexibility allowed to subsequent Cartesian philosophers either to emphasize experiments as decisive in science, or to relegate them to the status of mere expository devices.

2. The logical structure of theories: Descartes described the internal logic of his theories with terms such as 'deduction', 'induction', or 'demonstration', and he notoriously claimed to 'deduce' physics from a metaphysical foundation. If later Cartesians hoped to honour this tradition and to deduce physics from a philosophical foundation, they could realize their ambitions in a great variety of ways, depending on how they understood the term 'metaphysics', and how narrowly or loosely they interpreted 'deduction'.

3. The hypothetical character of scientific explanations: Cartesian science is often characterized as if it conflated obvious distinctions between purely formal systems in which demonstrative certainty is possible, and the hypothetico-deductive strategies which are unavoidable in empirical sciences. The demand for certainty, coupled

---

[4] I have argued for this claim in Clarke (1982).

with the almost palpable abhorrence of mere 'probability', is quite evident in Descartes's writing; it is most apparent in the rhetoric of demonstration and proofs. Paradoxically, perhaps, Cartesians also identified the hypothetical character of scientific explanation as one of its distinctive features, and helped to make acceptable the concept of physical theory as a system of interlinked hypotheses. Whether or not hypotheses were compatible with certainty remained the subject of on-going discussion.

4. The distinction of faith and reason, or the separation of philosophy and theology: Descartes invariably maintained a very proper, traditional attitude towards theologians as exponents of religious traditions, and towards the Catholic Church as an official and authoritative teacher of Christian beliefs. Although he consistently deferred to the authority of both, he was aware of the distinction between the mysteries of faith as objects of religious belief, and the philosophy-laden expositions which theologians and bishops tended to endorse as if they coincided exactly with the mysteries which they were meant to describe. This kind of distinction might have helped Descartes in publishing *Le Monde*, but on that occasion he succumbed to his own estimate of what was prudent or even safe in the circumstances. By the time he published the *Meditations* (1641), however, he was more confident of the need to separate Christian mysteries from philosophical theories. Thus, when challenged by Arnauld about the implications of his theory of matter for the Catholic doctrine of transubstantiation, he tried to accommodate the official teaching of the Church to his theory of matter and substance. Arnauld's challenge and Descartes's temerity in venturing into theological disputes did more to distort the subsequent history of Cartesianism than most of the substantive views in natural philosophy which he defended. The significance of the theological controversies which plagued Cartesianism in the seventeenth century is such that any sketch of the historical context of French science in this period must include frequent references to the perceived theological implications of proposed changes in philo-sophical theory.

Thus the situation which confronted would-be followers of Descartes at about the time when the first posthumous editions of his work were being prepared by Clerselier, at the beginning of the 1660s, was extremely complex. Descartes had given a lead in attempting to articulate the implications of the new sciences for philosophy and, by implication, for theology. His lead was bold, but ambiguous. Many of the central problems to which he turned his attention, from innate ideas and the nature of the soul to the role of hypotheses in human knowledge, remained very much a matter of debate even among Cartesians. At the same time, the general import of Cartesian thought was correctly perceived to be incompatible with traditional scholastic theology, and for that reason was fiercely opposed. Cartesians were subject to this type of theologically inspired condemnation as long as their philosophical innovations were linked with any form of religious unorthodoxy. What they had to fear was not limited to public disputation or even official denunciation; for example the abbé de Saint-Cyran, one of the spiritual leaders of the Jansenist movement, had been imprisoned without trial for four years despite the fact that he had earlier been a confidant of Richelieu.

Before elaborating further on the religious and political context in which the Cartesians undertook the articulation and defence of their inheritance from Descartes, it is appropriate to comment on the structure of educational facilities in France during this period and to identify some of the principal individuals involved.

Cartesians in France

The teaching of philosophy, including natural philosophy, in seventeenth-century France was not undertaken in the faculties of arts of the universities, as it had been in the Middle Ages, but in a great variety of *collèges de plein exercise* and private religious institutions which had gradually assumed responsibility for the preparatory training of students before they embarked on the study of law, medicine, or theology.[5] The philosophy courses were taught over a two-year period under four headings, logic, metaphysics, physics, and ethics, with logic always coming first as a foundation course and the other three sections usually following in the order in which they are listed. If one concentrates on the physics course in abstraction from the other parts of the curriculum, the historical evidence suggests that there was no significant change in these

[5] See Brockliss (1981*a*), Brockliss (1981*b*), Brockliss (1987), and Costabel (1964); the textook tradition in natural philosophy during the years 1600–50 is discussed in Reif (1969).

courses in France before the final decades of the century; they remained fundamentally scholastic both in content and style of presentation, although some of the professors began to take account of new phenomena which Aristotle had not discussed or of alternative explanations of physical phenomena which had been popularized in the writings of Pascal or Descartes.

The majority of colleges were operated by religious groups, in most cases by members of Catholic religious orders, although there were also some eminent Protestant colleges such as the Huguenot college at Saumur. The commitment of different religious orders to education was a direct result of their hopes of training young people in the true faith before they were exposed to the errors of other religious traditions. Among Catholic educators, the Jesuits were the dominant group in France, with fifty-eight colleges in operation by mid-century.[6] However their monopoly of college instruction was beginning to be challenged by members of the Oratory which, although only founded by Cardinal Bérulle in 1611, had already established twenty-seven colleges by the close of the century, most of them in the period 1614–30.[7]

There were a few sympathetic readers of Cartesian theories among the Jesuits, such as Père Ignace-Gaston Pardies (1636–73); there was even more interest in the Cartesian enterprise among the Oratorians and, despite official disapproval from their superiors, some of them modified the curriculum of studies so that their students were exposed to the new philosophy.[8] However, there were also many important contributors to the development of Cartesianism in France who had no affiliation with a teaching institution; in a way which paralleled the origins of the Royal Society in England, many developments in natural philosophy in France during this period took place almost entirely outside the universities and colleges. It is time to identify these contributors and to explain why we should classify some of them in retrospect as Cartesians while others are best described as non-Cartesians.

There is an obvious sense in which Christiaan Huygens was influenced by Cartesian physics and by Descartes's concept of what

---

[6] Brockliss (1981a), 157 n. 4. The evolution of scientific teaching in Jesuit colleges in France is discussed by De Dainville (1964).

[7] Costabel (1964), 69.

[8] Pardies's reaction to Cartesianism is summarized in Sortais (1929), 52–3, and his contribution to natural philosophy is analysed in detail in Ziggelaar (1971).

would count as scientific knowledge. In a similar way Edme Mariotte was one of the outstanding experimental scientists of the late seventeenth century in France and, like Huygens, was influenced by Descartes both in scientific work and in his 'logic' of science.[9] When one expands this list to include Claude Perrault, Leibniz, and the most prominent savants of the period, it becomes obvious that there was hardly any natural philosopher of that era in France who was not influenced by Descartes and by the Cartesian concept of scientific knowledge.

Yet, despite these obvious demarcation problems, it is possible to identify a number of prominent philosopher-scientists who were not merely influenced by Descartes but who endorsed his system as the appropriate replacement for the philosophy of the schools. These Cartesian supporters explicitly identified themselves as followers of Descartes, as exponents of his system, claiming to contribute nothing more to his intellectual legacy than an application of Cartesian insights to newly discovered experimental data. This does not mean that they merely repeated Cartesian formulae, nor that they always agreed on even the more important elements of Descartes's system. In fact, they engaged in heated disputes among themselves about almost all the issues which constitute their common heritage. But they disputed them within the general scope of Cartesian principles, and they defended their respective interpretations as developments of Descartes's system rather than as competing alternatives. Their dedication to a kind of 'pure' Cartesianism was challenged from two opposite directions. They were identified from a conservative perspective by scholastic philosophers and theologians as an unacceptable challenge to the traditions of university learning. Towards the end of the century, they were also challenged by those who had accepted the need for a new physics but were dissatisfied with any apparent attempts to accept Descartes's physics as the new orthodoxy, as if it contained the solutions to all their problems. Many of the new, creative scientists—such as Mariotte or Huygens—found themselves in this

[9] Some of the reasons for not classifying Huygens as a Cartesian are discussed by R. S. Westman in 'Huygens and the Problem of Cartesianism', and by A. R. Hall in 'Summary of the Symposium', both of which appear in Bos *et al.* (1980). The extent to which Mariotte's theory of science borrows from Descartes is evident in his *Essai de logique* (1678), in *Œuvres de M*^{r} *Mariotte*, ii. 609 ff. For a discussion of Mariotte's methodology, see Brunet (1947), Bugler (1950), and Rochot (1953).

category of sympathetic critics of Cartesianism who refused to be constrained by its fundamental principles or assumptions.

Among those who explained, defended, and eventually popularized Descartes in France, Jacques Rohault (1618–72) deserves pride of place.[10] Rohault was born in Amiens and, after completing his early education in his native town, he graduated in Arts from the University of Paris. Rohault spent the rest of his life in Paris. He was initially a teacher of mathematics, and numbered François Lamy (1636–1711), the later Benedictine teacher of Cartesianism at Saint-Maur, among his early pupils. He also initiated regular conferences in his home on Cartesian physics, and these seem to have begun as early as 1659.[11] Clerselier provides a description of the structure of these conferences. Rohault would first introduce the general principles of Cartesian physics; he would then explain how those principles provide explanations of various natural phenomena. Finally, he conducted detailed experiments which confirmed the results which he had predicted before doing the experiments. 'And in order that no doubt might remain, he added a number of good experiments as proofs, the results of which he had predicted (following on the principles which he had already established) even before he got to testing them.'[12]

Rohault's Wednesday conferences were held continuously for almost thirteen years. Among those who attended them were Huygens and a number of others who eventually became equally famous as proponents or critics of Descartes: Cordemoy, Malebranche, Simon Foucher, Desgabets, and Pierre-Sylvain Régis, Rohault's successor as chief Cartesian *conférencier* in Paris. Rohault also had amical relations with the Cartesian medical doctor, J.-B. Denis and he exchanged letters with Nicolas Poisson, who had sent him a copy of his *Commentaire ou remarques sur la méthode de Mr Descartes* (1671). Thus, together with his father-in-law, Clerselier, Rohault provided a focus for a Cartesian revival in Paris in the 1660s. It is not surprising, therefore, that when the archbishop of Paris (François Harley de Champvallon) wished to suppress the

---

[10] For a detailed biographical sketch of his life, see Pierre Clair, *Jacques Rohault 1618–1672: bio-bibliographie avec l'édition critique des entretiens sur la philosophie* (Paris, 1978).

[11] In the preface to vol. ii of Descartes's correspondence, published in 1659, Clerselier mentions that Rohault's Wednesday conferences were already under way in that year.

[12] Clerselier, preface to the *Œuvres Posthumes de Mr Rohault* (Paris, 1682).

spread of Cartesianism, he sent for Clerselier on 24 December 1671 and accused him and his son-in-law of being the principal culprits in disturbing the peace of the realm.[13]

Rohault's main publications were his *Traité de physique* (1671), and the *Entretiens sur la philosophie*, published in the same year. Much of his mathematical work was published posthumously by Clerselier, in 1682, as *Œuvres posthumes de Mr. Rohault*.

The other seminal work on Cartesianism which was published during the 1660s was the *Traité de l'esprit* of Louis de la Forge (1632–66).[14] La Forge had apparently studied at the Jesuit college of La Flèche and, after graduating ·in medicine, he established a practice at Saumur where he was acquainted with the Protestant scholar, Jean-Robert Chouet (1642–1731); Chouet was responsible for introducing Bayle to Cartesianism and, as already mentioned, was a major influence in bringing Cartesianism to Geneva.[15] La Forge had the distinction of editing Descartes's *L'Homme*, which was published in 1664 with supplementary notes from the editor; Clerselier mentions in the Preface that La Forge (together with M. de Gutschoven in Holland) was one of the very few who were capable of producing the detailed drawings required to illustrate various anatomical discussions in the work. *L'Homme* had been planned by Descartes in two sections which reflect his metaphysical dualism; the first part was devoted entirely to the human body, while the projected second part was intended to discuss questions about the human mind. Since part two was never written by Descartes, La Forge wrote his *Traité de l'esprit* as a substitute account of the Cartesian theory of mind.

The subsequent history of Cartesianism in France is the history of the assimilation and development of themes from La Forge and Rohault. The major beneficiary of their novel contributions was the Oratorian philosopher, Nicolas Malebranche (1638–1715). Malebranche was converted to Cartesian philosophy by reading Descartes's *L'Homme* soon after his ordination to the priesthood in 1664. His major contributions to philosophy were the *Recherche de la vérité* (1674–5), and the *Traité de la nature et de la grace* (1680).

---

[13] The archbishop's reprimand, delivered in the name of the king, is reported by Clerselier in a letter to Desgabets in Jan. 1672. See P. Clair, *Jacques Rohault*, p. 68.
[14] For biographical information on La Forge, see P. Clair, *Louis de la Forge: œuvres philosophiques avec une étude bio-bibliographique* (Paris, 1974).
[15] Heyd (1982).

He also cultivated a circle of mathematical collaborators who developed Descartes's mathematics in the direction of the new calculus. These included Jean Prestet, the Marquis de l'Hospital, Louis Carré, and Charles-René Reyneau.

Besides Malebranche, the Oratory also provided a number of other Cartesian supporters who deferred to St Augustine as their principal source of theological support, and to Descartes as their philosopher. These included Nicolas Poisson (1639–1710), already mentioned, and Barnard Lamy (1640–1715), the author of *Entretiens sur les sciences* (1683).[16] Lamy was a professor of philosophy at the college at Saumur, and subsequently in Angers where he encountered opposition to his Cartesian ideas. He was exiled in 1676, but eventually got another chance to teach at Grenoble, where *Entretiens* was published. He lived in Paris and participated in Cartesian controversies there between 1686 and 1689, when he was again disciplined by his superiors and sent into exile in Rouen; he remained at Rouen until his death in 1715.

It is significant that many prominent Cartesians were members of the same religious orders in France during the second half of the seventeenth century. Malebranche, Poisson, and Lamy were representatives not only of the new philosophy and theology, but also of new Oratorian initiatives in education which contrasted markedly with the traditionalist pedagogy of the Jesuits. At least one commentator explains the ferocity of the Jesuits' opposition to Cartesianism in terms of their loss of leadership in college education, especially at La Flèche where they were challenged in the same diocese by the Oratorian colleges at Saumur and Angers.[17] The Benedictines were another religious order which provided numerous supporters for the new philosophy; these included François Lamy (1636–1711) and Jean Mabillon of Saint-Maur (1631–1707).[18] The most notorious Benedictine defender of Cartesianism, however, was Dom Robert Desgabets (d. 1678).[19] Desgabets appears to have been more enthusiastic than wise in his unflinching public support for Cartesian ideas. He succeeded in drawing criticism even from his friends, as when he engaged in

---

[16] See Girbal (1964).   [17] Girbal (1964), 33 n. 1.

[18] The Benedictine reform of Saint-Maur and the role of the abbey of Saint-Germain-des-Prés is discussed in Ultee (1981).

[19] For Desgabets's contribution to Cartesian controversies, see Lemaire (1902) and Armogathe (1977).

correspondence with Poisson in 1668–9 over the merits of the latter's mechanics. Malebranche was singularly unimpressed by Desgabets's defence of the *Recherche* against criticism by Simon Foucher, and chided his supporter for not reading carefully the book he claimed to defend.[20] Even Arnauld and Nicole found Desgabets's theology so novel that they rejected it as an inaccurate expression of their position on the theology of the Eucharist.[21] As might be expected, most of the Benedictine's opposition came from various Jesuit supporters of scholastic philosophy; some of these objections are articulated in an anonymous tract, *Lettre d'un philosophe à un cartésien, ou l'on critique la physique et la métaphysique de Descartes*, which was published in Paris in 1672.[22] Desgabets replied in his *Résponse d'un cartésien à la lettre d'un philosophe de ses amis.*

Two other prominent members should be included in this preliminary list of Cartesian philosophers in France. Gerauld de Cordemoy (1626–84) and Pierre-Sylvain Régis (1632–1707) were not associated with religious orders, nor did they hold any official teaching positions in colleges; however, both of them contributed significantly to the articulation of Cartesian philosophy in the second half of the seventeenth century. Cordemoy was a lawyer at the *parlement* of Paris, and was among those who attended the return of Descartes's remains to Paris in 1667. He was also a participant in the conferences of Jacques Rohault. Despite his association with Cartesians and his public defence of Descartes's philosophy, Cordemoy should be recognized as a much more critical supporter than someone like Desgabets; his independence of mind is obvious in *Le Discernement du corps et de l'ame en six discours pour servir à l'éclaircissement de la physique* (1666), and in his other main contribution to Cartesian philosophy, the *Discours physique de la parole* (1668). Cordemoy's attempt to combine his obvious sympathy for Gassendi's concept of matter with Descartes's theory of an infinitely divisible matter is examined in Chapter 3 below.

Rohault's most outstanding protégé, and the one most committed

---

[20] Foucher's book was the *Critique de la recherche de la vérité* (Paris, 1675), to which Desgabets wrote in reply: *Critique de la critique de la recherche de la vérité* (1675).

[21] Lemaire (1902), 124.

[22] The anonymous author was possibly Père Rapin, SJ, or more likely Père Rochon of the same society.

to constructing a comprehensive Cartesian synthesis which would include the latest experimental results, was Pierre-Sylvain Régis. He came to study with Rohault as early as 1655, and later tried to emulate his mentor by providing similar conferences on Cartesian physics at Toulouse. After Rohault's death in 1672 he undertook to continue the tradition of Cartesian conferences in Paris; the results of his work were eventually published in 1690, after long delays, as *Système de philosophie, contenant la logique, la métaphysique, la physique et la morale*.

This preliminary survey suggests that there was a group of philosophers in France during the period 1660–1700 who were interested in Descartes's natural philosophy and who dedicated themselves to winning support for it in the intellectual community in France. They corresponded with Leibniz and Huygens and with members of the Royal Society; they interacted socially and professionally with many of the leading members of the Académie royale des sciences at that time. They even achieved their objective of winning widespread support for Cartesian natural philosophy as an alternative to what was standardly taught in French colleges. Yet, despite their eventual success and despite their unchallengeable contribution to our modern theory of science, they remained on the periphery of officially recognized French institutions until the beginning of the eighteenth century. One of the principal reasons for this lack of official recognition was the involvement of Cartesians in theological and political controversies.

Theological Controversy

As already indicated, the fortunes of Descartes's ideas in France were considerably influenced by a number of very divisive theological controversies in which Cartesianism became unavoidably involved. Among the central reasons why Catholic theologians took issue with Descartes, three in particular stand out as the main sources of debate between 1660 and 1700:

1. the implications of Cartesianism for the theology of the Eucharist;
2. the relevance of the machine model of animals for the immortality of the human soul;

3. the association of Cartesianism with Jansenism, and the consequent attribution to the Cartesians of all the objections, both theological and political, which were initially provoked by Jansenism.

Each of these sources of controversy deserves an extended discussion; for present purposes it is enough to summarize the reasons why Cartesians were accused of theological unorthodoxy and why they consequently experienced the kind of official disapproval which was predictable during Louis XIV's reign. The relevance of these controversies for the interpretation of Cartesian texts is discussed in the appropriate places in subsequent chapters.

1. The Catholic Church in France looked to the Council of Trent for its official teaching on the theology of the Eucharist. On 1 October 1551 the Council of Trent promulgated the following doctrine on the Eucharist: 'through the consecration of the bread and wine there comes about a conversion of the whole substance of the bread into the substance of the body of Christ our Lord, and of the whole substance of the wine into the substance of his blood. And this conversion is . . . properly called transubstantiation.'[23] At the same Session (XIII), the Council condemned those who claimed that 'the substance of bread and wine remains together with the body and blood of Our Lord Jesus Christ in the most holy Sacrament of the Eucharist'; instead the Council defended 'the total conversion of the whole substance of bread into the body (of Christ) and the whole substance of wine into the blood (of Christ), while the species of bread and wine alone remain (*manentibus dumtaxat speciebus panis et vini*)'.[24]

In adopting a formula with which to express its teaching, Trent intentionally avoided choosing between competing scholastic theologies of the Eucharist which had been proposed by partisans of different schools to the Council for official endorsement as Catholic dogma.[25] Thus, the Council never mentioned anything about 'real

---

[23] Bettensen (1963), 371.

[24] 'If anyone says that the substance of bread and wine remains in the most holy sacrament of the eucharist together with the body and blood of Our Lord Jesus Christ, and if he denies that unique and miraculous conversion of the whole substance of bread into the body [of Christ] and of the whole substance of wine into the blood [of Christ], while the species of bread and wine alone remain . . . may he be anathema', Denzinger (1960), No. 884.

[25] Cf. Armogathe (1977).

accidents' in the discussion of the Eucharist, opting instead for the more comprehensive and ambiguous term 'species'. Those who later taught theology in the scholastic tradition interpreted the Tridentine formula as if it had endorsed a theory of substances and accidents, so that the sacramental conversion of which Trent spoke required the accidents of bread and wine to be separable from their respective substances. On this theory, transubstantiation takes place when the substances of bread and wine are converted into the substances of the body and blood of Christ, while the accidents of bread and wine remain unchanged. This type of explanation assumes that the accidents of bread and wine can exist independently of the substances to which they naturally belong.

Descartes's account of matter unfortunately left no room for accidents which could exist independently of their proper substance. There was an urgent need, therefore, to explain how the Cartesian theory of matter, substances, and modes was compatible with the official teaching of Trent on the Eucharist. As already mentioned, Descartes had the temerity to become involved in this controversy in reply to objections from Arnauld, and he developed his account in two further letters to Mesland.[26] In subsequent years, the principal protagonists on the Cartesian side were Jacques Rohault and the Benedictine monk, Dom Robert Desgabets.

Rohault accurately identified the difference between Cartesianism and any theory which assumed the existence of scholastic accidents in his *Entretiens sur la philosophie* (1671): 'what are called accidents are nothing other than modes which cannot exist without a subject.'[27] Rohault also claimed that this theory was superior to the standard scholastic theology of the Eucharist, because his account explained how transubstantiation was possible whereas his opponents could only argue that, according to their philosophy, it was not impossible. Rohault's analysis relied on a distinction between primary and secondary qualities. The taste, colour, and all the other perceived qualities of bread and wine are secondary qualities which exist in the perceiving subject, and they are normally caused by what we call bread and wine. In the case of the Eucharist, transubstantiation means that what is actually present to the observer is no longer bread and wine, but the body and blood of

---

[26] Descartes, *Œuvres*, vol. iv. 161; 215. Descartes's role in the transubstantiation controversy has been examined in Laymon (1982) and Watson (1982).

[27] Rohault, *Entretiens sur la philosophie* (1671), ed. P Clair, p. 117.

Christ. Despite the change in substances, we continue to taste and otherwise perceive as if we were presented with bread and wine. The miracle of the sacrament consists, on this account, in the fact that the new substance is able to cause secondary qualities in us, as a result of divine intervention, which are normally caused only by bread and wine. Thus Cartesian philosophy explains, or at least is consistent with, the teaching of Trent. The 'species' of bread and wine remain, but they are not mysteriously detached from their proper subject, because the secondary qualities continue to exist in the very same subject (the perceiver) in which they normally exist. The only new and miraculous feature is that they are now caused by a different substance. 'There is nothing easier than to explain how the accidents of bread and wine subsist without the bread and wine because one need only say, simply, that when the bread and the wine are taken away, God continues to make the same impressions on our senses as they had made before they were changed (by transubstantiation).'[28]

Desgabets went even further than Rohault in his efforts to reconcile a corpuscular account of matter with the Tridentine formula about transubstantiation. He prepared his first version of a theology of the Eucharist in 1663, the very same year in which Descartes's writings were proscribed by Rome. In it he urged that God's revelation should be understood in a way which is compatible with reason: 'just as God cannot deceive when he speaks through revelation, neither can he deceive when he speaks through reason.'[29] To effect this kind of reconciliation between reason and revelation or between reason and theology's interpretation of revelation, and at the same time to maintain his commitment to the Cartesian concept of matter, Desgabets proposed an understanding of transubstantiation which did not require the problematic subsistence of accidents, such as colour or shape, independently of the matter of which they are mere modes of existence. Instead, the Benedictine philosopher suggested that the mystery of faith involved in this sacrament should be expressed in terms of the union of Christ, as a scholastic form, with the matter of bread and wine. The 'species' or appearances of bread and wine continue to be explained, even after transubstantiation, by the motions of small

[28] Ibid. 120.
[29] Quoted by Armogathe (1977), 92.

parts of matter. The only new feature after transubstantiation is that the matter in question is miraculously joined by God's power with the soul of Christ. On this account, the matter of bread and wine remains after the Eucharistic consecration, and it continues to subsist side by side with the added substances of the body and blood of Christ.

Desgabets's theological efforts were not warmly welcomed by his scholastic critics, nor even by those Port-Royal theologians on whom he might have counted for support. His theory was even more suspect than Rohault's because it implied that the substances of bread and wine remained unchanged by transubstantiation except for the new relationship with Christ. Desgabets was ordered by his superiors, at the instigation of the archbishop of Paris, to renounce his theology of the Eucharist and to desist from any further writing on the subject.[30] Most of the leading Peripatetic critics took issue with what they perceived as a rejection of the Tridentine teaching on the Eucharist. For example, Peter Daniel Huet objected in his *Censura Philosophiae Cartesianae* that the Cartesian Eucharistic theology was 'repugnant to many decrees of the holy faith' and the Jesuit critic, Gabriel Daniel, expressed his objections in Scotist categories in *A Voyage to the World of Cartesius*.[31] The fundamental source of all the objections was the assumption that Trent could not be understood, in an orthodox fashion, without first accepting the scholastic theory of substance and accidents in terms of which the theology of the schools had explained the Eucharist. Since Descartes's philosophy denied the possibility of detached accidents, any attempt to reinterpret the Tridentine formula about species was stubbornly resisted.

As a direct result of this controversy, Cartesian theology was proscribed by the Theology Faculty at Angers in 1675, and by the University of Caen in 1677.[32] In the case of Angers, it was Bernard Lamy who had precipitated the attack on Cartesianism, which was judged to be 'très pernicieux et à l'Église et à l'État'. Lamy lost his post teaching philosophy, just as Desgabets was removed from the prior's office at Saint-Airy-de-Verdun. The Benedictine and Oratorian orders forbade the teaching of Cartesianism in their schools, and the Theology Faculty at Paris continued to demand

[30] Lemaire (1902), 51.
[31] See Huet, *Censura*, 1st edn., p. 82; Daniel, *Voyage*, pp. 126–31.
[32] See Girbal (1964), 36–42.

that all professors sign a formal rejection of Cartesianism until the early part of the eighteenth century.[33]

2. A second, reasonably specific and widespread, objection to Cartesianism derived from concern about reductionism in explaining human thought. Christian anthropology and the Christian theology of the meaning of life depended on some concept of personal immortality, and this in turn was presented as if it presupposed the spirituality or immateriality of the individual human soul. Descartes had argued that the behaviour of non-rational animals could be explained without any reference to animal souls; more generally, that all explanations in terms of faculties and powers were pseudo-explanations. Opponents objected, with an astute anticipation of later developments in the history of philosophy, that, if the 'souls' of animals were reducible to mechanical causes, it was only a matter of time before human minds could be equally well explained in terms of stimuli, animal spirits, and brain functions.

Thus Daniel, in his *Nouvelles difficultez*, rebukes the Cartesians for explaining animals mechanically while at the same time making an exception for human beings: 'if that [i.e. mechanical explanation] is true, why is it that you, a Cartesian (whom I would like to assume is not an automaton) make an exception from the general rule for just one species of beings, of which all that you can see is a machine just like the bodies of other animals?'[34] Daniel develops his objection by wondering what would happen if God gave minds similar to ours to a dog, and if the Cartesian dog was faced with the unintelligible chatter of philosophers. In that case, the dog would argue that the noise-making human animals around him were only automata which could be mechanically explained, whereas the species of dogs is an exception to the general principle of mechanical explanation. Daniel's example is somewhat contrived and admittedly introduced in jest; however, the point is well made and the likely implications of any mechanical theory of explanation for the human soul are clearly underlined.

It was partly in response to these concerns that those who were less single-minded in their commitment to Descartes's philosophy continued to speak of the soul of animals in a non-reductionist way.

[33] For a history of the censorship of Cartesian views, see Bouillier (1868), i. 447–85, and McClaughlin (1979). The prohibition of Cartesianism in Jesuit and Oratorian colleges is discussed below (see n. 51).

[34] Daniel, *Nouvelles difficultez*, p. 100.

Thus Claude Perrault, in the introduction to *La Méchanique des animaux* (1680), defines an animal in explicit contrast with the Cartesians as 'a being which has feeling (*sentiment*) and which is capable of exercising the functions of a living being by a principle which is called a soul'.[35] Cartesians, however, were adamant that souls are redundant in explaining animal behaviour. Their objection was not confined to animal souls; it was more fundamentally an objection to the kind of explanation which required the use of substantial forms. Since the human soul was traditionally understood in scholastic philosophy as a substantial form, it was hardly unreasonable for critics to wonder about the eventual fate of human souls in a philosophical system which was in principle opposed to the use of substantial forms as theoretical entities.

3. By contrast with the first two objections which were quite specific, the third theological reason for the opposition to Cartesians in this period in France was the much more general objection that they either were, or they associated with, Jansenists. The assimilation of the two groups, as theologically heterodox and politically radical, was so complete in the eyes of opponents that Père Daniel attributes the following to Descartes in his *Voyage*: 'you should not see a Jansenist Philosopher that was not a Cartesian.'[36] This perception of collusion between Cartesians and Jansenists was not entirely erroneous, and it was one of the principal sources of opposition in France during a period when relations between the Church and the Court were of critical importance to both.

'Jansenism' is a comprehensive term which refers to a variety of interlinked theological, political, and religious views and practices. At the beginning of the seventeenth century, it denoted a theological view about the necessity of God's grace for salvation, and the effectiveness of this grace in those cases where it is bestowed freely by God. One interpretation of Jansen's theory, expounded at length in his *Augustinus* (1640), was that it compromised human freedom and that it was indistinguishable from the Calvinist theology of predestination. This disputed theology of grace was understood, therefore, as taking sides against the Jesuits in the

---

[35] Perrault, *Essais de physique*, iii. 1.
[36] *Voyage*, Eng. trans., p. 190. For a general overview of Jansenism, see Escholier (1968) and Sedgwick (1977). Weaver (1978) suggests that the Port-Royal reform was not as radical as its stormy history suggests. The relation between Jansenism and the Cartesians is discussed in Lewis (1950) and Gouhier (1978).

controversy between Michel de Bay (1513–89) and Luis de Molina (1535–1600). According to de Bay (Baius), grace was both a necessary and sufficient condition for genuinely meritorious religious actions; in contrast, Molina maintained that there was an irreducible element of human freedom involved in either seeking the help of God or in responding to his proferred grace. The dispute about the efficacy of grace was thus inextricably linked with complementary theories about human freedom; the Molinist view appeared to imply that the choice of the individual agent could not be completely subject to divine grace without thereby compromising human freedom. Since the Jesuits had publicly supported the Molinist view against de Bay, it was not surprising that any theology of grace such as Jansen's which appeared to revive de Bay's side of the argument would incur the official opposition of the Jesuits and of their supporters in Rome.

Jansenism also represented a revival of a rigorous view of devotional or religious life and, by implication, a rejection of many of the secular values which were prevalent at the Court. The belief in the efficacy of God's grace, in the personalized calling of each individual to respond to God's grace, and in the worthlessness of secular values was central to the rule of life adopted by members of the Port-Royal community. On this issue, there was nothing unusual about the Jansenists in France; they were part of a more comprehensive religious counter-reformation which included Cardinal Bérulle, St Francis de Sales, St Vincent de Paul, and many others. However, while the other contributions to religious reform in France were welcomed by Church and State, Jansenism became entangled in a web of ongoing disputes between Louis XIV, the Papacy, and the French episcopate which assured for its supporters the unrelenting opposition of all three.

After Louis XIV took full charge of the affairs of state on the death of Mazarin in March 1661, he significantly consolidated his power as absolute ruler. The drive towards absolutism had been under way in France since the beginning of the century; under Louis, it was accelerated and eventually realized to such an extent that religious unorthodoxy was as unacceptable as political opposition to the Crown.[37] The centralization of power in the Court involved ridding the kingdom of dissidents and redefining the relationship

---

[37] The historical development of French absolutism is summarized in Parker (1983).

between France and the Papacy. In response to religious dissidents, Louis moved against the Jansenists and the Huguenots. The Huguenots had enjoyed a measure of tolerance after the Edict of Nantes (1598); Louis now began to qualify the guarantees which it had provided and to deny to Huguenots various civil, educational, and religious liberties which were enjoyed by Catholics until, in 1685, the Edict was finally revoked.

Jansenism proved to be a more elusive opponent because it was a Catholic religious movement in a Catholic state. Louis needed the co-operation of the French Church and of the Papacy to identify his opponents and to help suppress them. The Sorbonne had already provided part of the solution to the king's dilemma. At the instigation of Jesuit opponents of Jansenism, the Sorbonne had isolated five propositions which were claimed to express the thought of Jansen, and these were forwarded to Rome for condemnation in 1649. On 31 May 1653, in a bull *Cum Occasione*, the five propositions in question were condemned by Pope Innocent X as heretical or false.[38] Within a very short time, Mazarin arranged for the bull to be endorsed by the French Church and to be enforced in France. The disputed propositions were confirmed as Jansenist by Pope Alexander VII, in a bull *Ad Sanctam Beati Petri Sedem* (1656); this condemnation was released in France in March 1657. The formal condemnations by Rome proved to be peculiarly inefficacious in France as long as Jansenist supporters believed that the condemned propositions did not accurately reflect their own beliefs about grace and redemption. In an effort to translate the Popes' condemnations into action, the king convoked a general assembly of the clergy which approved a formulary condemning the five propositions. This formulary was subsequently used as a touch-stone of orthodoxy; those who held positions of leadership in the Church were required to sign it to show their opposition to Jansenism. The enforced signing of this formulary gave rise to the

---

[38] The five propositions in question were: '1. Some commandments of God to men wishing and striving to be righteous are impossible with regard to the present strength that they possess; and they lack the grace by which they may become possible. 2. Interior grace is never resisted in the state of fallen nature. 3. For merit or demerit in the state of fallen nature freedom from necessity is not required in man but freedom from compulsion. 4. Semipelagians admit the necessity of prevenient interior grace for single acts, even for the beginning of faith; and they are heretics in this, that they wish grace to be of such a kind as human will can resist or obey. 5. It is Semipelagian to say that Christ died and shed his blood for all men.' Quoted from Bettenson (1963), 380–1.

famous distinction, drawn by Arnauld, between *droit* and *fait*.

The distinction conceded the right of the Church authorities to define the faith of the Christian tradition; but it also claimed that the factual question, whether or not certain propositions are found in Jansen's work, was a question which could only be settled by reason. Arnauld argued: it is a question of faith whether or not the condemned propositions are heretical, and on this issue the Papacy has exclusive competence; however, it is a question of fact to decide if Jansen or his followers ever endorsed such propositions, and the Papacy has no privileged role in deciding this issue. Thus Jansenists insisted on both acknowledging the authority of the Church and, at the same time, rejecting its claim that Jansen's theology of grace was heretical because they refused to concede that the five propositions accurately reflected their theology of justification.

The Court's efforts to rid the kingdom of Jansenism coincided with a parallel attempt to protect the State from papal influence. This was an issue on which the king and the French bishops could collaborate in a common cause. Thus M. Hardouin de Péréfixe, soon after his appointment as archbishop of Paris in 1664, formulated six articles expressing the views of the Paris Theology Faculty concerning the role of the king in Church affairs:

1. That it is not the teaching of the Faculty of Theology of Paris that the Pope has any authority over the temporal power of the king; . . .

2. That the king does not recognize and has no other superior in temporal affairs except God; . . .

3. That the subjects of the king owe him such fidelity and obedience that they cannot be dispensed from it for whatever reason;

4. That the same Faculty neither approves nor had it ever approved any propositions contrary to the king's authority, the true freedom of the French Church, or the canons in force in the kingdom; . . .

5. The Pope is not above a general Council; . . .

6. That the Pope is not infallible when he fails to win agreement from the Church.[39]

This intervention of the Theology Faculty provided a formal

[39] Statement of the Theology Faculty of Paris, 8 May 1663, in Jourdain (1888), i. 424.

expression of the views of Church–State relations which were eventually enshrined in the Four Articles of 1682, summarizing the Gallican claims of the Church in France to independence from the Papacy.[40]

Gallicanism provided an opportunity for the Court and the French episcopate to co-operate in pursuing their respective interests. The king needed theological support for his theory of political authority; the bishops, in turn, were dedicated to suppressing the challenge of Jansenism to their religious authority, and to do this they needed the co-operation of the civil powers. Rome was exploited by both sides. The Pope gave his support to the French episcopate against Jansenism in order to secure the allegiance of the bishops; when the same request was made by the king, it may have seemed like an ideal opportunity for the Pope to win concessions from the French Court in relation to its Gallican aspirations. The unfortunate Jansenists were therefore condemned by the French episcopate, the Papacy, and the king for different reasons. They enjoyed a short reprieve under the so-called peace of Clement IX who, in 1669, relaxed the demands for signing the formulary; for a period it was acceptable to sign the document with an implicit distinction between *droit* and *fait*. However even this measure of tolerance came to an end ten years later under Pope Innocent XI and Jansenist supporters once again experienced the full ire of their civil and ecclesiastical opponents. The persecution of the Jansenists culminated in the enforced closure of Port-Royal-des-Champs in 1709; armed representatives of the king physically evicted the remaining few nuns and relocated them in different monasteries in the vicinity of Paris. Two years later Louis had the buildings demolished.

One wonders in retrospect at the ferocity of the Court's diligence in extirpating heresy and at its political collusion with Rome in having the Jansenists declared heretical. One could hardly assume that Louis was primarily interested in winning acceptance for one of two competing theories of efficacious grace. Part of the explanation is provided by Jansenist sympathies with the Fronde; however, even this limited support was not shared by some of the most prominent Jansenists and it would hardly account for the continued harassment of dissidents well into the eighteenth century.[41] Likewise, the

[40] Cragg (1970), 24.
[41] The involvement of Jansenist sympathizers in the various Frondes is examined

extent to which Jesuit confessors could win the king's support in a theological controversy in which they were publicly involved—such as Père Jean Ferrier's intervention in 1671 in the condemnation of Desgabets—should not be exaggerated.[42]

Evidently, a major reason why Jansenists provoked the wrath of the king derived from the political implications of Jansenist theology.[43] Pascal's *Provincial Letters* illustrate this point clearly. For Pascal, there are many facts about which human reason alone is the final arbiter; neither the authority of the Church nor that of the king can overrule the human spirit's efforts to decide which facts to believe. Jansenism contained the seeds of a theory of individual conscience, of personal freedom, and of independence from human authority. Even if Jansenist convictions were ultimately supported by a theological theory of election by God, nevertheless they were convictions with obvious implications for any totalitarian rule, whether regal or clerical. Thus Dom Gabriel Gerberon argued, in 1688, that those human laws which conflict with the divine law should not be obeyed; and Arnauld had similarly defended the limits of obedience to civil authorities in religious matters, or to religious authorities in matters of 'fact'.[44] In the *affaire d'Angers*, Lamy had been accused of preferring democracy to the monarchy, and Malebranche was suspect for his theory of civil disobedience.[45] The subversive character of Jansenism can therefore be explained by reference to the king's understanding of the divine origin of his regal authority; in an absolutist religious state, religious dissent was tantamount to questioning the theologically based political authority of the Crown.[46]

Cartesians were correctly identified as sharing the Jansenist belief in the authority of human reason. They also shared the respect for

---

in detail in Golden (1981). Gérard Ferreyrolles disputes the extent to which Jansenists, especially Pascal, supported the Frondist position; see Ferreyrolles (1984), 33, 103–4.

[42] Lemaire (1902) 125–6.   [43] Cf. Tavenaux (1965).

[44] Both are quoted in Tavenaux (1965), 87, 90–1. For contemporary developments in political theory about the limited power of the king, see Skinner (1978), ii, Parker (1981), and Ferreyrolles (1984), 76.

[45] Girbal (1964), 39–42. Lamy had argued that, in a state of innocence before the fall, 'il n'y aurait point eu d'inégalité de conditions: c'est par une suite du péché qu'il y a maintenant une différence parmi les hommes, dont les uns commandent et les autres obéissent.' Quoted from Lallemand (1888), 126–7.

[46] The relation between the centralization of power in the Court and the demand for religious conformity is discussed in Parker (1983), esp. 42–64.

St Augustine which was the defining characteristic of Jansenist theories of free will, grace, and redemption. At the same time, most Jansenists showed a greater sympathy for Cartesian philosophical ideas than for those of their Jesuit opponents who assumed the role of defenders of scholastic orthodoxy. Given the established position of scholastic theology and the Jesuits' prominent role in defending it, all the theological disputes in which Cartesians became involved, including their association with Jansenism, developed into a confrontation between, on the one hand, the Jesuits and their supporters in Rome and, on the other hand, those such as the Jansenists or Cartesians who challenged the traditional scholastic theology.[47]

These theological disputes—concerning the theology of the Eucharist, the immateriality of the individual human soul, and Jansen's theology of grace—overlapped with equally acrimonious controversies about issues which we would classify today as philosophical; the foremost critics of Cartesianism on this front were also, as might be expected, the proponents of scholastic philosophy.

School Philosophy

The discussion thus far may give the impression that Cartesianism was opposed primarily for theological reasons, or for political reasons which were implicit in theological or religious views adopted by Cartesians. It is equally clear, however, that a major source of opposition was the entrenched philosophy of the schools. This is also the most explicitly recognized face of the opposition in Cartesian writing. For obvious reasons, neither king nor Church was usually identified by the Cartesians as their opponent, because the possibility of publishing any book depended on the king's *privilège* and on the Church's influence on censorship. Hence, when Cartesians wrote publicly about their opponents, they invariably identified them with the partisans of school philosophy.

Malebranche is probably sharper than his fellow sufferers when

---

[47] 'Those who were most anti-Jesuit could be identified as antiregular, Gallican, Jansenist and frondeur', Golden (1981), 99. Ferreyrolles gives a similar definition of the political stance of Pascal as the antithesis of the dominant Jesuit view; see Ferreyrolles (1984), 51–91.

he writes: 'it can be guaranteed concerning Aristotle that as his principles have been of no use for two thousand years, no phenomenon of nature will ever be explained by them, although his philosophy has been studied by the ablest people in almost all parts of the world'.[48] The inefficacy of Aristotle's system was not the real source of concern; what provoked such strong reactions was the appeal to Aristotle's authority to resolve questions which are open to rational investigation. Malebranche castigates this attitude in blunt terms: 'it is blindness, meanness of mind, and stupidity to surrender in this way to the authority of Aristotle, Plato, or any other philosopher'.[49] In a less aggressive style, La Forge had complained that many uncritically accepted a theology which relied on a 'confusion of scholastic entities which, in truth, are nothing but chimeras'.[50] Rohault objected in a similar vein, in the Preface to his *Traité de physique*, that the authority attributed to Aristotle was such that, in order for someone to cast doubt on scientific discoveries, it was enough to claim simply that Aristotle had said the contrary. The authority of Aristotle in defining what was orthodox continued after Rohault's death. In the Preface to a posthumous edition of Rohault's works, Clerselier objects to those who transform colours into real accidents and who even wish to make them into an article of faith, while those who adopt Rohault's explanation are treated as 'heretics'.

The reason why defenders of school philosophy were so adamant in their opposition to change is not explained adequately by the arguments which supported the competing theories, just as the Court's condemnation of theological heterodoxy is not explained by its interest in theories of grace. The universities in France were pillars of an established order. They might have coped well with philosophical or scientific controversies within an acceptable range, as long as authority was still recognized as a valid criterion in the arts or sciences. The Cartesian objection to the established schools was not so much that their teaching was mistaken, but that the teaching in question relied ultimately on authority for its justification. It hardly mattered that the father figure for the schools was Aristotle; anyone else would have been equally objectionable. Cartesians were accurately perceived, therefore, as challenging the assumption that scientific issues could be resolved by reference to

---

[48] *Search After Truth*, pp. 13–14.   [49] Ibid. 282.
[50] La Forge, *Traité de l'esprit*, p. 347.

anyone's authority, Aristotle's, the Church's, or the king's. What was at stake between the two rival approaches to learning was fundamental: should one rely on reason to decide scientific questions, or ought one defer to the authority of officially recognized teachers? The Cartesians challenged the very basis of traditional learning and, with it, the role of the universities as the embodiment of the received wisdom which was based on authority.

For this reason, they won the unflinching and bitterly implemented opposition of those who were engaged in teaching philosophy in French colleges. In some cases, the official exclusion of Cartesian theses from the curriculum could be explained by the desire to avoid controversy while still maintaining as much freedom as possible for professors. It was in this spirit that the sixth general assembly of the Oratory in September 1678 forbade teaching anything in their colleges which might 'be suspect of the opinions of Jansen or Baius in theology, or of Desquartes [sic] in philosophy'.[51] The Jesuits, however, were less ambivalent in their directions to their college teachers; as late as the fifteenth general congregation, in 1706, they listed thirty Cartesian theses which their professors were forbidden to teach.[52]

Cartesians reacted in two contrasting ways to the objections of scholastic philosophers. The most obvious reaction was scorn. Thus on many issues—such as the concept of explanation—Cartesians almost defined their contribution to philosophy by contrast with the scholastic counter-position. They presented their 'modern' ideas as the exact antithesis to an outmoded and intellectually disgraced authoritarian tradition. On the other hand, they also tried to present their philosophical system as a natural development of Aristotelian principles; one of the best ways of doing that was to publish the new philosophy in the style of scholastic manuals.

Rohault gave a lead in arguing that his philosophy was

---

[51] The prohibition on teaching Cartesian philosophy in Oratorian colleges was made by the sixth general assembly, 1678, which defended the right of members to hold or teach any doctrine which was not condemned by the Church. Thus the assembly 'ne défend d'enseigner que celles qui sont condamnées par l'Église ou qui pourroyent estre suspects de sentiments de Jansénius, de Baïus pour la théologie ou de Desquartes pour la philosophie'. Quoted from Lallemand (1888), 402. This regulation seems to be motivated by a desire to avoid controversy rather than to limit the freedom of its members. It coincides with an earlier injunction by the Oratorians in 1675 (quoted in Lallemand (1888), 122) which forbade the teaching of Descartes or any other 'new doctrine' against the 'orders recently given by the King'.

[52] Sortais (1929), 36–40.

compatible with that of Aristotle, although it differed in many respects from those who claimed to interpret 'the philosopher' with more authority than accuracy. Apart from some discoveries which had been made with the help of 'the telescope, the microscope and from certain experiments which . . . that ancient Philosopher did not think of doing . . . the Cartesians remain in agreement with everything which Aristotle had written; and they only differ from the Aristotelians in that they move from the metaphysical way of treating issues, to which Aristotle restricted himself, to a more physical and specific approach.'[53] Rohault's attempts to integrate Cartesian physics with Aristotelian metaphysics inspired one of his admirers to write a systematic account of the consistency of the two traditions. René le Bossu published his *Parallèle des principes de la physique d'Aristote & de celle de René Des Cartes* in Paris, in 1674. Le Bossu concedes that the task suggested by the book's title is more comprehensive than he can cope with; so he amends the project to compare 'the physics of the celebrated M. Rohault' with the first principles of Aristotle.[54] The results of Le Bossu's analysis reflect those of Rohault; that the metaphysics of Aristotle can be developed in such a way that it is consistent with the new physics.

Thus Cartesians responded to the established philosophy of the schools in two complementary ways, by claiming that their modern philosophy was vastly superior to what it hoped to replace and, at the same time, that it was a natural development of the principles of Aristotle and an adaptation of his metaphysics to recently discovered experimental results.

The development of experimental methods outside the context of the universities and colleges in France provided an independent and critical support for Cartesian claims. The contributions of both local and international experimental philosophers was given a new focus in France with the founding of the Académie royale des sciences in 1666.

Scientific Societies

It would be a serious misrepresentation of the history of natural philosophy in France during the seventeenth century to suggest that

[53] Rohault, *Entretiens* (1671), ed. P. Clair, p. 106.

[54] Le Bossu was a member of the Sainte-Geneviève community in Paris; the superior-general of 'the regular canons of the congregation in France' gave him permission to publish his book in 1674. It was published in Paris, by Michel le Petit, in the same year. See also Bouillier (1868), i. 435. The quotation above is from p. 9.

Cartesians struggled bravely, and alone, in the face of opposition from theological and political authorities in their efforts to provide an alternative to peripatetic philosophy. Cartesianism took its place among a great variety of disparate initiatives and theories which vied for official recognition from the Crown. Whereas the first half of the century produced many savants and scientific dilettantes but little successful science, the second half of the century was a period of significant growth both in mathematical expertise and in the application of mathematics to the solution of problems in physics and medicine.

The salon tradition in Paris provided an informal setting in which new ideas could be introduced to a wide public and made socially acceptable. The topics which were broached in these informal meetings were sufficiently disparate to include what we would now describe as classical literature, physics, physiology, philosophy, theology, and so on. The diversity of subjects seemed to titillate rather than weary the eager participants. This kind of eclecticism was much in evidence, for example, in the conferences organized at the Bureau d'Adresse by Théophraste Renaudot between 1633 and 1642. After the political instability caused by the Fronde, the Parisian appetite for scientific novelties was stimulated by a variety of overlapping scientific circles, most of which were less casual in their dedication to scientific research than Renaudot's Bureau. Thus, Clerselier devoted much of his time to collecting Cartesian manuscripts and preparing them for publication. Descartes's letters were published between 1657 and 1667, and the first edition of Le Monde appeared in 1664. As part of his efforts to propagandize Cartesianism, Clerselier helped arrange the weekly Wednesday conferences which were given by his son-in-law, Jacques Rohault. Rohault used these conferences to provide Cartesian explanations of diverse phenomena and to perform experiments within the general framework of Cartesian natural philosophy.

There were quite a number of informal academies in Paris and the provinces in France about the middle of the seventeenth century.[55] Two in particular deserve special mention, those of Montmor and Thévenot. Habert de Montmor was a patron of the sciences. He had provided a home for Gassendi during the last five years of his life; within two years of Gassendi's death in 1665, the informal meetings

---

[55] For the provincial academies, see Roche (1978); Brown (1967) is the standard history of scientific societies in France in the 17th cent.

which took place in the Montmor home were formalized into a distinctive, academic group. Samuel Sorbière was invited to draw up a constitution for the new academy. The rules included the stipulation that, at any meeting, the members would agree on two of their number who would present their views formally at the subsequent meeting. 'These opinions shall be read and produced in writing, in concise and reasoned terms, without amplification or citation of authorities.'[56] Besides, only those who could contribute to the advancement of learning were accepted as members, and the regular meetings were closed to non-members.

The Assembly being formed, no person shall be admitted who does not request it, and then only on the consent of two-thirds of the company present when the proposal shall be made. No person not a member of the Assembly shall be admitted into the place of the conference, which shall be entirely composed of persons curious about natural things, medicine, mathematics, the liberal arts, and mechanics, unless permission to introduce some person of merit has previously been requested.[57]

Montmor's ideal of organizing a centre for serious study was frustrated, partly by a lack of adequate resources, and perhaps more significantly by its failure to attract creative philosophers in sufficient numbers. Despite its collapse a few years after its foundation, it provided a common centre in Paris for savants of different traditions until 1664, when many of the members transferred the venue for regular meetings to the house of Melchisédech Thévenot. Thévenot can be rightly regarded, together with Montmor, as providing the context within which it was possible to found the Académie royale des sciences in 1666. It is especially clear that Thévenot's group helped formulate the policy, explicitly adopted by the fledgling academy, of separating science as much as possible from metaphysical and religious controversies. At Thévenot's, 'one never spoke of the mysteries of religion nor of affairs of state; and if one spoke sometimes of metaphysics, morals, history or grammar, etc. it was only in passing and only insofar as it was related to physics and the social behaviour of men.'[58]

The eventual founding of the academy, under the guiding hand of Colbert, was an official recognition on the part of the Court that

---

[56] Brown (1967), 75.   [57] Brown (1967), 76.
[58] McClaughlin (1975), 238. The early meetings of the Royal Society had a similar prohibition on discussing 'matters of theology and state affairs'; see Webster (1975), 54 ff.

scientific progress could no longer be left in the hands of amateurs. The history of its foundation and of its activities during the period before reorganization in 1699 is well documented.[59] In his introduction to the *Histoire de l'académie royale des sciences*, Fontenelle summarizes the spirit of the enterprise thus: 'The sterile physics which, for many centuries had remained at the same point, was abandoned. The rule of words and of terms is finished; what is needed are things; principles which can be understood are established and followed, and from this it follows that we make progress.'[60] The original members of the academy included many of the best mathematicians and physicists of the time, including Pierre Carcavi, Christiaan Huygens, Claude Perrault, Gilles Personne de Roberval, and, curiously, the Oratorian theologian and classical scholar, Jean-Baptise du Hamel, as its first secretary. The most outspoken representatives of various schools of thought, such as the Cartesian or Peripatetic, were noticeably absent from the list of those invited to join the academy.

The advisers to Colbert, the so-called Petite académie, had originally planned to include theologians and representatives of the various arts in the new academy, despite the obvious overlap with the Académie française. The Sorbonne objected to any theological organization which was not directly under Church control, just as the theologians had objected in the first year of publication of the *Journal des sçavans*, in 1665, to the apparent endorsement of theological opinions which were at variance with official teaching.[61] Both the academy and its official mouthpiece, the *Journal*, accommodated this type of objection by excluding theological and similarly contentious matters from their programme. Thus, although many of the early members of the academy were sympathetic to Jansenism, none of the Cartesian philosophers was invited to join the academy, nor indeed were any of their Peripatetic opponents.

However, the desire to avoid theological or metaphysical disputes only partly explains the criteria which were used in naming members to the academy before its reorganization in 1699, when Malebranche and Régis were eventually invited as associate members. The academies of Renaudot, Montmor, and Thévenot had each experienced a number of common problems which contributed to

---

[59] See Fontenelle, *Histoire de l'académie royale des sciences* (Paris, 1733), Maury (1864), Hahn (1971), Hirschfield (1981).

[60] Fontenelle, *Histoire*, p. 2.   [61] See Hirschfield (1981), ch. 1.

their early demise. One of the recurring problems was the exploitation of meetings by those in attendance to exhibit their rhetorical skills rather to provide any worthwhile contribution to knowledge. Unending terminological and scholastic discussions exhausted the patience of those who were seriously interested in the resolution of problems which had some relevant application to medicine or technology. Besides, Colbert was interested in a technologically productive academy which would not only glorify the reputation of the *roi soleil*, but would also help the national economy and provide technical assistance to the monarch in the conduct of domestic and foreign wars. This suggests a second criterion of selection for members of the new academy; only those who were primarily concerned with the resolution of scientific or mathematical problems were likely to contribute to Colbert's plans for the academy. With the possible exception of Jacques Rohault, none of the French Cartesians would have satisfied this criterion in 1666. Where there was room for doubt about the technological or medical applicability of their knowledge, there was good reason for excluding Cartesians in the interests of avoiding philosophical controversy. Besides, the king was not enamoured of the merits of Cartesians and the Theology Faculty of the University of Paris was so sensitive to any endorsement of Jansenist sympathisers that it was easier for all concerned if the Cartesians were excluded from the academy during its initial period of development.

Cartesians in Controversy

The historical context in which the French school of Cartesians initially developed is as complex as the theological and political controversies which dominated the reign of Louis XIV. Once the new Académie royale des sciences was founded, those who supported a Cartesian science found themselves in a very vulnerable position. They were publicly associated with Jansenism and other theological unorthodoxies, and were therefore condemned by Church authorities both in France and in Rome. Thus Malebranche followed the pattern established earlier by Descartes when the *Traité de la nature et de la grace* (1680) was put on the Index of proscribed books in 1690. At the same time, they were strongly opposed by the universities and colleges because they challenged the authority on which traditional learning depended. Thirdly, the Cartesians were frequently rebuked and censored by the king or his representatives because they disturbed the peace of the realm and, perhaps more importantly, because they espoused a doctrine which at least implicitly contained the seeds of a democratic theory. And finally, they were not even officially sanctioned by the newly established Académie which included most of the leading French scientists of the period, even though many of those who were favoured with the title of academy member, such as Huygens or Fontenelle, had been significantly influenced by Descartes.

In a word, there were no institutional supports for those who were committed to developing Descartes's philosophy and applying it to newly discovered experimental results. In spite of that, Cartesianism prospered. During the ferment of new ideas in France in the second half of the seventeenth century, when the established wisdom of the schools and the authority of theologians were successfully challenged, Cartesian supporters defended and propagandized a distinctive concept of natural philosophy which contributed significantly to the eventual acceptance of mechanical philosophy in France. It is this concept of natural philosophy which is examined in the following chapters.

2

Seeds of Truth

MOST of the early Cartesians repeated the suggestion, made by Descartes, that our minds are created with certain 'seeds of truth' already implanted in them, so that getting to know the world around us is a matter of drawing out the implications of these cognitive seeds in a manner which at least suggests the rigour of logical inference. There is no doubt that the metaphor about seeds of truth derived ultimately from Plato, and that it was adopted in the French Cartesian tradition as a direct result of the influence of St Augustine.[1] The consistent use of this metaphor has obvious implications for the Cartesian concept of natural philosophy. It raises the question: did the Cartesians believe in a substantive theory of innate ideas or innately given knowledge? If the answer is yes, then what theory of 'scientific knowledge', consistent with innately known ideas, did they develop?

Pierre-Sylvain Régis—one of the most orthodox exponents of Cartesian science—addressed this issue in his *L'Usage de la raison et de la foy, ou l'accord de la foy et de la raison* (1704), where he wrote 'all our ideas come to us through sensation'.[2] On first sight this is far removed from the standard interpretation of Descartes as someone who espoused innate laws of nature, innate ideas, axioms, and general notions, and who allegedly merited the lengthy refutation of the innateness theory which is found in Book I of Locke's *Essay Concerning Human Understanding*.[3] Whether Descartes deserved a Lockian response or not, the available evidence suggests that later French Cartesians were extremely reluctant about any substantive innateness theory, and that they

---

[1] For the influence of St Augustine on Cartesianism in the 17th cent., see Gouhier (1978). Descartes's use of innate ideas is examined briefly in Clarke (1982), 48–58.

[2] *L'Usage*, p. 21.

[3] The likely targets of Locke's argument against innate ideas are identified in Yolton (1956), ch. 1.

devoted considerable time and energy to disputes about the origin
of ideas in experience, the representative character of the resulting
ideas, and the reliability of acquired ideas as mediators between the
mind and objective reality. In other words, the Cartesian school in
France somehow maintained the language of *sémences de vérité*
while, at the same time, defending the theory that our ideas of
physical nature arise in the mind as a result of external stimuli.

While it is relatively easy to say what the Cartesians did not mean
by 'innate ideas', the problem remains of explaining the positive
implications of the metaphor about seeds of truth and the tenacity
with which it was defended in the face of consistently good
arguments on the other side of the debate. The best clue to
answering this question is found in the thesis which the Cartesians
thought they were rejecting. It was a thesis summarized in the
formula: *nihil est in intellectu quod prius non fuerit in sensu*. The
important word here was the first one, *nihil*; in explaining their
inability to accept the scholastic thesis and in constantly reiterating
the need for innate ideas, Cartesian natural philosophers were
merely spelling out the implications of their theory of matter,
especially their negative claims about the limited powers of matter.
In other words, the requirement that we have innate ideas is the
complement to Descartes's theory about the extremely limited
powers of matter, including the matter which constitutes our perceptual organs and our brains.

Before developing this line of interpretation, we should look at
how various Cartesians responded to the suggestion that our ideas
are innate.

La Forge and Rohault

The first move in exploiting Descartes's suggestions about ideas
came in 1664, with the publication of *L'Homme de René
Descartes . . . avec les remarques de Louis de la Forge.*[4] Two years
later, La Forge published a complementary volume on the human
mind, the *Traité de l'esprit de l'homme et de ses facultez et fonctions,
et de son union avec le corps.*[5] He anticipated that the two books

---

[4] In the 1664 edn., Descartes's text is on pp. 109–70; La Forge's commentary
occupies pp. 171–408. It is abbreviated as *L'Homme*.

[5] Henceforth abbreviated to *Traité de l'esprit*.

together would provide a complete Cartesian anthropology. The most obvious feature of La Forge's discussion is the attempt to establish a radical distinction between mind and matter, even more clearly than in Descartes. This effort is reflected both in the structure of his work and in the definition of *idée*. Thus, the *Traité de l'esprit* proposed to clarify the nature of the mind first, independently of any relationship with the body, and to broach the issue of dualism only at a later stage when the immateriality of mind had been established beyond doubt. 'For whatever the union [of body and soul] might be, it cannot prevent the soul from being what it is [viz. a purely immaterial substance].'[6]

To prevent any ambiguity about the immateriality of the mind, La Forge distinguished between the material images of the brain and the immaterial ideas which are present only in the mind. Descartes had ambiguously called both of them 'ideas' (in *Le Monde*); in the interests of clarity, La Forge adds a footnote to Descartes's text: 'the word idea can be understood in two ways, according to M. Descartes, namely for the inner form of our concepts, or for the way in which the [animal] spirits emerge from the gland . . .'[7] In the *Traité de l'esprit*, La Forge reserves the term *idée* exclusively for states of the immaterial mind, and calls the brain events which stimulate or accompany such ideas *espèces corporelles*.[8]

Once these distinctions are clearly drawn, the relationship between *idées* and *espèces corporelles* becomes immediately problematic, and a question arises about the possibility of having ideas without their physical counterparts in the brain. Descartes had distinguished three degrees of sensation: the physical effect of an external stimulus on our sensory organs, the perception (by the mind) of this physical effect, and the judgements which we spontaneously make on the occasion of such perceptions.[9] La Forge repeats these distinctions, with the caveat that the first is not, properly speaking, a sensation at all.[10] The physical stimulation of the senses is, therefore, the efficient cause of many of the ideas which occur in the mind. More accurately, it is God 'the author of the union of soul and body, [who causes] . . . all those ideas which

[6] Ibid. 111.   [7] *L'Homme*, p. 262.
[8] *Traité de l'esprit*, pp. 76, 158, 165.
[9] Sixth Replies to Objections, in *Œuvres*, vii. 436–7; *Philosophical Writings of Descartes* (Cottingham *et al.*), ii. 294–5.
[10] *L'Homme*, p. 262; *Traité de l'esprit*, p. 249.

we have without the use of our will, on the occasion of those species which are traced on the gland by some [external] cause'.[11]

The language of an *occasional* causal relationship first enters the Cartesian tradition in this context.[12] The principal reason offered by La Forge for the new terminology—a reason which was subsequently exploited by Malebranche—is that there is no *rapport* between *espèces corporelles* and ideas.[13] The incommensurability of the physical and the spiritual can only be overcome by a divine arrangement which unites body and soul in an otherwise unnatural union. At the same time, the metaphysical misgivings on La Forge's part about the way in which the mind–body union is achieved by God have no significant influence on his theory of sensation; physical stimuli are always followed by appropriate sensory perceptions. Despite their metaphysical incommensurability, mental ideas and physical brain-patterns are constantly conjoined by the power of God.

Any attempt on our part to explain this extraordinary mind–body interaction is recognized by La Forge as nothing more than a hypothesis. After lengthy discussion of the role of the pineal gland as the locus of the connection between body and mind, he comments: 'if there is any difficulty in accepting this opinion as a reliable truth, may I at least be permitted to use it as the most probable and intelligible hypothesis among all those which have so far been suggested for explaining all our animal functions.'[14] Even if the hypothesis fails, the certainty of mind–body interaction is assured by our 'sense' or our 'experience'.[15] In other words, the spirituality of the soul is certain, and the irreducibility of ideas to brain-states is equally certain. At the same time, we are convinced by our own inner experience that mind–body interaction of some kind takes place. To provide a coherent account of how physical stimuli result in spiritual ideas, we can do no better than speculate about mind–body interaction; whatever account we offer is unavoidably hypothetical.

The divinely established union of body and mind 'consists in a mutual and reciprocal dependence of the thoughts of one and of the motions of the other, and in the mutual interaction of their actions and passions . . .'[16] Thus, sensory stimuli result in spiritual

---

[11] *Traité de l'esprit*, p. 178.
[12] See Gouhier (1926), 89.
[13] *L'Homme*, p. 262.
[14] *Traité de l'esprit*, pp. 234–5.
[15] Ibid. 214–15, 224–7.
[16] Ibid. 210.

thoughts; and the mental activity of imagining something results in corresponding physical images in the brain. However, it is only with respect to the imagination or, more accurately, with respect to the brain when it functions as the organ of the imagination, that the Saumur physician is willing to endorse the scholastic axiom that all our ideas originate in sense.

It is for these reasons that it is true to say, not that *nihil est in intellectu quod prius non fuerit in sensu*, but rather that there are no species imprinted on the organ of the imagination which do not derive from some species which came through the senses; but please note that I am only speaking of corporeal species, and not of ideas of the mind.[17]

The obvious exception to ideas derived from sense are innate ideas.

When using the language of innate ideas, La Forge repeats Descartes's unsuccessful attempts to explain what he means by the term 'innate'. Descartes had claimed in *L'Homme* that the theory of innate ideas does not imply that a child is born with certain thoughts or ideas actually in his mind; innate ideas 'are acquired and they are not natural, if by the term "natural" one means that they are in the substance of the soul as in a reservoir, in the way in which we arrange pictures in a gallery to look at them whenever we wish'.[18] Innate ideas are only in the mind potentially;[19] the soul has such ideas in the sense that 'we are born with the faculty of producing them whenever we wish'.[20] Descartes had also claimed that innate ideas do not originate in the senses. The ambiguity of the Cartesian account of 'innateness' is left unresolved by La Forge when he quotes Descartes's response to Regius.[21] However, there is some progress in clarifying the innateness theory when the Saumur commentator suggests that, in an important sense, all ideas are equally innate; because there is no *rapport* between the physical motions of small parts of matter and the thoughts which they occasion in our minds, it must be the case that the principal and proximate cause of all our ideas is the mind itself. Apart from this claim about the irreducibility of thoughts to brain-states, most of the ideas which are relevant for physical science are assumed to have been generated in the mind on the occasion of appropriate sensory stimulation.

The innateness thesis, understood as the irreducibility of thoughts

---

[17] Ibid. 268.
[18] Ibid. 181; cf. also p. 293.
[19] Ibid. 181.
[20] Ibid. 293.
[21] Ibid. 181; also pp. 171–3.

to brain-states and the incommensurability of perceptions and sensory stimuli, is the metaphysical underpinning of the Cartesian distinction between primary and secondary qualities. Descartes had made this distinction in *Le Monde* about 1632; 'even though everyone is commonly persuaded that the ideas that are the objects of our thought are wholly like the objects from which they proceed, nevertheless I can see no reasoning that assures us that this is the case.'[22] The considerations which follow this text in *Le Monde* include the standard examples used by Galileo to show, for example, that a tickling sensation does not resemble any 'cause of tickling' and, more generally, that the properties of external objects do not resemble our sensations of them. It is relatively easy, on Cartesian assumptions about the mind, to support the conclusion that none of our sensations or ideas resembles the things which they denote.

Following the lead of Descartes and La Forge, the distinction between primary and secondary qualities is systematically developed by Jacques Rohault in his *Traité de physique* (1671). Rohault repeats the occasionalist theory of perception which had been introduced by La Forge; 'such is the nature of our soul, that particular motions of the body to which it is united, are the occasions of particular perceptions in it [*i.e. the soul*].'[23] However, the metaphysical issue of incommensurability is not a foremost consideration in Rohault's *Traité de physique*, and he seldom discusses it. Instead, he exploits the Cartesians' insight about the unrepresentative character of secondary qualities to highlight the foolishness of scholastic inferences, based on perceptions, to judgements about the physical causes of perceptions. The Preface to the *Traité de physique* explains that he has committed a large part of Book I to explaining qualities. 'The reason of which is, because . . . hereby we are seasonably freed from a popular error . . . viz. the ascribing their own sensations to the objects which cause them, and the considering these sensations as qualities in the objects.'[24]

---

[22] *Œuvres*, xi. 3; Eng. trans., *The World*, by M. S. Mahoney, pp. 1–3. For the non-resemblance of brain-patterns or ideas and their causes, see also *Œuvres*, vi. 109, 130, 131.
    [23] I quote Rohault's *Traité de physique* from the Eng. trans. of John and Samuel Clarke, *A System of Natural Philosophy* (1723), 2 vols. To avoid possible confusion with Regis's *Système* or La Forge's *Traité de l'esprit*, all references to this work by Rohault will include the French title, *Traité de physique*. The quotation above is from i. 248.   [24] Ibid., unpaginated preface.

The distinction between sensations and their objective causes is reinforced in the discussion of heat, cold, taste, sound, and so on, in Book I of Rohault's *Traité de physique*. For example, in explaining heat and cold, the author writes:

These two words have each of them two different meanings: For first, by *heat* and *cold*, we understand two particular sensations in us, which in some measure resemble those which we call pain and pleasure, such as we feel when we touch ice, or when we go near a fire. Secondly, by *heat* and *cold*, we understand also the power which bodies have to raise the forementioned sensations in us.[25]

The same distinction is repeated for taste, with the Lockian qualification that it denotes 'something, I know not what, in the meat and drink in which the power of raising this sensation . . . consists'.[26] Likewise for smells, sounds, and light; in each case there is a distinction between what can be directly experienced, and what can be described initially only in terms of the powers of certain objects to cause sensations in us.[27]

The distinction between primary and secondary qualities immediately confers a unique and exclusive epistemic role on experience: 'After what has been observed when we spoke of tastes and smells, it is mindless to say that sound, taken in the former sense of the word [i.e. as a sensation], cannot be described, nor known any other way but by experience.'[28] It follows just as evidently that whatever is claimed about the powers which cause our sensations will have to be based on some type of inference from our sensations. The hypothetical and relatively uncertain character of these inferences is discussed further below.

Thus the theory of ideas which was launched as the official Cartesian doctrine by La Forge and Rohault contains the following elements: (*a*) the mind, as a non-material substance, is the exclusive locus of all thoughts, perceptions, or sensations, of anything of which we are directly aware in our experience. (*b*) the immateriality of the mind makes it incommensurable with any sensory stimuli. Therefore what would otherwise be classified as a causal relationship between sensory stimuli and sensations must be redescribed in the language of occasional causes. The correspondence of types of sensory stimuli with types of mental ideas is arranged by God.

---

[25] Ibid. i. 151.
[27] Ibid. i. 179, 183, 196–7.
[26] Ibid. i. 169.
[28] Ibid. i. 183.

There is an important sense, then, in which the events which take place in our sensory organs are not an adequate explanation of the ideas which arise in the mind. (c) the qualitative disparity between ideas and perceptions on the one hand and, on the other, what we must hypothesize as their occasional causes both facilitates the development of a non-Aristotelian physics and introduces new problems about the representative character of ideas.

This account of ideas was also endorsed by other supporters as orthodox Cartesianism. Gerauld de Cordemoy devoted his two major publications to the distinction of body and soul, and to the irreducibility of human language to the 'natural signs' used by animals. The *Discernement du corps et de l'ame* was published in 1666, and was followed two years later by the *Discours physique de la parole*. Despite the distinctiveness of the soul as non-material, the union of body and soul is said to be 'much greater and more perfect than that of two bodies'.[29] The closeness of the union is sufficient to support a necessary connection (even if it is occasional) between some thoughts and brain-states. 'Natural signs are those by which, because of the necessary connection which obtains between the passions of the soul and the motions of the body, one can know the different states of the soul externally.'[30] The 'necessity' of this connection does not make the coincidence of brain-states and their corresponding ideas any less occasional than in Rohault or La Forge. Hence, for Cordemoy, the word 'sound' may mean either of two distinct things; 'one is the manner in which the air, striking the nerve of our ear, shakes our brain; and the other is the sensation of our soul on the occasion of that agitation of the brain.'[31]

Claude Gadroys (1642–78) maintains an equally disjointed picture of problematic relations between two incommensurable substances, mind and body. 'Since thought is spiritual and motion is material, in themselves they have no *rapport*. They are only related because God willed it . . .'[32] Once these incompatible elements are joined by God, however, 'the mere motion of a body can stimulate a sensation in the soul'.[33] Gadroys claims, in line with the other Cartesians, that the words traditionally used to describe the

---

[29] *Discernement, Œuvres*, ed. P. Clair (1968), p. 146.   [30] Ibid. 235.
[31] *A Philosophical Discourse Concerning Speech*, ed. Karl Vitti (1974), p. 98.
[32] *Discours sur les influences des astres, selon les principes de M. Descartes* (1671), p. 123. On p. 131 Gadroys says: 'there is no proportion between the material and the spiritual.'   [33] Ibid. 120.

resulting sensations are ambiguous between our inner sensations and the objective causes which stimulate them in the mind, that is, between primary and secondary qualities.[34] The Oratorian priest, Nicolas Poisson, published his commentary on Descartes's method in 1671, in which he also tried his hand at clarifying the independent status of ideas.[35] Poisson's objections were aimed at what he took to be the naïve empiricism of school philosophy. He rejected the principle that 'nothing enters into the mind which has not passed through the senses' because, among other things, it was one of the Sacramentarians' assumptions when they claim that the bread used in the Eucharist is just what it appears to be, namely bread.[36] As in Rohault's theology of the Eucharist, Poisson depends on the claim that our ideas of secondary qualities do not correspond to the primary qualities which cause them in order to challenge the apparent data of our senses when we seem to see bread after the conclusion of the liturgy. From the perspective of the faith, what we see is not bread at all, despite its appearances.[37]

Thus most Cartesians agreed about the main features of their theory of ideas, including the ontological irreducibility of ideas to brain-states and the complementary thesis about the unrepresentative character of our perceptions *vis-à-vis* their likely causes. The only exception to this near unanimity about ideas was Nicolas Malebranche.

Malebranche and his Critics

Nicolas Malebranche was, like Poisson, a member of the Oratory. He made one of the most original and controversial contributions to the theory of ideas which was developed by the Cartesian school in France. Malebranche's theory develops from Descartes's definitions of matter and mind, and he attempts to work out the logical

---

[34] *Système du monde* (1675), p. 215.

[35] *Commentaire ou remarques sur la méthode de Mr Descartes* (1671).

[36] Ibid., unpaginated preface.

[37] Poisson develops what looks like a scholastic theory in order to distinguish different levels of abstraction in our ideas. At one end of the scale are perceptions of the colour or shape of an object actually present to our senses. At the other end of the scale are the ideas of God, of the angels, of substance, or of existence, because these involve a degree of metaphysical abstraction which is not present in merely perceiving the properties of some object. See *Commentaire*, p. 138.

implications of these suggestions. The most basic feature of the relationship between the mind and matter is that they are reciprocally incommensurable. Malebranche argues that mind and matter have no *rapport*,[38] have no essential or necessary *rapport*,[39] and have no *proportion* between them.[40] Whatever these claims mean, they cannot imply that there is no relation between ideas and brain-states because, as will be clear from passages cited below, Malebranche accepts that there is a relation of occasional or physical causality between the two disparate kinds of entity. One should also note that there is a very significant difference between a contingent and a necessary *rapport*, and that this distinction figures prominently in Malebranche's discussion of causality (see below, Chapter 4).

The *Traité de la nature et de la grace* helps clarify what is meant by the term *rapport*, when it claims that 'there is no *rapport* between the finite and the infinite'.[41] This presumably means that the finite and the infinite have no common factor and are therefore incommensurable. In a similar way, Malebranche's understanding of the concepts 'mind' and 'matter' is such that each one is defined by the negation of the defining features of the other, and in this sense they have no common property by which they may be compared. If they were left to what one might call their natural condition, therefore, nothing which occurs in matter would affect the mind and vice versa. God has joined the mind of each person with a body in such a way, however, that the two parts of the new composite being operate harmoniously together. Since the two complementary substances have no natural *rapport*, their union can only have been established by the will of God.[42] It follows that this

---

[38] I quote Malebranche's *Recherche de la vérité* from the Eng. trans. by T. M. Lennon and P. J. Olscamp (1980) (abbrev. as *Search After Truth*). The reference above is from vol. i of his *Œuvres complètes* (1962), p. 142, and from *Search After Truth*, p. 102. See also *Recherche*, iii. 226 (*Search After Truth*, p. 669), and *Conversations chrétiennes*, iv. 28. There are few monographs in English on Malebranche; those available include Church (1931), Connell (1967), Radner (1978), and McCracken (1983). The situation is not significantly better for books written in French; among those worth consulting are Robinet (1955) and Rodis-Lewis (1963).

[39] *Conversations chrétiennes*, in *Œuvres complètes*, iv. 78; and *Dialogues on Metaphysics*, Eng. trans. by W. Doney (1980), p. 179.

[40] *Search After Truth*, p. 223 (the French text uses the term *proportion*). Cf. *Meditations chrétienes et métaphysiques* (1683), in *Œuvres complètes*, x. 38–9, for Malebranche's attempt to explain the crucial term *rapport*.

[41] *Œuvres complètes*, v. 11.

[42] *Search After Truth*, pp. 183, 575; *Dialogues on Metaphysics*, p. 281.

divinely arranged union cannot be discovered by reason,[43] and that as soon as the union is dissolved 'God will no longer have the self-imposed obligation of giving us sensations that must correspond to brain traces'.[44]

This occasionalist coincidence of brain-states and their corresponding ideas is, on first sight, the standard Cartesian theory. Malebranche gave it a new twist at this point and thereby provoked a lengthy debate about the status of ideas which involved Antoine Arnauld, Simon Foucher, and Régis among his critics. The principal source of disagreement among Cartesian philosophers was the Oratorian's distinction between objective ideas and subjective modifications of the individual mind. This distinction is central to the *Search After Truth* and is often repeated in texts such as the following:

When we perceive something sensible, two things are found in our perception: *sensation* [in French, *sentiment*] and pure *idea*. The sensation is a modification of our soul, and it is God who causes it in us. . . . As for the idea found in conjunction with the sensation, it is in God, and we see it because it pleases God to reveal it to us. God joins the sensation to the idea when objects are present so that we may believe them to be present and that we may have all the feelings and passions that we should have in relation to them.[45]

Why did Malebranche introduce a distinction between ideas (in the mind of God) and the mental states of the individual perceiver? The initial motivation came from his concern about the failure of mental events to represent accurately the physical causes which trigger them in the mind. 'There is nothing in the objects of our senses similar to the sensations [*sentiments*] we have of them. These objects correspond to their ideas, but . . . have no affinity with our sensations.'[46] On this point he was simply repeating the standard Cartesian theory of a radical dissimilarity between primary and secondary qualities.[47] By focusing on secondary qualities, Malebranche was persuaded to disqualify them completely as a basis for objective human knowledge. He explained his understanding of *sentiment* by repeating Descartes's distinction between different uses of the term which denote various stages in the causality of a particular perceptual experience. Thus the term *sentiment* may apply to: (*a*) the

---

[43] *Search After Truth*, pp. 182, 365–6.   [44] Ibid. 309.
[45] Ibid. 234.   [46] *Dialogues on Metaphysics*, p. 71.
[47] *Search After Truth*, pp. 54–5, 441–2; *Dialogues on Metaphysics*, p. 63–75.

action of an external object on the human sensory faculties; (b) the physical effect (passion) caused by the external stimulus in any sensory organ, for example, the motion of the tympanum in the ear; (c) the mental perception of this physical effect, for example, the experience of sound or colour which occurs in the soul as a direct result of mind–body union; and (d) the natural or spontaneous judgements which we are likely to make on the occasion of having such experiences.[48] The need for a category of pure ideas emerged from Malebranche's analysis of the epistemic value of sensation in the sense of (c) above. He argues that, if Descartes's arguments about secondary qualities are well founded, then we never have any reason to believe that the states of the soul which are caused as a direct result of sensory stimulation are a reliable guide to claims about objective states of affairs.

Given this analysis of sensations, the Oratorian metaphysician argues as follows. We must assume that a non-deceiving God makes it possible for us to have objective, reliable knowledge. Therefore we should examine the various ways in which God might realize this objective and we should choose the theory which seems to be most plausible. Malebranche proceeds to list the alternatives available, and he excludes each one in turn until only one remains, namely, the hypothesis that we can come to have objective knowledge by means of the ideas which are in God's mind. Among the options excluded in the course of the argument are the following: (a) that ideas are modifications of each individual mind which are occasioned by external stimuli, and (b) that ideas are innate in the mind of each individual.

Malebranche argues against the standard Cartesian theory of ideas as follows: all changes in a finite being are finite. Hence, mental events are finite. The idea of extension is infinite. Therefore the idea of extension is not a mental event.[49] This argument is so obviously fallacious that one must assume the real motivation for Malebranche's theory lies elsewhere. The stumbling block in accepting some variation of Descartes's theory was not just the 'infinity' of some of our ideas; it was much more the assumption, already mentioned, that subjective mental events cannot represent objective states of affairs in a manner which would guarantee access to knowledge which is objective, true, and timeless.[50]

---

[48] Search After Truth, pp. 52–3.   [49] Œuvres complètes, xvii. 1. 283.
[50] Cf. Search After Truth, pp. 238–9.

The argument against innate ideas is directed at a very un-sophisticated version of the theory, according to which human minds are created by God with a supply of ideas already fully formed and present in the mind of each person, like a store of pictures. Malebranche's objection also assumes that all our ideas are innate, rather than a special subset of them which might be central to human knowledge. The argument against innate ideas, understood in this way, relies on a principle of simplicity. Malebranche argues that any theory about the origin of our ideas must invoke God, at some stage, as cause of our ideas or as guarantor of their veracity. Given that God is involved one way or the other, we should assume that he acts in the simplest way possible. However, if God provided each individual with an almost infinite supply of actual innate ideas, he would be duplicating a process which could be accomplished more economically by an alternative method, namely, by providing each individual with access to a single set of ideas in the mind of God. If one must choose between innate actual ideas in this sense, and ideas in the mind of God, Malebranche argues that we should endorse the latter theory for reasons of simplicity.

Since all other alternatives fail, Malebranche concludes that we must assume that God has the ideas we need for objective knowledge, and that we know things as they really are by somehow knowing God's ideas.[51] In the course of explaining and defending this suggestion, Malebranche had occasion to make some telling criticisms of Cartesian theory. For example, he insisted against Arnauld's objections that there is a distinction between 'having a sensation' of something and having an idea of it; thus there is an obvious difference between having an idea of sorrow in the sense of feeling sad on the death of a friend, and merely thinking about the concept of sorrow in a philosophical discussion.[52] But these insights do little to minimize the radical character of Malebranche's central claim about human knowledge to the effect that objective knowledge of reality is possible only because of the correspondence between two parallel systems of ideas, the mental events in the mind of the perceiver and ideas in the mind of God. The unreliability of the former and the unacceptability of a theory of innate ideas made

---

[51] This may be an adaptation, on Malebranche's part, of scholastic theories of angelic knowledge. For a full discussion of this interpretation, see Connell (1967).
[52] Œuvres complètes, vi. 55.

recourse to God's ideas seem the only available access to objective, certain knowledge.

Despite the radical change from orthodox Cartesianism which is involved in the introduction of quasi-angelic ideas in God's mind, and the theory that reliable human knowledge presupposes some kind of access to such divine ideas, Malebranche continues to endorse the standard Cartesian understanding of sensation, and of the coincidence of sensory events with perceptual events in the mind. Thus, he argues in the *Search After Truth*:

We are not pure intelligences. All the dispositions of our soul produce certain dispositions in our body, as the dispositions of our body excite similar dispositions in our soul. It is not that the soul can receive absolutely nothing except through the body, but that it is so united to the body that it cannot receive any change in its modifications without the body also receiving some change. True, it can be enlightened or receive new ideas without the body necessarily playing some role; but this is because pure ideas are not modifications of the soul, as I have proved elsewhere. Here I am only speaking about sensible ideas, for these ideas involve a sensation, and every sensation is a mode that moves and concerns the soul.[53]

This leaves us with two quite different accounts of what takes place in the mind. There are the sensations or perceptual events of which Descartes, La Forge, and Rohault spoke. These are genuine spiritual events in the mind, and they are accompanied by corresponding physical events in the sensory organs and in the flow of animal spirits. Secondly, there is Malebranche's new category of pure ideas which properly belong in the mind of God and are somehow involved in any instance of human knowing that is objectively true.

This raises questions about the relationship between the two complementary types of idea, and about the respective role of each in any coherent account of scientific knowledge. Malebranche fails to integrate the two sources of knowledge into a unified account. In fact, at the conclusion of Books I–III of the *Search After Truth*, he suggests that we keep the distinction constantly in mind between the two types of knowledge. One kind of knowledge depends on God's ideas, whereas the other is based on sensations. Accordingly, we must distinguish between the objective condition of external objects and the ways in which they affect our senses.

Our sensations and imaginings must be carefully distinguished from our

[53] *Search After Truth*, p. 599.

pure ideas, and the former must guide our judgments about the relations external bodies have with our own, without our using them to discover the truths they always confound; and we must use the mind's pure ideas to discover these truths, without using them to make judgments about the relations external bodies have with our own, because these ideas never have enough scope to represent them exactly.[54]

The distinction between 'knowledge in relation to us' and 'knowledge of objective states of affairs', corresponding to perception-based versus idea-based knowledge, assumes the possibility of a purely theoretical science based on ideas. For example, Malebranche argues that if one could know all the motions and figures of the human body and of a piece of fruit, one could then calculate whether or not eating the fruit would cure a sick man. However, he also thinks that it is impossible for us to have such detailed knowledge. Faute de mieux, we have just to eat the fruit and see what happens.[55] By contrast, an ideal 'rational medicine' would be the best possible, and would not rely on the experimental results of eating the fruit.

Descartes's dualism of mind and body has thus been cultivated by Malebranche into yielding a corresponding dualism of two kinds of knowledge. One is an ideal science which relies exclusively on pure (divine) ideas, while the other is based on the data of perceptual experience. Yet, despite this extreme separation of science from experiential data, there is still no room even in Malebranche's theory for innate ideas.

Antoine Arnauld (1612–94) wrote *Vraies et fausses idées* (1683) in response to Malebranche's theory of ideas. Arnauld well expressed the likely reaction of many modern readers when he said that he never heard such a ridiculous theory as the suggestion that we see all things in God.[56] Among the many objections he puts to Malebranche, the most fundamental is that God's ideas are redundant in explaining human knowledge.[57] Malebranche's model of a mind which is thinking of A involves the following three distinct elements: (i) A, the object; (ii) the idea of A, or what Arnauld calls an *être représentatif*; and (iii) some mental act on the part of the human thinker by means of which he is aware of the relevant *être représentatif*. If the perceiver's mind must be modified in some way to distinguish those minds which are thinking of A from those that

[54] Ibid. 263.
[56] *Œuvres complètes*, xxxix. 237.
[55] Ibid. 263.
[57] Ibid. xxix. 222–6.

are not, then this mental modification can play the role of the idea of *A* and, by Occam's principle, an *être représentatif* is redundant. Besides, the extra entities introduced by Malebranche not only fail to explain how we have ideas; they derive, in Arnauld's view, from the intentional entities of scholastic philosophy and this must have been about the worst thing one could say of any dedicated Cartesian.[58] By contrast, Arnauld's own theory is quite clear: 'I give notice, once and for all, that *idea* and *perception* are only the same thing in my dictionary.'[59]

Arnauld also makes some telling comments on the logic of Malebranche's argument in favour of the vision-in-God theory. He frequently charges his Cartesian opponent with ambiguity. The claim that 'we do not perceive objects which are external to us *par eux-mêmes*' is ambiguous between two readings: it may mean that objects cannot cause ideas in us by their own power or agency, a thesis with which Arnauld is sympathetic; or it may mean that objects can only be perceived if some kind of representative entity mediates between us and the object. To understand it in this second way is to beg the very question at issue, rather than to make an uncontentious claim with which others agree.[60] Malebranche's ambivalence about the meaning of *par eux-mêmes* is reflected in a corresponding ambiguity in his use of the terms *idée* and *pensée*. Sometimes these words mean what everyone is already agreed on, that is, that we have ideas when we think; at other times, however, they camouflage the introduction of new entities which mediate between our mental acts and the objects of which they are the ideas.

Simon Foucher (1644–96) was one of the first of his contemporaries to outline objections to the *Search After Truth*; in fact, he rushed his *Critique de la recherche de la vérité* into print even before the second part of the *Search After Truth* was published. Foucher focused his objections on the lack of resemblance between ideas and objects and, on the basis of their non-resemblance, he challenged the alleged capacity of such ideas to represent objects. The lack of resemblance follows immediately from the Cartesian theory that matter and spirit have nothing in common; without any possibility of common properties, therefore, non-material ideas could not possibly 'resemble' physical objects: 'these [external] objects contain nothing which is similar to what they produce in us,

---

[58] *Œuvres complètes*, xxxix. 190–7.   [59] Ibid. xxxix. 207.
[60] Ibid. xxxix. 210–16.

because matter is incapable of having modes of existence which are similar to those of which the soul is capable; . . . [therefore] one must also agree that the soul cannot contain anything which is similar to those modes which are found in matter.'[61] Unfortunately, the same conclusion applies equally in the case of Malebranche's ideas. Whatever their mysterious nature, they are also incommensurable with matter and therefore bear no resemblance to its changing conditions. This argument can also be reversed; if 'pure ideas' could somehow represent objects without resembling them, then so could modifications of an individual's mind:

If it is possible that ideas, which are not at all similar to certain objects, can represent them, then there is no reason to claim that the modes of being which we receive through the senses fail to represent the objects which cause them, no matter how dissimilar they may be. Either our ideas can represent, without being similar, or they cannot![62]

Foucher's point about the lack of resemblance of ideas to the objects they represent is well taken; indeed, the alleged relation between God's ideas and creatures in the Augustinian tradition never implied that creatures 'resemble' God's ideas. The motivation for demanding some kind of resemblance relation should be sought elsewhere; as John Yolton has argued, it had much more to do with the emerging optical theories of the seventeenth century than with any intrinsic requirements of a theory of ideas.[63]

The controversy within the Cartesian tradition about Malebranche's ideas in God involved not only Arnauld and Foucher, as already mentioned, but also Pierre-Sylvain Régis. In his contribution to the debate, Régis returns to a theory of mind and ideas which could have been copied almost verbatim from Descartes. Régis's basic assumption about ideas is that mind and matter are so closely united, that mind is almost 'confounded and mixed' with the body.[64] This physical union of body and soul is not remotely like a pilot in a ship;[65] rather, it 'consists in the actual dependence of all the thoughts of the soul on some motions of the body, and of some motions of the body on some thoughts of the soul'.[66]

---

[61] *Critique de la recherche de la vérité*, pp. 45–6.　　[62] Ibid. 51.

[63] The influence of optical images on perceptual theories in the 17th cent. is examined in detail in Yolton (1984*a*).

[64] *Système de philosophie* (1690), i. 121. Régis's principal work is abbreviated to *Système* in subsequent references.

[65] Ibid. 122, 123.　　[66] Ibid. 122.

The theory that we see all things in God could only be endorsed, therefore, in a very weak sense; namely, that God is the primary cause of all the thoughts which we have.[67] God's primary causality is compatible with physical objects exercising a genuine causal influence on our minds; those objects which stimulate our sensory organs can be said to be truly efficacious in causing our ideas. It is not a valid objection against this theory to say that physical objects are so dissimilar to ideas that they could not cause them; if that were the case, Régis argues, God could not cause anything which is not similar to himself. Experience shows that many things do indeed cause effects which are like themselves, as when one fire causes another fire; however, some causes give rise to dissimilar effects, as when a fire causes a heap of ashes. So there is no a priori reason why physical stimuli may not cause non-physical ideas in the mind.

The causal relation between ideas and physical stimuli is known by expérience.[68] How this relation is possible and how the soul is united with the body are issues we cannot explain, except by assuming that God is able to unite such apparently incommensurable substances by genuine causal connections. 'One must also think that ideas and sensations of the soul depend necessarily on four principles, namely: on God, as their first efficient cause; on objects, as their exemplary cause; on the action of objects on the organs of the body, as their secondary efficient cause; and on the soul itself, as their material cause.'[69]

Régis's commitment to an experiential basis for all ideas is underlined in his opposition to Malebranche's entendement pur, and by the weak version of innateness which he defends. As in Arnauld's Vraies et fausses idées, ideas are nothing more for Régis than states or conditions of the individual's mind. 'I say that the ideas which the soul uses to perceive bodies are nothing but simple modifications of the mind . . . the ideas which the soul needs in order to know God and other spirits are not different from its own substance.'[70] These mental states are inextricably bound up with corresponding physical states of the brain; therefore, not only are there no 'pure ideas' in Malebranche's sense, but there is no pure understanding either.

[67] Système, Bk. ii, part 11, ch. 14, pp. 184–8: 'In what sense can one claim that we see physical bodies in God?'
[68] Ibid. 124.
[69] Ibid. 169.   [70] Ibid. 190, 191.

It is certain that, according to the laws of the union of body and mind already established, such a so-called pure intellection is incompatible with the nature of the soul . . . the hypothesis of modern philosophers who admit a pure understanding, that is an understanding which acts independently of the body, can have no solid foundation. . . . It is therefore without any basis that modern philosophers assert that there is anything in the understanding which has not passed through the senses . . .[71]

To be consistent with this position, Régis must adopt a very weak version of innateness; that is exactly what he does. 'All our ideas come to us through sensation, with this qualification; some of them come immediately, and others come only mediately, that is, by reflection . . . In the same way the idea of God comes through sensation . . . sensible objects are the efficient cause of the idea of God which is insensible . . .'[72] The ideas which come immediately through sensation are the experiences of heat, light, etc.; from these we infer or construct our concepts of distinct physical objects such as a fire, a lamp, etc. This inferential move is a function of the imagination. Régis is willing to admit that we do not get an idea of God or of our own soul directly through sensation and, for that reason, one could call such concepts innate. On the other hand, he is quick to qualify this concession lest it imply the absurd thesis that we are born with some ideas already formed in the mind. 'When I say that the ideas of God, of the soul and of the body are innate, I do not thereby mean that they are independent of the body; I only mean to say that these ideas are always in the soul explicitly or implicitly . . .'[73] The implicit presence of some ideas in the soul is another way of saying that the mind, by reflecting on its sensory experiences, can generate the idea of a spiritual mind and that the idea of God can be constructed, in turn, from the idea of the soul. The starting-point of the process of acquiring the idea of God is— however it may be further explicated—the sensory experiences which Régis thinks demand the concept of mind–body interaction for their adequate explanation.

Thus the controversy within Cartesianism about the merits of Malebranche's theory was concerned with the plausibility of introducing a new type of idea, in God's mind, as a necessary prerequisite for objective knowledge of the world. All the contributors, including Malebranche, agreed that there is no place in the

[71] L'Usage, 16, 106–7.   [72] Ibid. 21 and 15.
[73] Ibid. 27. Cf. Système, i. 171, for simple ideas which are 'born with the soul'.

Cartesian account of ideas for any actual, innate ideas in the human mind. At the same time, they also agreed that all genuine ideas are, as non-material events, irreducible to and incommensurable with the physical events in the human body which occasion their occurrence in the mind.

Innate Ideas

The extreme reluctance of all the Cartesians, from La Forge to Régis, to consider any substantive innateness theory leads one to suspect that they possibly misnamed whatever intuition they hoped to express in the rhetoric of innate ideas. Descartes's analogy about a predisposition to suffer from gout was generously quoted to imply that the mind has innate ideas only in potency, or that it is created in such a way that it has a disposition to acquire certain ideas when appropriately stimulated by the relevant secondary causes.[74] The talk about potential ideas, while it helped avoid naïve pictures of innate ideas built into the mind from birth, failed to provide any positive explanation of what was meant by a theory which was defended consistently in the Cartesian tradition against all sides. The failure to get the message across even to sympathetic readers is partly explained by the suggestion that only some ideas—such as the idea of God or of the soul—are innate and that our ideas of physical objects are either not innate at all or, at least, are not as innate as the idea of the soul. Unfortunately, this was a misleading cue for readers because the fundamental inspiration of the innateness theory implied that all human ideas must be innate. This comprehensive claim about all ideas is found in Descartes, La Forge, and each of the Cartesians who have been examined to this point; however, the clearest statement of the thesis is found in Antoine le Grand.

Le Grand was a Belgian ex-patriate who assumed the mission of translating French Cartesian philosophy into a form which would be intelligible to his London audience; so while he is not strictly a French Cartesian, he is a reliable interpreter of official Cartesian

[74] Cf. Rohault's use of the term 'innate' to describe the power of an illuminated body to cause our sensations of light; innate light is contrasted with 'secondary' or 'derivative' light which is the effect this innate power has on the medium through which it is transmitted (*Traité de physique*, i. 197).

theory. His works can be easily recognized as a rather uncreative, *haute vulgarisation* which merely repeats the most common theories or philosophical theses which had been defended by mainland European Cartesians. The English translation of the *Institutio Philosophiae* (1672) was included in a compendious survey of Cartesian philosophy, *An Entire Body of Philosophy*, which was published in London in 1694. In Part IX, chapter 4, Le Grand introduced the question 'whether there are any innate or inbred ideas in the Human Mind'.[75]

Before answering this question in the affirmative, he repeats the Cartesian distinction between adventitious, fictitious, and innate ideas, where 'adventitious' means 'those which are receiv'd from things transmitted by the Senses'.[76] One is very surprised, in the subsequent discussion, to find that these same adventitious ideas are used as a primary example of innate ideas!

For to begin from things most obvious, it is most certain, that the ideas which we perceive by any sense, are inbred, and can no way proceed from the things themselves by any similitude. For he that well understands, by what way the perception of pain, for example, is excited in the soul, will easily be convinc'd, that the idea of pain hath no more affinity with that nervous disposition of parts, by whose means the soul frames an idea of pain, than that deprav'd affection hath an affinity with a sword, by which a wound hath been inflicted into a body; . . . and consequently when the sense of pain, and other perceptions . . . are excited in the Minds by no other species, which have affinity with them, it must needs be affirm'd, that these sort of ideas which have no affinity, are innate or inbred to it.[77]

The context of this argument is clear. If even adventitious ideas which derive from sensory experience are necessarily innate in some sense, then *a fortiori* those ideas which do not appear to originate in sensory experience at all, such as the concept of consciousness, must also be classified as innate.[78] In other words, the acts of awareness which Cartesians call ideas are irreducible to the sensory stimuli and motions of animal spirits which cause or occasion their occurrence in the mind. The ultimate justification for this almost self-evident truth was the metaphysical incommensurability of mind and matter.

---

[75] *Entire Body of Philosophy*, p. 327.   [76] Ibid. 327.
[77] Ibid. 327. Cf. ibid. 8, where the ideas 'of all other things that are not material, are inborn in us' in potency.
[78] See *Entire Body of Philosophy*, pp. 7, 23, 57, where the ideas of the self and of God are said to be 'born with us'.

It follows from the irreducibility of mental states to brain-states that our acts of awareness do not resemble the physical events which occasion their occurrence. It is in this sense, fundamentally, that our senses 'deceive' us. The slogan 'the senses deceive' was understood by the French Cartesians to mean, not that our senses deceive but that perception provides data for the perceiver which can be exploited in either of two directions: critically to construct a science, or uncritically to reinforce natural prejudices. The philosophy of the schools was taken as a paradigm example of the latter option. The ambiguity of 'the senses do/do not deceive' is cultivated by Descartes's followers in France as an orthodox expression of the master's own thought.[79] For example, Malebranche writes, with equal conviction for both parts of the disjunction: 'The senses always deceive you'; and 'We are deceived not by our senses but by our will, through its precipitous judgments.'[80] To unravel the apparent inconsistency here Malebranche endorses the Cartesian analysis of the term *sensation*.[81] As already indicated above, Cartesian usage allows the same term to denote both the following: (*a*) the perceptual experiences of which one is aware when appropriately stimulated by external or internal physical causes; and (*b*) the judgements which we are likely to make, in a precipitous or uncritical way, on the occasion of having sensations in the sense of (*a*). The so-called 'natural' judgements by which we judge 'that our sensations are in objects' are the principle source of error.[82] Such natural judgements are under the control of the will; therefore there is no error at all in our sensory perceptions, as such, but only in the judgements which the unsophisticated are likely to make as a result of sensations.

The prevalence among Cartesians of this doctrine of hasty judgement based on sensations, understood as naïvely projecting our sensations on to external objects, is easily understood in terms of their opposition to school philosophy.[83] The offenders against

[79] For Descartes's apparent ambivalence about the reliability of the senses, see Clarke (1982), 34–5.

[80] *Meditations chrétiennes*, x. 103, and *Search After Truth*, p. 23.

[81] See also Le Grand, *Entire Body of Philosophy*, p. 283.

[82] *Search After Truth*, p. 69. See also ibid. 7, 34, 46–7, 52–3, and *Dialogues on Metaphysics*, pp. 117, 283.

[83] See La Forge, *Traité de l'esprit*, pp. 100–1, 159, 205, 348, 325; Gadroys, *Système du monde*, pp. 311–13; Le Grand, *Entire Body of Philosophy*, p. 7, where he speaks of the 'precipitancy and inconsiderateness in judging [which] is commonly attributed to the senses'; Régis, *Réponse à Huet*, pp. 6–7, and *Système*, p. 175.

due caution were usually identified as children or scholastic philosophers;[84] and since children were hardly the source of philosophical
error, the main target for charges of *naïveté* was scholastic
philosophy. Those who 'embrace the maxim of Aristotle, that there
is nothing in the understanding which was not first in the senses',
allow themselves to be deceived.[85] The scholastic axiom, *nihil est in
intellectu quod prius non fuerit in sensu*, was objectionable because
of the first word *nihil*; when taken literally, it meant that there was
nothing in the mind which had not come through the senses, that
the senses are the exclusive source of all knowledge. In other words,
the senses are not only a primary occasion for sensory perception,
but the qualitative character of sensory stimulations determines the
limits of all subsequent ideas.

This is quite explicit in Régis's replies to objections from Huet.
Huet defended the thesis, in his *Censura Philosophiae Cartesianae*,
that there is nothing in the soul which was not first in the senses,
and that the idea of God cannot be innate. Régis's *Réponse à Huet*
(1691) involves distinguishing the immateriality of the mind from
the physical activity of the sensory organs. Although perceptions
arise in the mind only on the occasion of sensory stimulation,
nevertheless it remains true that the resulting mental states or ideas
cannot be adequately explained in terms of the appropriate sensory
stimulation. To the extent that ideas transcend their physical
(occasional) causes, ideas are innate in the mind. However, the idea
of God is not innate as an actual idea, but only as an idea in
potency.[86]

This is one meaning of the term 'innate' in the Cartesian tradition.
It is a negative thesis to the effect that (mental) ideas are not
reducible to the sensory stimulations which occasion them and,
more generally, that human knowledge is not limited to the
perceptual qualities which are experienced as secondary qualities by
the mind. The mind brings its own contribution to bear on these
data and whatever this extra contribution is must, in some sense, be
given with the mind itself. This is the sense of innateness which is
summarized in the handbook of Cartesian logic, the *L'Art de penser*
of Port-Royal:

[84] See Malebranche, *Dialogues on Metaphysics*, pp. 135, 137.
[85] Le Grand, *Entire Body of Philosophy*, p. 4.
[86] Huet's defence of the senses as the locus of sensation and his rejection of the
innate idea of God are found in the *Censura*, pp. 51, 52–3; the replies by Régis are in
his *Réponse à Huet*, pp. 173–8, 181–6.

It is therefore false that all our ideas come from our senses. On the contrary, one could say that no idea which is in our mind owes its origin to our senses, except as an occasion insofar as the movements which take place in our brain—which is all that our senses can cause—provide an occasion to the soul to form diverse ideas which it would not otherwise form, even though these ideas almost never resemble anything which takes place in the senses or in the brain. Besides, there are many ideas which do not depend in any way on a physical image, and therefore cannot be related to our senses without an obvious absurdity.[87]

A second source of disquiet for Cartesians, apart from the Peripatetic theory of sensory knowledge, was the suggestion implicit in some extreme forms of Jansenism that the human mind was totally incapable of any learning apart from what is revealed by God or what is made possible by his grace. In contrast with this pessimistic theory, Cartesians hoped to assert the autonomy of the mind and of its rational faculties and its innate power of making some progress in search of truth without the need for any special intervention by God to cure the intellectual diminishment caused by Original Sin. One way of expressing the natural powers of human reason was in terms of the metaphor of 'seeds of truth'.

This attitude is especially clear in those who applied themselves to articulating a Cartesian method of study, such as Bernard Lamy in the *Entretiens sur les sciences* (1683). Lamy repeatedly claims that the human mind is already equipped with certain 'seeds' of knowledge, and that the task of the teacher is merely to draw out this innate knowledge by appropriate stimulation. 'Experience shows that we have the seeds of all truths and the principles of all the sciences in us; so that there is no richer library where there is more to read and to learn than the heart of man, that it is say, what he has in himself.'[88] These innate principles include the fundamental rules of logic.

We find inside ourselves many truths the clarity of which is so great, that we could not doubt them for a moment. Nature has given us these to be like the seed of all the sciences. There is no one, for example, who does not know that something cannot both be and not be at the same time. . . . It is nature which makes us consent to such clear propositions; thus they are true, because nature does not deceive us.[89]

[87] A. Arnauld and P. Nicole, *La Logique ou l'art de penser* (1662), ed. F. Girbal and P. Clair (1981), p. 46.
[88] Lamy, *Entretiens sur les sciences*, p. 88.   [89] Ibid. 95–6.

Lamy goes on to explain that all reasoning involves deducing the truth or falsity of one proposition from the truth-value of another proposition which is already known for certain. Therefore, in order to reason one must have some *maximes incontestables*.[90] The surprise is found in the examples given of maxims or first principles from which reasoning can begin, for they include inductively confirmed generalizations: 'In physics, *expériences* which are repeated and always confirmed serve as maxims.'[91]

This empirical basis for physics seems at first sight incompatible with Lamy's claim that God has put the first principles of all the sciences in our minds, so that all we need to do is to draw out the implications of these principles:

> God has put into man the seeds of knowledge, that is, some primary truths from which the others flow as streams from their sources. . . . Experience shows that since God has given to the soul the principles of the sciences and a mind with which to understand them, one only has to make use of this help, and to pay attention to these primary truths from which all the others flow as from their source.[92]

These claims are almost like a refrain in the Cartesian tradition, and their meaning can only be gleaned from the context in which they were so frequently repeated. Part of their meaning for Lamy lies in a rejection of the axiom *nihil est in intellectu quod prius non fuerit in sensu*, when he argues that some of our knowledge does not originate in sense. 'In geometrical figures, it is the mind which sees an infinity of properties, relations and proportions which are not sensible, and which the senses cannot make known.'[93] That is the negative thesis about innateness already discussed. The positive side of the claim, however, is a defence of the powers of reason to discover truths which lie beyond the limitations of sensory data, but which are not revealed by divine revelation either.

This effort to delineate the innate powers of human reason was required in opposition to those who wanted to subjugate reason to the alleged teaching of revelation. Any attempt to overthrow the hegemony of theology had to include the claim that the human mind can know certain principles on its own, and that it is certain that it can know them. Rohault had tried to separate the respective spheres of theology and philosophy by distinguishing their basic

---

[90] Ibid.
[92] Ibid. 63, 65. See also p. 239.
[91] Ibid.
[93] Ibid. 88.

principles. 'It is certain that theology and philosophy have different principles; theology is based on authority and revelation, while philosophy relies only on reason. From which it follows that one can discuss one without the other.'[94] Lamy similarly identifies the maxims of theology: 'Theology draws its maxims from Scripture and tradition, or from the unanimous agreement of the Fathers [of the Church].'[95] This claim to autonomy on the part of human reason was expressed in the Cartesian tradition, following St Augustine and Descartes, in terms of seeds of truth which are naturally in the soul.

In fact, both parts of the innateness thesis were urged against exactly the same opponents. The Jesuit critics of Cartesianism argued for the limitations of human reason as a complementary thesis to the need for divine revelation. They defended both the axiom that there is nothing in the mind which has not come through sense perception, and the claim that theology should dictate the limits within which philosophy can operate. The theory of seeds of truth represents a Cartesian attempt to make some space between these twin limitations on human reason. Negatively, we are not limited to what we learn through the senses; positively, human reason can discover some truths which are so certain that we must accept them first in our efforts to interpret revelation.

This interpretation of the innateness theory may have the appearance of salvaging it against standard objections only at the expense of trivialization. However, none of Descartes's followers in France showed any enthusiasm for a thoroughgoing theory of actual innate ideas or axioms in the human mind. What they claimed to defend was the autonomy of human reason and its independence of sense in constructing a science of natural phenomena. It remains to be seen, in subsequent chapters, how they exploited this autonomy in the construction and defence of physical science. The conclusion to be drawn, at this stage, about the innateness theory is that there are no indications in the Cartesian school that physical science should be based on completely a priori foundations with which the mind is innately endowed. The indications are rather more ambiguous, both with respect to the value of empirical evidence and the availability of independent 'rational' evidence. This ambiguity about innateness permeates the theory of science

---

[94] Rohault, *Entretiens*, p. 111.
[95] Lamy, *Entretiens sur les sciences*, p. 96.

which is explicit in Cartesian methodology, and which is implicit in the scientific theories to which the French Cartesians gave their approval. In brief, 'innateness' was a code-word for a number of related theses about the autonomy of human reason in constructing a viable science of nature: (*a*) that our ideas are non-material and therefore irreducible to physical events; (*b*) that they do not necessarily resemble their occasional causes; (*c*) that human knowledge is not confined to the perceptions of secondary qualities which are made available through the senses; (*d*) that there are some epistemically privileged truths which are not discoverable by sense at all, such as the rules of valid inference. The positive, complementary thesis in each case is a claim about the cognitive resources of the human mind. These resources are what the Cartesian tradition meant by seeds of truth.

In focusing on the incommensurability of mind and matter and on the consequent inability of our senses adequately to explain human knowledge, I have implicitly assumed a theory of matter which made it seem self-evident to Cartesians that ideas could not possibly be caused by material objects or events. This metaphysical perspective on innate ideas coincides with what Leibniz claimed to be doing in his *New Essays on Human Understanding*. The *New Essays* were written during 1704–5 in response to Locke's *Essay*, although they were only published much later in 1765. In the course of completing his response to Locke, Leibniz wrote to a friend in the Berlin court, Isaac Jaquelot, in 1704: 'My remarks on the work of Mr Locke entitled *Essay Concerning Human Understanding* are almost finished . . . I am above all concerned to vindicate the immateriality of the soul which Mr Locke leaves doubtful.'[96] For Leibniz, as for the Cartesians, the immateriality of the soul implies that ideas could not possibly be caused by sensory stimulation; indeed, if ideas could be adequately explained in that way, then the immateriality of the soul would be in jeopardy. It is only those who have a confused idea of matter and spirit who continue to talk (like Locke) as if God might be able to superadd thinking to a material substance:

When people have only confused ideas of *thought* and *matter*, which is usually all they do have, it is no wonder that they cannot see how to resolve

[96] Nicholas Jolley provides convincing evidence to show that Leibniz's primary objective, in writing the *New Essays*, was to defend the immateriality of the soul. The quotation above is found in Jolley (1984), 102.

such questions. . . . the inner nature of matter shows well enough what it is naturally capable of. And it shows that whenever God gives matter organs suitable for the expression of reasoning, it will also be given an immaterial substance which reasons; . . . To maintain that God acts in any other way, and gives things accidents which are not 'ways of being' or modifications arising from substances, is to have recourse to miracles and to what the Scholastics used to call 'obediential power'.[97]

Leibniz's response to Locke helps to highlight the fundamental issue on which the Cartesians had disagreed with their scholastic counterparts with respect to the causality of ideas in the human mind. In a word, it was the impotence or barrenness of matter which made it appear self-evident that the mechanical processes which take place in sensation could not possibly explain the origin of ideas in the human mind. The impotence of Cartesian matter and the spirituality of the human soul demand that some other account be provided of how human minds come to have ideas. The language of innate ideas was the Cartesian way of expressing the creativity, originality, or autonomy of the mind in response to sensory stimulation.

This metaphysical interpretation of the language of seeds of truth is made more plausible when one considers, in some detail, the extent to which Cartesian matter was denuded of all the powers which it would need to help explain thinking. This is taken up in the next chapter.

[97] S. W. Leibniz, *New Essays*, trans. R. Remnant and J. Bennett (1981), pp. 378–9.

3

The Concept of Matter

THE Cartesian distinction between the objective causes of our perceptions and the sensory experiences on which we rely for knowledge of the natural world—a distinction which was subsequently given its canonical expression by Locke in the language of primary and secondary qualities—emphasizes the unreliability of perception as a basis for natural philosophy. The predominance of this sceptical insight is in danger of overshadowing the complementary thesis about the assumed reliability of our ideas of primary qualities. Both claims about the relative reliability of different types of ideas were put to use by Descartes in the *Principles*, when he claimed that 'size, figure, etc., are known in a very different manner from colours, pains, etc.'[1] Some of the reasons for claiming that our perceptions of colour or pain are epistemically unreliable were discussed in Chapter 2; the ways in which we can discover the fundamental properties of natural phenomena remain to be seen. However this knowledge is to be acquired, Descartes assumed that we could successfully identify various fundamental properties or primary qualities in material things, and that these basic properties would provide a way of explaining all the other properties which we perceive in nature.

There is nothing exclusively Cartesian about this approach to natural philosophy in the seventeenth century. All the corpuscularian philosophers of the period adopted a similar strategy which relied on a distinction between primary and secondary qualities, and which contrasted our objective knowledge of the former with our subjective experiences of the latter. The significant differences between alternative philosophies of science depended on the methods used to identify primary qualities, and on variations in the selection of primary qualities which were considered adequate to explain natural phenomena.

[1] Descartes, *Principles*, i. 31, art. 69.

For example, when Robert Boyle introduced his list of primary qualities in *The Origin of Forms and Qualities according to the Corpuscular Philosophy* (1666), he explicitly acknowledged that his description of matter as extended, impenetrable, and so on was a hypothesis, and that the fruitfulness of the hypothesis provided a reason for accepting it.

I may, Pyrophilus, furnish you with some general apprehension of the doctrine (or rather the *hypothesis*) which is to be collated with, and to be either confirmed or disproved by, the historical truths that will be delivered concerning particular qualities . . . here we have a fair occasion to take notice of the fruitfulness and extent of our Mechanical hypothesis.[2]

The general structure of Boyle's introduction of a very small number of primary qualities, as an hypothesis in need of confirmation, does not prevent him from using independent, conceptual considerations to justify each of the primary qualities which he is willing to accept. For example, he argues that local motion is required to explain the diversity of properties which we experience in matter; likewise, the fact that each corpuscle is a finite body implies that it must have some definite, measureable shape. However, one also gets the impression that the empirical and conceptual arguments are presented in Boyle's exposition almost as a redundant exercise in deference to the requirements of scientific method; the concepts used to describe the primary properties of matter are assumed to be so evident and unproblematic that they only needed to be mentioned for everyone to accept them as an uncontentious basis for a mechanical philosophy of nature.

This suggests that two related issues need to be investigated in order to understand the Cartesian concept of matter in the second half of the seventeenth century: (*a*) which primary qualities were predicated of matter, and (*b*) what reasons were advanced for trusting our ideas of those primary qualities as a reliable account of natural phenomena? In general, the Cartesian presentation of primary qualities is less explicitly hypothetical than Boyle's, and it relies more heavily on conceptual and metaphysical considerations about the nature of matter. Descartes had exploited both empirical and conceptual strategies to articulate his understanding of matter, and the concept which emerged from his efforts dominated the

[2] Stewart (1979), 18, 48.

conceptual history of Cartesianism for the remainder of the seventeenth century.

This chapter discusses those qualities which Cartesians were willing to predicate of matter at rest, while Chapter 4 examines the concept of force and its role in explaining motion. If these 'internalist' considerations which guided the formulation of the Cartesian concept of matter are placed in a wider historical context, it is easier to appreciate the extent to which Cartesian matter was totally inert, devoid of forms, powers, or other suspect properties which are precluded by the metaphysical and conceptual parsimony of the system within which matter was defined. In this respect, Cartesians were responding not just to popular beliefs in the demonic powers of witches and their chosen instruments of evil, but to the decadent scholasticism of the colleges in which philosophy held a pre-eminent place on the curriculum. The emancipation of natural philosophy from scholastic constraints, the presentation of the new sciences as controlling and exploiting nature to the advantage of man, and the requirement that human souls be insulated from the possibility of mechanical explanation all coincided in the rigorous use of Occam's razor in identifying the primary qualities of matter.[3] In fact, given the sharpness of the distinction between matter and mind it became more imperative than ever before to classify qualities as belonging either to a spiritual substance or a material substance; consequently, the properties of material things could not overlap in any way with properties which are more appropriate to spiritual substances.

In the process of denuding matter of most of its powers, there was a significant evolution in the concept of 'occult powers' in which the term 'occult' ceased to mean 'hidden' and became instead a derogatory term to describe those hidden powers which mechanical philosophers found unintelligible.[4] As a result, proponents of a mechanical philosophy objected to two different kinds of qualities in physical phenomena. One kind included all those accidental forms which were used by scholastic philosophers in explaining our perceptions of physical phenomena; the reasons for excluding such forms or qualities are discussed below in Chapter 6. The second type of objectionable quality comprised those with spiritual or

[3] Cf. Easlea (1980), for a discussion of the connection between witchcraft, magic, and the new mechanical philosophy.

[4] Hutchison (1982) analyses this development.

sensory connotations, because the spiritual or sensory was to be explained by reference to the activity of spiritual substances rather than material substances. Therefore, the kinds of qualities which were available for explaining physical phenomena were very limited. At the same time, it was irrelevant that these qualities might be occult in the sense of being outside the scope of direct or immediate perception by unaided human sensory faculties. As already suggested above, Cartesians did not believe that we perceive any physical phenomenon directly or immediately; the ideas we have are the result of the interaction of external stimuli with our sensory faculties and there is nothing especially problematic for mechanical philosophers about the causal activity of physical stimuli which are not perceived by unaided senses.

Thus the challenge facing Cartesian philosophers in the mid-seventeenth century was to identify (preferably) a small number of qualities in matter by reference to which all natural phenomena could be explained; in their choice of primary qualities, they excluded any which they thought should be predicated of spiritual rather than material substances, and likewise they excluded anything which resembled scholastic forms. The implementation of this programme defined the limited categories within which all Cartesian explanations had to be expressed; it also provided one of the main sources of reluctance in accepting a dynamic concept of force.

Matter as Extension

To clarify the concept of matter one needs to identify those basic qualities in terms of which all the observable properties of physical phenomena can be explained. Descartes approached this question by means of a thought experiment. We can imagine material bodies without weight or hardness, and we could even imagine that they lose their ability to affect our senses; but we could never conceive of a physical body which is not extended. 'From this it follows that the nature of matter does not depend on any such properties, but consists solely in the fact that it is a substance which has extension.'[5] It does not follow from this type of argument that matter has no other primary properties apart from extension, nor that any of the

---

[5] *Principles*, ii. 41, art. 4.

others are reducible to extension. Nevertheless, Descartes claims in a subsequent article of the *Principles* that 'all the properties which we clearly perceive in it [i.e. matter] are reducible (*reducuntur*) to the sole fact that it is divisible and its parts movable'.[6] The inference from 'extension is essential to matter' to 'extension is the essence of matter' was the single most important factor in the subsequent history of Cartesian physics in France; no other assumption so significantly influenced the development of Cartesian physics than the uncritical repetition of the axiom that matter had no other intrinsic properties apart from those which could be explained in terms of extension.

Of course the Cartesians also included a concept of local motion in their conceptual repertoire, and this concept played a major role in scientific explanations; the way in which 'motion' is defined and explained is discussed in the next chapter. Even though motion was a very important factor in the explanation of natural phenomena, however, the concept of matter had to bear a significant explanatory burden in the Cartesian enterprise. This may seem like a vain hope, given the conceptual restrictions on describing what looks like a homogeneous substance called matter. The persistent attempts by Cartesians to wrestle as much as possible in scientific explanations from the concept of extension needs to be examined in some detail.

As is well known, Descartes's definition of matter in terms of extension implied that there is no real distinction between matter and space, and that the concept of a perfect vacuum is a contradiction in terms. The same definition of matter also implies that every part of matter, irrespective of its size, must be divisible in principle. This does not mean that God could not create parts of matter which are so small that we would be incapable of subdividing them further; but even if God chose to do this, such 'physically indivisible' particles would still be divisible in principle.

Descartes also argued that we cannot discover by purely speculative considerations what types of particle exist; God might have chosen any one of an indefinite number of alternative ways of dividing matter into movable parts. We are free, therefore, to hypothesize anything we wish in this context, on one condition: that our hypothesis agrees with the available evidence.

We noticed earlier that all the bodies which compose the universe are

---

[6] Ibid. ii. 50, art. 23.

formed of one [sort of] matter, which is divisible into all sorts of parts and already divided into many which are moved diversely and the motions of which are in some way circular, and that there is always an equal quantity of these motions in the universe; but we have not been able to determine in a similar way the size of the parts into which this matter is divided, nor at what speed they move, nor what circles they describe. For, seeing that these parts could have been regulated by God in an infinity of diverse ways, experience alone should teach us which of all these ways He chose. That is why we are now at liberty to assume anything we please, provided that everything we shall deduce from it is entirely in conformity with experience.[7]

Descartes takes advantage of this methodological licence to postulate the existence of three types of particle which are initially distinguished by their size and shape; they are also distinguished at a later stage by their relative speeds. The smallest, invisible particles are called the first element, and the others are correspondingly named in order of size.[8]

   The rejection of empty spaces between particles gives rise to obvious difficulties in explaining the relative density of different bodies. The model of a sponge was used at this juncture to show how the same quantity of matter, i.e. the matter out of which a sponge is composed, may have more or less volume depending on whether it is immersed in water. When not immersed in water, the pores of the sponge are filled with some matter, such as air. In a similar way, every physical body may be more or less porous and hence more or less solid; but whatever condition it is in, it never presupposes any genuinely empty spaces. By rarefaction, therefore, Descartes understands the dispersion of the parts of a body so that its outer surface encloses a greater extension, just like the sponge in water; and by condensation he understands the contraction of the surface of a body so that it includes fewer pores than before. 'Thus rarefied bodies are those with many spaces between their parts which are filled by other bodies. And rarefied bodies only become denser when their parts, by approaching one another, either diminish or completely eliminate these spaces; if the latter ever occurs, then the body grows so dense that it cannot possibly become denser.'[9]

   The sponge metaphor cannot provide Descartes with an account

---

[7] *Principles*, iii. 106, art. 46.   [8] Ibid. iii. 110, art. 52.
[9] Ibid. ii. 41–2, art. 6.

of density. As long as there are no spaces between the parts of matter, there is no room for more or less compacted bodies. The only way out of the difficulty would be if the different types of particle differed in relative density; in that case the densities of bodies could be explained by the ratios of the three particles from which they are composed. But that avenue is also closed, as long as matter is defined exclusively in terms of extension. This is consistent with the claim that the quantity of matter contained in any body is determined only by its volume.

We shall recognize as well that it is not possible for there to be more matter, or material substance, in a vessel when it is full of lead, gold, or another extremely heavy and hard body, than when it contains only air and is thought to be empty; because the quantity of matter does not depend on the weight or hardness of its parts, but on extension alone, and this is always the same in a given vessel.[10]

Without any empty interstices, the quantity of matter in equal volumes is always equal. Despite this conclusion, Descartes introduced the concept of solidity in order to explain our experience of moving bodies of equal size with more or less facility; even bodies of the same size sometimes require varying degrees of effort to move them equal distances at the same speed, and this suggests that the bodies themselves differ in some respect which is relevant to their resistance to motion. The concept of solidity was designed to explain this phenomenon. By the solidity of a star, for example, is meant 'the quantity of the matter of the third element, of which the spots surrounding it are composed, in proportion to its volume and surface area'.[11] The significant point about matter of the third element is that a body with a high proportion of such elements has fewer interstices, so that there is less foreign matter entering and leaving its pores when it is in motion. Its solidity, therefore, determines how it will move in any given medium. A solid body with a relatively non-porous surface will be less easily moved than a porous body through which the surrounding medium can easily penetrate.

There are two important features to notice in this approach to articulating the concept of matter. The most obvious one is that Descartes is not at all bashful about the invisibility of the particles which he postulates. Given a notice between postulating something

---

[10] Ibid. ii. 48, art. 19.   [11] Ibid. iii. 151–2, art. 121.

invisible and something unintelligible, he opts for the first alternative
without any hesitation.

It is less consistent with reason to imagine something unintelligible, in
order to appear to explain rarefaction by a merely verbal device, than it is to
conclude, from the fact that bodies become rarefied, that they contain pores
or interstices which grow larger and that some new body approaches to fill
these pores; even though we may not perceive this new body through any
of our senses.[12]

There is an implicit criterion of intelligibility assumed here in
deciding which kinds of entity may to be postulated, or what types
of explanation amount to nothing but 'a merely verbal device'. In
the discussion of empty spaces, Descartes assumes that the concept
of a vacuum is logically incoherent and that any explanation of
rarefaction which depends on such a concept is unintelligible.

More generally, Descartes's whole discussion of small parts of
matter is based on the following criterion of intelligibility: that the
kinds of properties which these particles exhibit are exactly the same
as those which we experience in familiar physical objects. The only
difference between small invisible particles and large-scale visible
ones is size.[13] Therefore all the properties of small particles can be
described in the concepts usually used to describe rivers, plants, or
planets. This kind of conceptual empiricism has significant implications for later Cartesian science.

In short, the kinds of properties which may be predicated of
Cartesian matter are limited to those which can be described by
analogy with macroscopic physical bodies. They may not include
any which have connotations of scholastic properties or those
which are more appropriately predicated of spiritual substances,
such as the capacity for sensation or self-motion; they must be
consistent with the fundamental metaphysical assumptions of the
Cartesian system; and there is no objection to their being occult in
the sense of being too small to be perceived directly by means of
unaided human perceptual faculties.

Descartes's extremely restrictive categories for describing matter

---

[12] *Principles*, ii. 42, art. 7.
[13] 'In the analogies I use, I only compare some movements with others, or some
shapes with others, etc.; that is to say, I compare those things which because of their
small size are not accessible to our senses with those which are, and which do not
differ from the former more than a large circle differs from a small one.' Descartes,
Œuvres, ii. 367–8.

in terms of extension became so entrenched in subsequent Cartesian writing that their defence almost amounted to theoretical intransigence. With the one exception which is discussed below, no other writer in this tradition proposed any significant amendments to the properties of matter, although there was considerable tolerance for variations in the descriptions of the size, shape, and number of basic particles. The only serious challenge to the orthodox account of matter came from Gerauld de Cordemoy, in the first of six discourses 'on the distinction and union of body and mind', in which he suggested a distinction between the concepts of 'body' and 'matter'.[14] The amendments suggested by Cordemoy are partly inspired by an earlier revival of atomism in France which found expression especially in the work of Descartes's contemporary, Pierre Gassendi (1592–1655); however, they were equally justified by conceptual difficulties in Descartes's concept of matter.

Descartes had defined a substance as 'a thing which exists in such a way that it needs no other thing in order to exist'.[15] When the concept of substance is applied to Cartesian physical objects it is ambiguously used to refer to the whole of matter, to distinct physical objects, or even to their invisible parts. Since any part of matter is divisible, it follows that a material substance is divisible into two substances, and so on indefinitely; this suggests that new substances may be created by the division of physical objects, and that the concept of a substance has lost its traditional connotations of individuality and unity. To Cordemoy, at least, the concept of an indefinitely divisible substance conflated two incompatible concepts.[16]

A second objection to defining matter as an extended substance derived from Descartes's difficulty in explaining the distinction between two contiguous bodies which are at rest. Since nothing separates two such bodies, there is no basis for any real distinction between them unless they move relative to each other. Cordemoy thought there was an obvious distinction to be made here, even among bodies at rest. Some distinction between bodies and matter was therefore required in order to cope with these difficulties. Cordemoy suggested that a body is 'an extended substance'. Each atomistic body has its own characteristic shape or figure, and 'since

---

[14] G. de Cordemoy, *Discernement du corps et de l'âme*, in *Œuvres philosophiques*, pp. 95–189.

[15] *Principles*, i. 23, art. 51.   [16] *Discernement*, p. 99.

each body is only one substance, it cannot be divided. Its figure cannot change; and it is necessarily continuous in such a way that it excludes every other body. This is called impenetrability.'[17]

With this definition of 'body', it is a simple step to define matter as a collection of bodies.[18] Ordinary physical objects, which are clusters of atomic bodies, exhibit the properties which misled Descartes into assuming the indefinite divisibility of matter; physical objects are divisible until we reach a limit in what Cordemoy calls 'bodies' and, since these are invisible, it might appear that matter is divisible indefinitely. The distinction of 'bodies' and 'matter' also allows Cordemoy to amend Descartes's rejection of empty spaces between the parts of matter. 'The bodies which compose . . . masses are not everywhere so close to each other that they do not leave some spaces in different parts. . . . It is not necessary that these spaces be filled; one could imagine the situation where there is no other body between bodies which do not touch each other.'[19] Thus Cordemoy rejects Descartes's argument to the effect that the sides of a vase would collapse if all the matter which it contained were removed. He sees no difficulty in thinking of two bodies subsisting 'so far from each other that one could put a great number of bodies, or none at all, between them, without one body approaching or receding from the other'.[20]

Cordemoy's attempted integration of atomism with Descartes's account of matter was rejected by most other members of the Cartesian school. Desgabets perhaps exaggerated its significance by describing Cordemoy's position as a 'schism', or as nothing less than 'heresies against the philosophy of Descartes'.[21] However, it is also clear that the Benedictine defender of Cartesian orthodoxy captured, in his use of the term 'heresy', an important nuance which is relevant to the subsequent history of the concept of matter. With the exception of Cordemoy, the discussion of matter among later Cartesians achieved the kind of unanimity which is characteristic of a religious dogma.

[17] *Discernement*, pp. 95–6.
[18] Ibid. 96. René le Bossu also objected to Descartes's conflation of the concepts of body and matter, in his *Parallèle des principes de la physique d'Aristote & de celle de René Des Cartes* (1674), p. 237: 'The new philosophy is less exact; by forming definitions on the basis of knowledge which is too general and common, it has given rise to objections to the effect that it confounds together [the concepts] mathematical body, physical body and matter.'
[19] *Discernement*, p. 103.
[20] Ibid. 104.   [21] Lemaire (1902), 79, 80.

The orthodox Cartesian account of matter is redefined by Jacques Rohault, in his *Traité de physique*, where he presents the Cartesian concept of matter dressed up in the trappings of Aristotelian categories. The irenic preface of the book goes to great lengths to urge that the system of philosophy being presented to the public is a better reflection of genuine Aristotelian thought than most scholastic philosophy:

> I have taken all the general notions from Aristotle, either for the establishing the principles of natural things, or the chief properties of them: And I have rejected a vacuum and atoms . . . which I think are things contrary to what is firmly established by Aristotle; . . . though there seems to me to be a just ground to doubt of the truth of some qualities and powers commonly ascribed to some bodies, yet I do not think that there is the same reason to doubt of their being composed of insensible parts, or that I can be deceived in affirming that all these parts have their particular figure and bigness.[22]

The official deference towards Aristotle is reflected even in Rohault's definition of matter in terms of extension. Part I, chapter 6 of the *Traité de physique* explains that the principles of natural things include their matter and form, although Aristotle's third category, 'privation', is claimed to be redundant. Matter is the common stuff which survives, for example, when a piece of wood burns and is converted into flames; it is 'this, whatever it be, that subsists under these two Forms'.[23] However, 'we have not yet made any great advances in the knowledge of the things of nature' when we have simply said that 'something, we know not what, is common with other things' in the transformation of a physical body into something else.[24] Descartes's concept of matter is introduced at this point, without acknowledging its source, as a natural development of an Aristotelian insight.

Rohault repeats the standard line of argument about extension as the essence of matter. He lists many of the generally accepted properties of matter, such as hardness, liquidity, heaviness, and so on, most of which we do not 'perfectly understand'; 'yet we

---

[22] *Traité de physique*, i, preface (unpaginated).
[23] Ibid. i. 21. Cf. Le Grand, *Entire Body of Philosophy*, p. 94, where he defines matter as extension and then claims that it is the same notion as the 'first matter' about which the Peripatetics dispute.
[24] *Traité de physique*, i. 22.

understand enough of them, to know, that they are none of them inseparable from matter, that is, it may exist without any of them.'[25]

But when we consider matter as extended into length, breadth, and thickness, as having parts, and those parts having some figure, and that they are impenetrable, we do not judge in the same manner of these, nor think them mere accidents of matter. For as to extension, it is certain, that we cannot separate the idea of that, from any matter whatsoever; . . . as to the parts of matter, we apprehend them to belong to it so necessarily, that we cannot imagine any portion of it so small . . . [that it is not divisible].[26]

The impenetrability of matter is established by means of a similar thought experiment. If a piece of matter 'has all that is necessary' to constitute one cubic foot of matter, and if another cubic foot is added to it, the resulting body cannot be less than two cubic feet. Otherwise the addition of the second body either destroys some matter, or it implies the denial of the initial assumption, viz. that the first body contained all that was necessary to constitute one cubic foot.

The value of this type of conceptual analysis as a method of defining basic concepts is justified by Rohault in a different context in which he defends his concept of substance. There he claims to be defining, not what a substance is absolutely or independently of our ideas, but rather what we mean by our concept of a substance. A substance is 'a thing which *we conceive* to subsist of itself'. The reason for this is that 'we know things from our ideas only, and we ought always to judge according to our thoughts'.[27] A similar qualification should be entered, therefore, in respect of the definition of matter; our concept of matter is such that we cannot imagine or conceive of it not being extended and impenetrable, but our idea may not correspond to the way things are, absolutely. The most we can hope to do is to analyse our concept of matter.

The definition of matter in terms of impenetrable extension is developed in the context of clarifying two other concepts; the concept of hardness, and the notion of a vacuum. The hardness of a body is distinct from its solidity and its impenetrability. Solidity is explained along the usual Cartesian lines, using the metaphor of a sponge. The 'hardness' of a body, however, corresponds to our experience of resistance when pressing against its surface, in the

[25] *Traité de physique*, i. 23.   [26] Ibid. i. 23.
[27] Ibid. i. 15.

sense in which steel is hard and putty is soft. Rohault rejects the Aristotelian explanation that hardness is due to condensation and softness to rarefaction; he concludes from the experiment of freezing water that water both expands and hardens on freezing. As an alternative he suggests that 'to be hard, is to be composed of particles which are so at rest among themselves, that their connexion and order, is not disturbed by any matter that moves between them'.[28] The hardness of a body is distinct from its impenetrability because even the softest body is composed of impenetrable matter, even if the body as such is not impenetrable. While any particular piece of matter may change its shape and may (at least in theory) be divided indefinitely into smaller parts, the total volume of matter is not subject to change nor can individual parts of matter be compressed to occupy a smaller volume than before. The only justification for this analysis is the identification of matter with extension; if a given extension were to contract (or expand) then it would no longer be the same extension!

There is a similar combination of experimental evidence and conceptual analysis used in defending the conclusion that a perfect vacuum is impossible. Descartes claimed to have proposed to Pascal the famous Puy-de-Dôme experiment which showed that the height to which liquid rises in a closed barometric tube is inversely proportional to the height above sea-level at which the experiment is conducted.[29] Both Descartes and Pascal concluded from the results of the experiment that nature's abhorrence of a vacuum was irrelevant to explaining the rise of liquid in evacuated tubes; they disagreed, however, in their description of the apparent vacuum which is formed above the liquid in the inverted closed tubes. By the time Rohault discussed vacua, Pascal's work was already well known and the details of his experimental strategies were repeated with minor amendments by various Cartesians in the interests of confirming Descartes's objections to the possibility of a vacuum.[30] For example, Rohault argued that the fear of a vacuum was not a cause of water rising in a tube from which the air had been drawn by a suction pump; if it were, then the fear should operate as long as

---

[28] Ibid. i. 121-2.

[29] The disagreement between Pascal and Descartes about interpreting the results of the Puy-de-Dôme experiment is summarized in Mouy (1934), 35-45.

[30] See B. Pascal, *Expériences nouvelles touchant la vuide* (1647), in *Œuvres de Blaise Pascal*, ii. 55-74.

the vacuum is created. However, experiments show that the water only rises approximately thirty-one feet, despite evacuating a much longer glass tube of air. Rohault argues that 'whence we ought to conclude that the fear of a vacuum . . . is not at all the cause of the waters ascending, since it does not agree with experience'.[31] Rohault argued that it was the weight of air alone which explained the rise of liquids in evacuated tubes; but this raised the problem of explaining what was in the upper part of such evacuated tubes when there appeared to be neither air nor liquid in them. The identification of matter and extension implied that the evacuated space must be filled with some kind of matter; at the same time, the rise of the liquid in the tube also implied that whatever matter is involved must be less 'heavy' than the column of air which supports the raised height of liquid. This question underlines the problematic status of the Cartesian concept of density or solidity. The most attractive account of the space above the liquid in an inverted closed tube would involve either a vacuum or small parts of matter which are separated by empty spaces; however, both explanations are precluded by the identification of space and matter, and hence Cartesians were required to hypothesize that the space above the column of liquid is completely filled with some kind of matter which is less heavy than the air in the surrounding environment. Hence the need for an account of relative 'heaviness' without a corresponding concept of density.

The division of matter by Rohault into various kinds of particles is borrowed from Descartes. Rohault relies on experiments to support the assumption that some particles are unobservable. The microscope has shown, he contends, that a mite is a small animal with legs, tendons, etc., and that we would never have imagined the existence of such small parts without optical aids to our vision. This suggests that the invisibility of particles to the unaided eye is no objection to their reality. We are free, then, to endorse Descartes's reasons for hypothesizing the existence of three kinds of particle. Rohault gives the impression of even greater certainty than Descartes that the threefold division of particles is correct, despite its hypothetical origins. He admits that God may not have divided matter in this way in the beginning; however, despite what God might have done at the time of Creation, matter

---

[31] *Traité de physique*, i. 57.

is now divided into those three sorts of matter which I have described; it being certain, that they necessarily follow from the motion and the division of the parts of matter which experience obliges us to acknowledge in the universe. So that the three elements which I have established, ought not to be looked upon as imaginary things, but on the contrary, as they are very easy to conceive, and we see a necessity of their existence, we cannot reasonably lay aside the use of them, in explaining effects purely material.[32]

Rohault's choice of elementary particles is explicitly made in opposition to Aristotelian elements and also to those suggested by chemists. The scholastic elements are rejected because they are defined in terms of secondary qualities, the dry, wet, hot, and cold. The chemists' particles are excluded for two reasons: they reduce things to their sensible elements while ignoring the insensible parts which compose them, and many of their elements are merely names which are not supported by any genuine understanding of what the names denote. For example, sulphur is said to be a 'fat inflammable substance', but if we ask what this substance is, the chemists reject our question as being inappropriate. 'So that their science extends no further than to give names to things whose natures they understand not.'[33]

In summary, Rohault's concept of matter was articulated both on the basis of conceptual analysis and experimental results. The conceptual analysis dominated the choice of all his basic categories, such as extension, solidity, hardness, and impenetrability. At the same time, he was willing to speculate about the extent to which we could confirm our hypotheses about the properties of invisible particles of matter by experiments. This combination of conceptual restraint and experimental openness represented the new orthodoxy for the Cartesians in France. Malebranche followed his lead in defining matter exclusively in terms of extension: 'the body is only extension in height, breadth, and depth, and all its properties consist only in (a) motion and rest, and (b) an infinity of different figures.'[34] The same point is made more explicitly in the *Dialogues on Metaphysics*:

Whatever can be conceived by itself and without thinking of another thing . . . that is certainly a being or a substance; Now, enter into yourself, and do you not find that you can think of what is extended without thinking of some other thing? Do you not find that you can perceive what is extended

[32] Ibid. i. 116–17.   [33] Ibid. i. 110.
[34] *Search After Truth*, p. 49.

by itself alone? Hence, extension is a substance and in no way a state or manner of being. Hence, extension and matter are but one and the same substance. . . . Modifications of extension consist entirely in relations of distance.[35]

The infinite divisibility of extension or matter is supported, by Malebranche, by reference to both experimental and conceptual arguments similar to those of Rohault. In Book I, chapter 6, of the *Search After Truth*, he refers to current microscopic work on small animals, and this inclines him to believe that each animal or plant contains, in the form of seeds of reproduction, minuscule versions of the same animals or plants, which in turn contain further seeds, and so on *ad infinitum*. This suggests that matter can be divided into parts which are so small that we would never have imagined them before the invention of the microscope. It also shows that we cannot rely on our senses to determine any lower limit to the size of these seeds; hence we may assume that matter can be indefinitely divided into ever smaller particles. Besides, even apart from such empirical considerations, 'we have clear mathematical demonstrations of the infinite divisibility of matter'.[36]

The infinite divisibility of matter was already a standard Cartesian thesis by the time Malebranche endorsed it in the *Search After Truth*. For example, Arnauld and Nicole had included similar considerations in the Port-Royal Logic almost thirteen years earlier. The Jansenist authors discoursed at length about worlds within worlds in a grain of sand; they also admitted that 'all these things are inconceivable (*inconcevables*). Yet one must agree that they are true, because one can demonstrate the divisibility of matter to infinity, and because geometry provides proofs of this thesis which are as clear as any of the truths which it discovers.'[37] The proof quoted was that, in a right-angle triangle where the two sides enclosing the right angle are each one unit in length, the length of the hypotenuse is incommensurable with that of the other sides. If the sides were not infinitely divisible, then by repeated subdivision one could reach a point where the smallest parts of each length could be counted, and they would no longer be incommensurable.

---

[35] *Dialogues*, p. 27. Le Grand expresses the same sentiments in *Entire Body of Philosophy*, p. 94: 'Matter is a body, in as much as it is a body or a substance extended in length, breadth and depth; wherefore a material and a bodily thing are synonymous terms, and do not differ, save by our mode of considering them.'
[36] *Search After Truth*, p. 26.   [37] *Art de penser*, p. 297.

In other words, the incommensurability of some geometrical lengths logically implies the infinite divisibility of extension.

Similar arguments persuaded all other Cartesian contributors to this debate; their conviction about the infinite divisibility of matter was such that they even proposed Aristotle's prime matter as an early version of their own theory.[38] At the end of the century, Antoine le Grand could summarize the debate of the previous sixty years as follows: if something is extended then 'it must have distinct parts, and what is conceiv'd to have such parts, must be conceiv'd Divisible'.[39] Apart from the usual mathematical arguments which support this conclusion, Le Grand claims that it is warranted by the observations of 'the famous Rohault' about the almost infinite divisibility of gold. Finally, the divisibility of matter is required by the principle of simplicity: 'beings are not to be multiplied without necessity',[40] and there is no necessity to postulate the existence of atoms which are such that even God could not further subdivide them.

A similar survey of the Cartesian theory of elementary particles of matter shows no significant change before the end of the century, when we find Le Grand still maintaining the explanatory power of the traditional three elements: 'it remains next to shew that these three elements of the world, are sufficient to explain all natural effects whatsoever, and that therefore there is no need of feigning any other.'[41] Despite the continued allegiance to Descartes's three elements, a slightly more tolerant attitude towards chemists had also developed, as is evident in the comments of Régis in 1690:

It should be acknowledged, however, that if one wishes to get as close as possible to the true principles of nature [i.e. the primary elements], one could not adopt a more reliable way than chemistry; because even though the division which it makes among substances is unsophisticated, nevertheless it provides a very good idea of the nature and shape of the particles which enter into the composition of bodies which are mixed, large and palpable.[42]

This is hardly an enthusiastic endorsement of the chemists of the late seventeenth century; perhaps it is more a reflection of Régis's

---

[38] Régis, Système, i. 284: 'one must add that primary matter is the same as extension, considered as the immediate subject of the modes in which consist the first forms of purely material being.'

[39] Entire Body of Philosophy, p. 97.

[40] Ibid. 96, 97.   [41] Ibid. 101.   [42] Système, ii. 333–4.

moderate empiricism in natural philosophy rather than a revision of the Cartesian concept of matter. It coincides with the spirit of Book III of his *Système, La Physique*, which begins with a reminder that 'only sensible experience can make us certain of the existence, number and structure of these [invisible] bodies'.[43]

Solidity, Elasticity, and Rigidity

As already mentioned, one of the results of defining matter in terms of extension was the inability of Cartesian physics to give a coherent account of density. In its place one finds repeated efforts to exploit the explanatory resourcefulness of the concept of 'solidity'. The fifty-year period following the death of Descartes saw few innovations on this question; by the end of the century, the Cartesians' concept of solidity was not significantly different from that originally proposed by their founding father. Claude Gadroys is typical in this respect. In *Le Système du monde* (1675) he tackled the problem of bodies being differently affected by the application of equal forces, a phenomenon which we know from experience.

I think, therefore, that the force of a body which is moving only depends on its solidity; and that the solidity consists in having many parts at rest with respect to each other under a small surface. To understand this, let us take two round bodies each of which is one foot in diameter, and let us suppose that one is composed of intertwined branches and that the other is made of lead. It is certain that there is no more matter in one than in the other, since matter only consists of extension and they both have the same extension. However, since the lead has more parts at rest than the wood because it is more compact, it follows that when the ball of lead moves, almost all its parts co-operate together in the same motion. Since the forces of each [part] are united, the whole [cluster of parts] has more force to continue its motion in a straight line; whereas in the body made of branches, there are very few parts which are co-ordinated in the same motion, because there is a quantity of air with diverse motions between the parts. I claim that this air breaks the effort of the solid parts, and since the forces [of the parts] are disunited, the whole body has less force to continue its motion in a straight line.[44]

It is clear from this explanation of solidity that there is no question of the relative packing of more or less matter into equal volumes.

---

[43] *Système*, ii. 2.   [44] *Système du monde*, pp. 170–1.

Instead, the term 'solidity' refers to the different reactions of bodies with an equal quantity of matter to equal impressed forces, where the different results are explained exclusively in terms of the effect of 'foreign' matter filling the pores of a body and failing to be co-ordinated in the motion of the host body.

This concept of solidity survived, with only minor amendments, until the close of the century. For example, Régis returned to the same concept in a series of definitions which are introduced in Book I of *La Physique*, as a preamble to the discussion of collision rules. Among the concepts defined, he distinguished absolute solidity and relative solidity as follows:

A solid body with absolute solidity is one which contains more matter under a small surface area; all spherical bodies are solid with an absolute solidity, because they contain more matter under their surface. A solid body with relative (*respective*) solidity is one which contains more of its own matter within its surface than another body of equal size. A ball of lead is a body which is more solid, in this sense, than a ball of wool of equal size.[45]

Régis goes on to say that a great number of difficulties could be avoided if this distinction were kept in mind; for example, 'lightness depends on absolute solidity, whereas weight depends on relative solidity'.

Régis's concept of solidity, like those of Descartes or Gadroys, is designed to focus on the extent to which a surrounding medium, such as an ether, affects the condition of another body in motion or at rest. Those bodies which are very porous (i.e. not solid in the relative sense) are easily penetrated by extraneous matter; the net effect of this penetration is that their ability to accelerate or decelerate is affected by the motion of the surrounding medium more than other bodies of comparable size which are less porous. Likewise, the motion of a spherical body will be less inhibited by the surrounding medium than a cubic body of the same material, because the effect of the medium is transferred through a body's surface, and therefore the proportion of surface area to quantity of matter is an obvious factor in calculating the retarding effect of the medium.

Whether these considerations provide a satisfactory account of the motion of particles in a surrounding medium or not depends on

---

[45] *Système*, ii. 42.

other factors, which can only be discussed in the light of the Cartesians' theory of the transfer of motion from one body to another. This is taken up in later chapters.

The concept of elasticity suffered a fate similar to that of density. It might have been expected that a scientific tradition which placed so much emphasis on collisions between particles of matter would require some concept of elasticity to account for the results of impacts. Despite the desirability of such a move, however, the Cartesians steadfastly opposed the introduction of elasticity as a primary quality of material bodies. One of the reasons for this conceptual restriction was the standard objection to scholastic qualities; 'elasticity' had connotations of a pseudo-explanation. If one suggested that bodies are reflected on impact with others because they have a property called 'elasticity', it seemed as if one was merely inventing a name for the phenomenon to be explained and assuming that one had thereby provided an explanation. However, a little less conceptual intolerance might have allowed the temporary introduction of 'elasticity' pending its eventual explanation in terms of some other properties. Descartes had already faced this issue in his disagreement with William Harvey about the mechanism involved in the beating of the heart. Harvey was willing to settle for a characteristic power of contraction in muscles, including the heart, but this smacked of what Le Grand later called scholastic 'gibberish'.[46] Thus Descartes set the course which his followers unanimously adopted: there was no room, not even a temporary haven, in the Cartesian concept of matter for a property called 'elasticity'.

This does not mean that the Cartesians refused to discuss the phenomenon of elasticity. For example, Poisson provides a clear indication, in his *Commentaire ou remarques sur la méthode de Mr Descartes* (1671), that he is familiar with elastic phenomena. 'Air has an elastic power (*une vertu élastique ou de ressort*) as M. Boyle shows by a thousand experiments, and as can be seen rather well from a balloon filled with air; because one can feel with one's finger that it gives way, and that it recovers as soon as one stops pressing it.'[47] Régis is even more explicit in his definition of elasticity in his *Physics*: 'A flexible elastic body is one which, having changed its

---

[46] *Entire Body of Philosophy*, p. 56.
[47] *Remarques*, p. 66. Cf. Descartes's discussion of the elasticity of air in *Principles*, iv. 204, art. 47.

shape as a result of a collision or by the pressure of another body, recovers its original shape as if by its own power. A bow or the blade of a sword are flexible, elastic bodies.'[48] There was no difficulty for Cartesians in accepting the obvious fact that some bodies were more elastic than others; the question at issue was whether or not to accept elasticity as an independent property of matter (apart from extension and motion), and whether such a concept might have a role in explaining the results of collisions between bodies in motion.

Elasticity was a paradigm of how Cartesians attempted to integrate experimental results from the work of others into a conceptual framework which was strained by the challenge. Both Huygens and Mariotte had done innovative experiments on elastic collisions, and it was impossible for the French Cartesians of the late seventeenth century not to know of their results. For example, in the *Traité de la percussion ou choc des corps*, Mariotte described experiments of dropping elastic bodies from different heights in order to measure their relative deformation (indicated by an imprint on grease at the point of impact); these experimental results had been presented to the Académie royale des sciences in 1673, and were published two years later.[49] Despite widespread publication of Mariotte's results, one finds a typical Cartesian response in Régis's discussion of impact rules, in which he argues that elasticity is irrelevant to explaining the results of collisions between hard bodies.

One might say that, in reflections, there is always a new cause which communicates to the body which is reflected enough force to return to where it came from; and that it is the elasticity of bodies which makes them reflect and that, without it, they would not be reflected. But we reply that this idea cannot be sustained, for two reasons: 1. Because it is contrary to the general law of nature which requires that a body never loses its motion except insofar as it communicates it to another body. For we certainly know that a body which is reflected does not communicate its motion to that which causes its reflection because, if it did, it would no longer have the force to reflect; 2. Because it is repugnant to experience which shows that a balloon, when compressed against a wall, never reflects as much as when one throws it against the wall, because it lacks the force which is involved in throwing it.[50]

[48] *Système*, ii. 360.
[49] See Mariotte, *Œuvres*, i. 27. See also Leibniz, *Specimèn Dynamicum* (1695), ed. L. E. Loemker (1969), 446–7.   [50] *Système*, i. 351.

Despite this argument against elasticity as a contributory cause of motion after collisions, Régis accepted Mariotte's results to the effect that many 'soft' bodies are deformed on impact with a 'hard' body. However, for the orthodox Cartesian, collisions involving a temporary deformation of the colliding bodies is only a more complex example of the phenomenon which he wishes to explain in an idealized impact. Régis's rejection of elasticity as an explanatory concept is motivated by the need to defend the possibility of reflection, on impact, even between two 'perfectly hard' or inelastic bodies. If that could be done, then the elastic characteristics of some bodies would have to be explained in terms of the internal motions of different parts of a body relative to others, without any need for an extra property called elasticity.

Descartes had attempted a similar reduction of elasticity, in Part IV of the *Principles*, where he argued that the property of 'springing back . . . generally exists in all hard bodies whose particles are joined together by immediate contact rather than by the entwining of tiny branches'.[51] Thus the elasticity of a bow was explained in terms of the tendency of subtle matter to force a passage through the invisible pores of certain (elastic) bodies:

Since they have innumerable pores through which some matter is constantly being moved (because there is no void anywhere), and since the shapes of these pores are suited to offering free passage to this matter (because they were earlier formed with its help), such bodies cannot be bent without the shapes of these pores being somewhat altered. As a result, the particles of matter accustomed to passing through these pores find their paths less convenient than usual and push vigorously against the walls of these pores in order to restore them to their former figure. . . . although this force is very tiny in the individual globules of the second element, the united and concerted force of all the very many globules . . . is sufficiently great to restore the bow to its former shape.[52]

This type of explanation raises the obvious difficulty: why should the particles which are displaced from the pores of an elastic body force their way back to their original location and, by doing so,

[51] *Principles*, iv. 242, art. 132.
[52] Ibid. 242. A similar account of the elasticity of air is given in part iv, art. 47; in this explanation, there is a reduction in the agitation of the particles of air and a corresponding increase in the quantity of motion in the surrounding 'heavenly globules'. Why does the system not reach an equilibrium at that point, and why should the air particles recover exactly the same amount of motion as they had originally?

reopen the pores and thereby cause the bow to recover its original shape?

Jean-Baptise de la Grange, a scholastic critic of Cartesianism, gave an added twist to this type of objection in his *Les principes de la philosophie* (1675). La Grange imagines a situation where a Cartesian ether is flowing from west to east, and an archer bends a bow so that the convex side is facing west. If bent in this way, the pores of the wood will open to a greater extent on the convex side than on the concave side. The ether should rush into these pores, and this should have the effect of preventing the bow from springing back to its original shape.[53] There is no answer available, in the Cartesian account, to this type of objection. Subsequent attempts to explain elasticity were little more than variations on Descartes's basic theme.

Thus Descartes distinguished the hardness and the elasticity of bodies and provided different accounts of each property. The hardness of a body is caused by the state of rest of its constituent particles relative to each other and their resistance to being moved; elasticity, on the other hand, is explained as an effect of the motion of subtle matter when it flows through the pores of a body and thereby forces it to recover its original shape after deformation. Malebranche rejected the hypothesis that bodies at rest have any force to resist motion, for reasons which are discussed in Chapter 4 below, and therefore rejected Descartes's explanation of hardness. At the same time he agreed that elasticity is not an irreducible primary quality. Malebranche attempted to explain both hardness and elasticity in terms of the same model, a model suggested by the experiments of Otto de Guericke on evacuated hemispheres. These experiments showed that if two hollow hemispherical shapes are sealed together and then evacuated, two teams of horses pulling in opposite directions cannot separate them; however, as soon as air is allowed to re-enter anyone could easily separate the two hemispheres by hand. This suggested that it was the force of the surrounding air which resisted the separation of the two hemispheres.

Malebranche argued that all bodies are surrounded, in a similar way, by very fast-moving subtle matter. The force of this matter in motion, rather than any intrinsic properties of a body, explains why

[53] La Grange, *Les principes de la philosophie, contre les nouveaux philosophes Descartes, Rohault, Regius, Gassendi, le P. Maignon, &c.*, pp. 358–9.

bodies are hard; they are compressed and kept that way by the surrounding medium. Likewise, if an elastic body is deformed in any way, the surrounding medium will force it to recover its shape:

> Now, as there are always a great many parts of this invisible matter that enter and circulate in the pores of hard bodies, they not only make them hard, as we have just explained, but furthermore they are the reason why some spring back and return to their original shape, others remain bent, and still others are fluid and liquid. . . . It appears obvious to me that the cause of the elasticity and stiffness of certain bodies is the same as what gives them the force of resistance when we want to break them apart, for in the end the force we use actually to break steel differs only insensibly from that by which it is bent to the point of almost breaking.[54]

Malebranche's hypothesis is no more successful than Descartes's because it fails to explain why the subtle matter which surrounds a deformed, flexible body should force its way through the pores of such a body rather than displace other parts of subtle matter in the environment. Evidently some kind of attractive forces between the constituent parts of an elastic body would be an ideal candidate for explaining elasticity; but any mention of attractive forces was anathema to Malebranche: 'there is not a single argument or experiment that clearly demonstrates the notion of attraction.'[55] This question is given detailed discussion in the next chapter.

The ontological parsimony of the Cartesians might be compared with the efforts made by some of their contemporaries to explain the phenomenon of elasticity. Claude Perrault (1613–88), a prominent member of the Académie royale des sciences, considered weight, hardness, and elasticity as the principal properties of bodies. In the opening chapter of the *Essais de physique* (1680), weight is said to be the most basic of these three properties since it is used to explain both hardness and elasticity. There is no significant difference, for present purposes, between Perrault's explanation of weight and that of the Cartesian tradition; the weight of a body is caused by the external impact of a fast-moving ether. In explaining elasticity, Perrault says ambivalently: 'elasticity is the same power [as hardness] by which the parts of matter are re-united when they have been separated and distanced a little from each other . . . the causes of elasticity, in my opinion, are an internal disposition which makes the parts capable of uniting easily when they are close to each

---

[54] *Search After Truth*, pp. 523, 524.   [55] Ibid. 500.

other, and also an external power which causes them to come together.'[56] The 'external power' is the force of the surrounding ether, as in Malebranche's theory. The 'internal disposition' is explained as follows:

The internal principle which is the disposition of particles of matter [to reunite] depends on their shape; to the extent that their shape is suitable for joining them together, then it is difficult to separate them, because if their surfaces are smooth the bodies can be fitted together more closely. Thus the more polished and flat the surfaces are, the more difficult it is to separate the parts of a body.[57]

It is the vagueness of this inner disposition which attracted Cartesian objections. Either it is nothing more than an effect of the size, shape, and surface of the particles in question, in which case it is equivalent to the Cartesian theory; or it includes an implicit reference to some kind of attractive force between particles, in which case Perrault should be more explicit about the kind of forces involved.

Christiaan Huygens, another member of the Académie, made significant contributions to the mathematical analysis of 'hard body' collisions. Some of his results were published in summary form in the *Journal des sçavans* in 1669, and in the *Philosophical Transactions* of the Royal Society in the same year.[58] The systematic presentation of his theory of collisions is found in *De Motu Corporum ex Percussione*; all the essentials of this work had been written by 1656 although it was only published posthumously in 1703.[59] While Huygens devises his theory for idealized, 'perfectly hard' bodies, he avoids discussing the explanation of the elasticity which permits bodies to reflect on impact. However, he does address this question briefly at the beginning of his *Traité de la lumière* (1690):

[56] Perrault, *Essais de physique ou recueil de plusieurs traitez touchant les choses naturelles*, i. 3–4.

[57] Ibid. i. 15–16.

[58] 'Règles de mouvement dans la rencontre des corps', *Journal des sçavans*, 18 Mar. 1669, pp. 21–4 and the 'Extrait d'une lettre de M. Hugens à l'auteur du journal', pp. 19–20; 'Summary Account of the *Laws of Motion*, Communicated by Mr. Christian Hugen in a Letter to the *Royal Society*, and since printed in *French*, in the *Journal des Scavans of March 18, 1669 st. n.*', in *Philosophical Transactions*, 4: 46 (12 Apr. 1669), 925–8.

[59] The final text was edited by B. de Volder and B. Fullenius and published in Leiden in 1703. The history of the text is discussed in the editor's introduction to the text published in Huygens, *Œuvres complètes*, xvi. 4–27.

there is nothing to hinder us from estimating the particles of the ether to be of a substance as nearly approaching to perfect hardness and possessing a springiness as prompt as we choose. It is not necessary to examine here the causes of his hardness, or of that springiness, the consideration of which would lead us too far from our subject. I will say, however, in passing that we may conceive that the particles of the ether, notwithstanding their smallness, are in turn composed of other parts and that their springiness consists in the very rapid movement of a subtle matter which penetrates them from every side and constrains their structure to assume such a disposition as to give to this fluid matter the most overt and easy passage possible. This accords with the explanation which Mr. Des Cartes gives for the spring . . . But though we shall ignore the true cause of springiness we still see that there are many bodies which possess this property . . .[60]

For Huygens, hardness was primarily a property of the small particles into which matter is divisible, whereas ordinary physical bodies which collide are more or less hard.[61] By assuming that the hard constituent parts of a body are arranged so as to provide an easy passage for the subtle matter which penetrates physical bodies, Huygens is endorsing the same kind of mechanical explanation of elasticity as Descartes, with the minor amendment that the hollow pores may have a variety of different shapes.

Scholastic explanations of elasticity fared no better. For example, La Grange writes about elasticity as 'the way in which the parts of a body are united together'.[62] When he tries to explain this in more detail, the resulting theory is almost equivalent to Descartes's, except for the use of small vacua in the pores of a bent elastic rod. 'When one bends a body this causes many small vacua to appear in it; it is easy to understand that the weight of the air would push the body to recover its shape in order to fill these little vacua, and that the greater the number of evacuated pores, the greater the force with which the body is affected.'[63] This account is objectionable to Cartesians for obvious reasons; it assumes the concept of a vacuum and, implicitly, some kind of natural force which causes matter to fill evacuated pores in elastic bodies.

---

[60] Œuvres complètes, xix. 472, and the Eng. trans. by S. P. Thomson, p. 14.

[61] Cf. Huygens to Leibniz, 11 July 1692, in Œuvres complètes, x. 299–300.

[62] La Grange, Les principes de la philosophie, p. 376.

[63] Ibid. 375. Cf. the explanation of the elasticity of a bow which was proposed by Honoré Fabri, in his Physica (1669), i. 42 ff.; according to Fabri, when an elastic body is deformed the air which is trapped in its pores is compressed and thus the air has a genuine potentia motrix to cause a deformed body to recover its original shape.

THE CONCEPT OF MATTER

The rejection of elasticity as an independent parameter in the Cartesian description of matter might suggest that the only primary qualities allowed were the size, shape, and position of small particles of matter. However, there was at least one other property required in order to generate the reductionist explanation of elasticity, namely, rigidity. This concept appears so discreetly, under the rubric of 'extension and its modes', that it almost fails to be recognized as an independent, irreducible property of matter.

As already indicated, Descartes introduced three types of material particle which were distinguished by their size, shape, and relative speeds. The shape of a part of extended substance may appear to be a purely mathematical property; but if shape is given a definite role in physical explanations, one needs to explain why a body retains its shape or figure when it collides with other bodies. In Part II, article 55 of the *Principles*, Descartes suggested that there is no bonding among parts of a solid body apart from their state of rest relative to one another: 'our reason certainly cannot discover any bond which could join the particles of solid bodies more firmly together than does their own rest.'[64] The question of bonding between different particles of matter distracts from the more basic question of bonding within any given particle. This question arises because some of Descartes's particles had *inflexible* shapes; since any particle is infinitely divisible into smaller particles, it remains to be explained why the parts of any particle should maintain a rigid spatial relationship among themselves.

The most notorious inflexible particles in the Cartesian repertoire are the 'grooved' members of the first element which are put to extensive use in explaining magnetism in Part IV of the *Principles*. These are 'small cylinders with three grooves which are twisted like the shell of a snail'; besides, 'those coming from the South Pole must be twisted in exactly the opposite direction from those coming from the North'.[65] There are corresponding grooves in the earth which only accept particles moving in a particular direction.[66] This implies that the pores of the earth or of magnets are also rigid. Descartes's account of these inflexible pores relies, in part, on the branched structure of the particles from which iron ore is formed.[67] Unless these branched particles are rigid, their initial shape is irrelevant to explaining why some particles can pass more easily

---

[64] *Principles*, ii. 70, art. 55.
[65] Ibid. iii. 134, arts. 90, 91.
[66] Ibid. iv. 243, art. 133.
[67] Ibid. iv. 196–7, art. 33; iv. 244, art. 136.

through some pores rather than through others; likewise, unless the grooved particles of the first element are rigid, their grooves are irrelevant to explaining why they can only pass in one direction through certain types of channels and not through others. Hence the concept of inflexibility or rigidity must be introduced to describe one of the basic properties of matter.[68]

The introduction of rigidity as a property of material particles raises a number of problems. Descartes had assumed that the three different types of matter are not intrinsically different from each other, and that one type could be converted to the other by addition or division. That is what one might expect if matter is defined in terms of extension. In order to explain the rigidity of a branched particle of the third element, for example, he must rely on the principle introduced in Part II of the *Principles*, namely, that the condition of rest of sub-particles is an adequate explanation of their bonding into one larger particle. But this seems to be nothing more than a postponement of the problem. In a situation where all the different kinds of particles are constantly colliding with each other, why are some very small particles privileged in being unaffected by the surrounding flux? What makes them combine together rigidly as constituents of a relatively large particle with a branched shape? It seems as if there is no answer to this question available, and Descartes might have preferred to assume 'rigidity' as an independent quality of some fundamental particles.

This difficulty did not escape the notice of Malebranche, who discussed it in some detail in Book VI (Part II), chapter 9, of the *Search After Truth*. The Oratorian philosopher focused on the following problem. Assume that small parts of matter are bonded together by means of minuscule, invisible bonds. Since these bonds are material, they in turn must be capable of subdivision. How do we explain the bonding together of the parts of a bond, so as to provide the kind of rigidity which is exhibited by rigid bodies? 'The knot of the question now is to know how the parts of these tiny bonds or branched parts can be as tightly united together' as in the accompanying figure in his text.[69] No mere reference to the 'nature' or 'essence' of a bond will do, for the usual Cartesian reasons. Nor would it help to suppose that the bonds are indivisible; Malebranche argues that these hypothetical bonds must be classified as material

---

[68] *Principles*, iv. 198, art. 36.   [69] *Search After Truth*, p. 512.

substances and are therefore further divisible. The only way out of the dilemma would seem to be to acknowledge that the bonds are inflexible; but this runs counter to our experience. If the bonds were inflexible, then in order to break a piece of iron it would be necessary to do the impossible; we would have to bend the very large number of inflexible bonds which compose it! Malebranche settled, *faute de mieux*, for an explanation of bonding in terms of the impact of the surrounding medium.[70]

In summary, Cartesian natural philosophers in France in the seventeenth century were unanimous in their commitment to a mechanical explanation of natural phenomena, and were almost unanimous in their adoption of Descartes's definition of matter in terms of its extension. The viability of mechanical explanations depended in a crucial way on the properties which they were willing to predicate of matter. Apart from force and motion, which are examined below, Cartesians were adamant that many of the features which might initially seem to be fundamental properties of matter are reducible to other more basic properties, and that the list of so-called primary qualities excludes hardness, density, weight, or elasticity, all of which must be explained in terms of small parts of matter in motion. This mechanical research programme encountered many difficulties from the very beginning; indeed, even in constructing dynamic models which might explain elasticity or hardness, it was necessary to assume at least one other property in material particles, namely rigidity, if one is not to embark on an infinite regress in explaining why parts of extended substance remain together through an indefinite number of collisions with the surrounding medium.

The resolve with which Cartesians controlled the list of potential primary qualities of matter is partly explained by their concept of explanation which is discussed in more detail below, and partly by the strict separation of matter and spirit which has already been mentioned. It is also clear that the invisibility of the hypothetical particles which played such an important role in mechanical explanations did not give rise to any theoretical qualms on their part; hypothetical particles could be occult to human powers of perception as long as they satisfied other criteria which were

---

[70] Malebranche's rejection of the inertial force of particles at rest as a possible explanation of bonding presupposes his more general thesis about inertial force which is discussed in Ch. 4 below.

demanded by the Cartesian programme. The confidence displayed by Cartesians in identifying the primary qualities of matter and, at the same time, in excluding alternative proposals suggests a degree of reliability in our ideas of primary qualities which has not been adequately explained.

Ideas of Primary Qualities

One of the issues that has failed to emerge explicitly in the disputes about various primary qualities is the relationship between our ideas and the objective properties which they purport to denote. This is an especially important question for a tradition which put so much emphasis on the extent to which our perceptions are unreliable guides to the way the world is. It is also an issue which must be faced, sooner or later, in assessing the Cartesians' attitude towards scientific realism. It is important, therefore, to take a preliminary look at some of the assumptions being made in identifying various primary qualities about the objective validity of our ideas.

Our ideas of primary qualities cannot resemble anything in physical objects or events. This non-resemblance follows from the metaphysical incommensurability of mind and matter; as already indicated in Chapter 2 above, Simon Foucher exploited this point with telling effect against Malebranche. Despite that type of objection, Descartes endorsed a theory of simple ideas and simple natures in the *Regulae*, and it was assumed in this theory that there was some kind of realistic correlation between the two. Granted, the theory of simple ideas was not a peculiarly Cartesian construction;[71] however, it was an essential component of a theory of scientific knowledge which hoped to avoid instrumentalism. For this reason, it was cultivated more or less in its original, ambiguous form by most of the French Cartesians of the seventeenth century.

Thus Régis distinguished, in his *Logique*, between simple and complex ideas: 'There is this difference between simple and complex ideas, that simple ideas are always real, that is to say, that they

---

[71] See e.g. Locke, *An Essay Concerning Human Understanding*, ii. 2. i, in which the 'simplicity' of ideas is explained, and ii. 7. ix, in which he claims that primary qualities are perceived by means of simple ideas. 'These I call *original* or *primary* qualities of body; which I think we may observe to produce simple *ideas* in us, viz. solidity, extension, figure, motion or rest, and number.' Stewart (1979, 1980) provides an analysis of Locke's mental atomism.

always conform to their original or to the real existence of things; whereas complex ideas do not always enjoy this conformity.[72] There is no attempt here to explain how simple ideas can be identified, nor does Régis clarify the apparent implication that the term 'simple' is used in an absolute sense. Instead he just repeats the ambiguity which was evident in Descartes's earlier suggestions.

The assumptions which are not made explicit by Régis include the following; that our ideas can be analysed into their constituent parts, and that this kind of analysis eventually terminates in ideas which (unlike parts of matter) are so simple that they are incapable of further analysis. The ideas of extension, of thought, of truth, etc., fall into this category. All other ideas are complex, either in the sense that they are generated by a combination of simple ideas, or at least that they are capable of being analysed into simple ideas, whatever their psychological origin. In combining simple ideas into complex ideas, there is always the possibility that there is nothing in reality corresponding to compound ideas, such as the idea of a mermaid. By contrast, simple ideas are those which correspond to the unanalysable properties of actually existing things. These assumptions on Régis's part are consistent with a distinction between primary and secondary qualities; even though sensations are veridical, they only make known to us how external objects affect our sensory organs rather than how the objects are in themselves. 'One ought to reason from sensations in the same way as from simple ideas, with this difference however; ideas always represent something in objects which causes the ideas, whereas sensations represent nothing like that. They only lead us to consider the way in which external objects affect our senses.'[73]

The same contrast is expressed in terms of the relative certainty of ideas and sensations:

The certitude of the senses and that of reason are absolute and metaphysical, that is, they are such that one could never be mistaken in their regard. One must add that although the senses are as reliable as reason, their certitude does not depend on the same principle [as reason]. For it is certain that the certitude of reason derives from the essential connection between ideas and their exemplary causes, while the certitude of the senses depends on the essential connection between sensations and their efficient causes, which are very different.[74]

[72] *Système*, i. 59.   [73] Ibid. i. 61.
[74] Ibid. i. 148.

The final sentence here presumably means something like the following: there is logical connection between ideas and their exemplars, whereas the degree of certainty which results from sensations depends on a successful identification of the external causes of our sensations. This glosses over the problem of successfully identifying primary qualities by means of simple ideas. If the primary qualities of bodies are not given in sensation, if they must be inferred in some sense from our experience of their effects on our sensory organs, then our knowledge of primary qualities is hypothetical and no expression of trust in the reliability of sensation can camouflage the inferential character of the resulting knowledge.

Alternatively, Régis may be proposing a dual system of knowledge similar to Malebranche's, in which indubitable knowledge of possible worlds based on ideas exists side by side with a hypothetical knowledge of the actual condition of the universe, which is based on sensations. Given his opposition to Malebranche's theory of 'pure understanding', it is hardly likely that he would have endorsed a separation of human knowledge into two mutually incommensurable subdisciplines.

There is a more useful suggestion for identifying primary qualities in Poisson's commentary on Descartes's method. As a gloss on the third rule of scientific method, which recommended beginning with those things which are simple and easy to understand, Poisson suggests that the most simple notions are those which 'are easiest to justify'.[75] This has the ring of a genuinely hypothetical approach to natural philosophy. On this reading, simple ideas can be identified, not by any of their intrinsic psychological characteristics nor even by reference to a special degree of innateness, but primarily by reference to their explanatory role in a successful science of nature.[76] In other words, the simplicity of simple ideas is relative to our theories; those ideas are simple which play the role of unanalysed concepts in a successful theory. If this were true, then the arguments used to defend particular ideas as fundamental explanatory concepts in natural philosophy would throw more light on the methodological concept of a simple idea than the explicit philosophical discussion of their

---

[75] *Remarques*, p. 73.
[76] In contrast, cf. Locke, *An Essay Concerning Human Understanding*, ii. 2. i, where he talks about the 'uniformity of our sensations' as an identifying criterion for simple ideas.

epistemically privileged role in human knowledge. The reasons why Cartesians adopted some fundamental scientific concepts have been discussed in this chapter, and also the reasons given for rejecting others; the next chapter concentrates on another basic concept, the concept of force. In examining the reasons given by the Cartesians for their choice of primary qualities, it should become clear that an adequate explanation of their choice is as complex as the variety of factors which explain their fundamental metaphysical world-view and their concept of explanation.

4

Causality, Motion, and Force

THE previous chapter concentrated on a Cartesian description of matter and some of its primary properties, without any account of how changes in these properties come about. The explanation of changing properties is a question to which the Cartesian tradition devoted considerable ingenuity. In addressing this question, Cartesians discussed the concepts of motion and of force and, in the process of analysing these concepts, they developed a characteristic theory of occasional causality.

The seeds of a theory of occasional causality had been planted by Descartes, when he argued that an adequate explanation of any physical phenomenon must include some reference to two distinct types of cause. One is 'universal and primary . . . the general cause of all the movements in the world';[1] this primary cause is God. Secondly, one needs to identify the particular causes 'by which individual parts of matter acquire movements which they did not previously have'.[2] The dual character of causal explanations applies to all phenomena, including the occurrence of ideas in the mind of an individual. 'Our ideas or notions, since they are real things . . . come from God.'[3] At the same time, our adventitious ideas are also caused in some sense by sensations, or by the physical stimulation of our sensory organs by external objects. The dual causality of every event provided Descartes with an opportunity to comment on the complementary roles of primary and secondary causes. 'One can say that one thing comes from another in two senses: either the latter is its proximate and principal cause without which it could not exist, or it is only its remote and accidental cause, which provides an occasion to the principal cause to produce its effect at one time

[1] *Principles*, ii. 57–8, art. 36.
[2] Ibid. ii. 58.
[3] *Discourse on Method*, *Œuvres*, vi. 38.

rather than at another.'[4] This passage introduced, for the first time, the language of occasional causes into the Cartesian tradition; La Forge's commentary on this text in his edition of *L'Homme de René Descartes* (1664), initiated a tradition which resulted in a comprehensive theory of occasional causality.

La Forge's use of the term 'occasional cause' was originally intended to underline a problem in any Cartesian account of causality, namely, the disparity between material causes and mental causes.[5] The scholastic tradition was generally content to distinguish primary and secondary causes, and to argue that all secondary efficient causes depend on the concurrence of God's creativity both to maintain them in existence and to support their causal efficacy. The introduction of the new terminology of occasionalism presupposed the scholastic account of secondary causes in so far as they depend, in an essential way, on God's concurrence; however, it also emphasized the inefficacy of secondary causes when they are considered independently of God. For this reason it is not surprising when La Forge claims that occasionalism is a doctrine which derives from St Augustine;[6] the reference to Augustinian origins prepares the reader for a possible Jansenist influence on La Forge's assessment of the relative significance of God and secondary causes in explaining both human behaviour and the apparent activity of inanimate causes. In fact, the stage was set for a complete reversal of roles in primary and secondary causes. What we might spontaneously call the proximate or primary efficient cause is downgraded to being a mere occasion for the exercise of God's causal power. The importance of this reversal is not yet clear in La Forge; it only emerges as a fully developed theory in Malebranche.

The metaphysical concerns about the role of primary and secondary causes coincided with the reluctance of Cartesians to attribute any properties to matter which were not reducible to extension and its properties; it also coincided with the strict separation of material and spiritual substances. The crucial extra ingredient in Cartesian explanations of natural phenomena, over and above the fundamental properties of matter already listed, was

---

[4] *Notae in Programma*, in *Œuvres*, viii, part II, 360. Gouhier (1926), 89, mistakenly attributes this passage to La Forge, who quotes it from Descartes in his *Traité de l'esprit*, p. 172.

[5] See *L'Homme*, pp. 268, 277; *Traité de l'esprit*, pp. 96, 178.

[6] Ibid. 96-7.

motion. Since motion was to enjoy a privileged place in the
categorial repertoire of the Cartesians it was imperative that its
status be explained clearly and that any account of how something
begins to move or changes its state of motion be consistent with the
background metaphysics of causality. While Cartesians were willing
to attribute local motion to physical bodies, they baulked at the
suggestion that mere material objects could be causes of motion in
any genuine sense of the term. As a result, matter remained inert
and inactive despite its passive capacity for being moved by
something else; the source of motion, the locus of motive force, had
to be some non-material substance to which the power of moving
physical bodies could be attributed without compromising the
Cartesian categories of substance and modes and the strict
separation of powers between material and spiritual substances.

Motion and Force

The discussion of motion and various kinds of force centred on the
explanation of local motion and on the extent to which a moving
body can cause a second body to move by transferring some of its
motion or its motive force to the other body. Here, as usual, La
Forge provides the first step in the reinterpretation of Descartes. He
distinguishes two meanings of the term *mouvement*. In one sense,
motion is a mode of a body 'which is not distinct from the body to
which it belongs, and which can no more pass from one body to
another than other modes of matter [can]'; in this first sense, motion
is 'the transfer of a body from the promixity of those which
immediately touch it and which are considered to be at rest, to the
proximity of some other bodies'.[7] The second sense of 'motion' is
the motive force (*force de mouvoir*) 'which transports a body from
one place to another . . . [and which is distinct from] the body which
it moves . . .' These two senses of the term are as distinct as cause
and effect; the motive force causes the relative motion of a moved
body.

Once this distinction is made La Forge proceeds to argue that, in
contrast with motion in the first sense, motive force is not a
property of physical bodies at all.

[7] *Traité de l'esprit*, p. 238.

If the force which moves [a body] is distinct from the thing which is moved, and if nothing except bodies can be moved, it clearly follows that no body can have the force to move itself. For if that were the case, the force would not be distinct from the body, because no attribute or property is distinct from the thing to which it belongs. It follows that, if a body cannot move itself, it is evident in my opinion that it cannot move another. It must be the case, therefore, that every body which is in motion is pushed by something completely distinct from itself which is not a body.[8]

The Saumur physician supports the real distinction between motive force and body by an analysis of the distinction between the two concepts, 'force' and 'extension'. Just as the concept 'thought' does not include the concept 'extension', so likewise the concepts of force and extension are really distinct; thus force must belong to something which is not extended, to some 'incorporeal substance'.[9] If one wished to maintain the contrary—that force is merely a mode of a physical body—such a mode would not be really distinct (in Descartes's sense of a real distinction) from the body to which it belongs, and therefore it could not pass from one body to another in collisions. In order to be transferable, force must be really distinct from physical bodies.

The understanding of substance and modes, and of what counts as a real distinction, which is assumed at this point in the argument is borrowed from Descartes. In Book I, article 56, of his *Principles of Philosophy*, Descartes distinguished between a substance and a mode as follows: 'we understand by *modes*, exactly the same thing as we understand elsewhere by *attribute* or *qualities*.'[10] What this means is explained in the discussion of modal distinctions in article 61. There are two kinds of modal distinction, the first of which obtains between a substance and its various modes. We recognize this type of distinction from 'the fact that we can indeed clearly perceive a substance without the mode which we say differs from it, but cannot, conversely, understand the mode without the substance itself'.[11] Modes are said to be not really distinct from the substance to which they belong, because a real distinction (as opposed to what is called a rational distinction) between two things implies that 'we can clearly and distinctly understand one without the other'.[12] As an example of this type of modal distinction, Descartes uses the relation between motion and the substance which is moving. He

[8] Ibid. 238.   [9] Ibid.   [10] *Principles*, i. 24–5, art. 56.
[11] Ibid. 27.   [12] Ibid.

argues that we cannot understand motion without thinking of it as the motion of some substance or other although it is possible, conversely, to think of a substance which is not in motion. Thus motion is a paradigm of what Descartes means by a mode; we cannot conceive of it existing apart from the substance to which it belongs.

In a similar way, La Forge classified motion as a modal entity which is not really distinct from some physical substance in motion. The contentious question is whether force should also be classified as a mode of physical substances. The argument against this suggestion was as follows: if force were a mode of physical substances, it would not be really distinct from them and therefore could not pass from one body to another. However, our experience of collisions suggests that a body which is struck in a collision often acquires a motive force which it previously lacked and that the striking body loses some of its initial force. Thus we cannot conceive of forces as modes of physical bodies because it is counter-experiential.

La Forge also briefly considered the possibility that the 'real qualities' of scholastic philosophy might be used to describe the metaphysical status of forces. This view assumed that the force of a moving body could be subdivided with one part of the force remaining in the original body and the other part being transferred to the body with which it collides. For a Cartesian, however, this involved a confusion between substances and qualities, because only substances can be divided in such a way that their parts are separable. La Forge concludes: since force is neither a substance nor a mode of physical substances, we must assume that motive force is really distinct from the material substances which it moves and that, in a collision, the force of one body causes the creation of a new force in the body which it strikes.[13]

This argument based on modes and substances was supported by a thought experiment about the causation of motion. Suppose God were to withdraw all the motion from the universe, could we conceive of individual parts of matter beginning to move themselves or other bodies in their immediate vicinity? 'It is easy to decide that they could not because extension, in which the nature of body in general consists and which is the only quality which it would keep

---

[13] *Traité de l'esprit*, pp. 238–9.

in this situation, is not active.'[14] Besides—and this seems to be the ultimate test—even if matter somehow acquired motion, it could not continue to maintain it without the concurrence of God's creative power. We may conclude, writes La Forge, 'that it is God who is the first, universal and exclusive cause of motion'.[15]

La Forge attributed this theory of force to Descartes;[16] however, there are new elements in La Forge's account which represent a significant devaluation of the role of secondary causes. In Descartes's world every substance owed its continued existence to God's creative power; despite that, we are encouraged to believe that physical substances are genuine secondary causes. In fact, the analogy between existence and power is straightforward. Just as physical substances derive their existence completely from God without thereby ceasing to exist in some genuine sense of that term, so likewise physical substances derive all their causal power from God without thereby ceasing to be genuine secondary causes; their parasitic causal power mirrors their parasitic existence. Why could La Forge and later Cartesians not accept an account along these lines? The intuition which dominates the revised Cartesian theory of forces is that the modes of any substance are inseparable from it. Thus La Forge had argued that the motion of one body cannot be communicated to another; if force were likewise a mode of a moving body, it would be equally inalienable. However, efficient causality in a Cartesian world is explained exclusively in terms of collisions between parts of matter and the impact of one particle on the speed and direction of other particles. The only way in which La Forge thought he could accommodate this reality within Cartesian metaphysical categories was by locating all forces in God as their primary cause, and by classifying collisions as mere occasions on which God would redistribute motive forces between different bodies. It follows that since moving bodies do not possess their own motive forces as proper modes, physical bodies are not genuine secondary causes. Paradoxically, in order for forces to be transferable from one body to another on collision they cannot belong to either body as a proper mode. Thus the transferability of force from one body to another reduces collisions to occasions for the exercise of God's power.

A similar argument was developed axiomatically by Gerauld de

---

[14] Ibid. 240.
[15] Ibid. 241.   [16] Ibid. 242–3.

Cordemoy in the *Discernement du corps*. As already indicated in Chapter 3 above, Cordemoy argued that matter is composed of small, indivisible corpuscles called bodies, and that macroscopic physical objects are aggregates of bodies. The principle reason for the revision of Descartes's theory was Cordemoy's concern about the implied divisibility of substances. Once the concept of matter was amended and physical objects were understood as clusters of indivisible material substances, it sharpened the problem which had been highlighted already by La Forge, that is, the problem of attempting to transfer modes from one substance to another. If the whole of matter could be designated ambiguously as one substance, then the transfer of motion from one physical body to another could be described metaphysically as a redistribution of a modal property within the same physical substance. However, if each physical body is a cluster of distinct substances, then of course any attempt to transfer motion from one body to another must be described, in Cordemoy's language, as the translation of the modes of one substance to another—which is conceptually impossible.

The argument against the transfer of motion is found in the fourth discourse, 'On the First Cause of Motion'; it is based on a series of definitions and axioms:

Definitions
1. To cause the motions of bodies means nothing other than to move the bodies in question.
2. To have motion means only to be moved.

Axioms
1. Whatever a thing can lose without ceasing to be itself, it does not have of itself.
2. Any body can lose its motion . . . without ceasing to be a body.
3. One can think of only two kinds of substance, namely *Spirit* . . . and *Body*. Therefore one must think of them as the causes of everything which occurs . . .
4. *To move* or cause motion is an action.
5. An action can be continued only by the agent which initiated it.[17]

It follows from the first two axioms that motion cannot be an essential attribute of any material substance, because a body can lose its motion without ceasing to be a body. This implies that the first mover cannot be a body, for the first mover must possess the power

---

[17] *Discernement*, pp. 135–6.

to cause motion as an essential attribute. Since (by the third axiom) there are only two kinds of substance available, it follows that the first mover must be a Spirit and, by the final two axioms, that the same spirit which caused motion initially is ˌthe cause of the continued motion of any body.

Cordemoy presumably sees this conclusion as the logical outcome of Descartes's views on the identity, in God, of creation and conservation. Descartes held that there is only a rational distinction (rather than a real distinction) between God's creating the universe and conserving it in existence from one moment to the next. The identity in reality between God's creation and conservation applies not only to substances but also to their modes, such as motion. What is new here is not the emphasis on God's concurrence; it is the suppression of forces as redundant theoretical entities in the explanation of efficient causality in physical nature. If God is the exclusive cause of motion and if the continued motion of moving bodies is also explicable only by reference to his causal agency, then there is no need to go any further in our attempts to explain why physical bodies begin to move or why they change speed in various circumstances.

'Force' in Malebranche

Malebranche read both La Forge and Cordemoy, and they provided the main features of a theory of causality which included the following elements: the passivity of matter, defined in terms of its principal attribute, extension; the necessity for God's causality in any account of efficient causality; and finally, the conceptual difficulties in thinking of force as something which could be a cause of motion and yet be capable of being transferred from one body to another, given that it is not a substantial entity which is capable of division or redistribution. Malebranche used all these considerations together with his own arguments, most notably his reflection on the simplicity of God's action and the inconceivability of force as a distinct type of entity.

The Oratorian metaphysician repeats the distinction of the two senses of the term 'motion' which are found in La Forge; one of them is force, while the other is translation from one relative place to another.[18] He also assumes 'that locomotion is the principle of generation, corruption, alteration, and generally of all the changes that occur in bodies'.[19] Thus any viable theory of causality will have to provide an account of the communication of motion from one body to another; there may be other types of efficient causality operative in nature, but no theory of causal agency could fail to address the problem of the transfer of motion between colliding bodies.[20] Our observations of colliding bodies reveal various constant conjunctions between types of event with which we are all familiar: 'when I see one ball strike another, my eyes tell me, or seem to tell me, that the one is truly the cause of the motion it impresses on the other, for the true cause that moves bodies does not appear to my eyes.'[21] Malebranche claims that we cannot decide by inspection whether the impact of a moving body is the true cause of the subsequent motion of a second body with which it collides: 'it is useless to open one's eyes to judge the efficacy of creatures.'[22] The efficacy or otherwise of creatures as causes can only be decided by reason, because the criteria for identifying authentic causes are not applicable by observation. This presupposes some distinction between apparent causes and true causes.

Malebranche explains a 'true cause' as follows: 'By a true cause I understand a cause which acts by its own force . . .'[23] The identification of true causes depends therefore on deciding whether, in any particular case, a putative cause acts by its own force. This in turn could be converted into a slightly different and perhaps more practicable criterion; if there is a necessary connection between a cause and its effect, then the cause in question must act through its own force. 'A true cause as I understand it is one such that the mind perceives a necessary connection between it and its effect.'[24] Evidently, this calls for some account of 'necessary', and the attempt to explain this concept leads Malebranche into a conceptual cul-de-sac.

For Malebranche, those truths are necessary 'which by their

---

[18] *Search After Truth*, p. 37.
[19] Ibid. 660.   [20] Ibid. 661.
[21] Ibid. 660. See also pp. 224–5.
[22] *Méditations chrétiennes*, *Œuvres complètes*, x. 60.
[23] *Œuvres complètes*, v. 66.
[24] *Search After Truth*, p. 450. See *Œuvres complètes*, x. 61: to decide whether a causal relation is true or occasional, one needs to discover if 'there is a natural and necessary relation (*rapport*)' between the assumed cause and its effect.

nature are immutable, or have been fixed by the will of God'.[25] This implies that the laws of physics are necessary because they are defined precisely in terms of God's will. It is not surprising then when the *Search After Truth* concedes that: 'Mathematics, meta-physics and even a large part of physics and morals contain necessary truths.'[26] Why, then, do the necessary relations expressed in scientific laws fail to denote true causal connections? One can only assume that Malebranche was seduced into ambiguity by the language of necessity and that he demanded logically necessary relations, instead of merely physically necessary connections, as a condition for causal relations. The most obvious example of this occurs in discussing the connection between brain-states and ideas. The 'mind and body have no essential relation (*rapport*) one to the other'.[27] This means that it is logically conceivable that different brain-states could have been joined by God with the occurrence of different perceptions in the mind. In other words, it is exclusively God's free choice and not any intrinsic powers or properties of brain-states which explains the constant conjunction of types of idea and types of brain-pattern. This is another way of emphasizing the complete dependence of secondary causes on God's will. The force of this argument relies, therefore, on the assumption that God does not share his power with secondary causes. Malebranche seems to assume that either God is involved in causal relations, or that physical causes adequately explain the laws of nature, but that there is no room for a third option in which God shares his power with secondary causes. The analysis of necessary relations fails to provide an independent reason for rejecting this third option. One must look elsewhere for the fundamental source of Malebranche's opposition to the efficacy of secondary causes.

The second line of argument proposed against the autonomy of secondary causes is that we cannot conceive of the independent force of secondary causes. What is at issue here is whether or not apparent secondary causes have the power or force to act of themselves. In denying this thesis, Malebranche clarifies the point at issue:

There is no relation of causality between mind and body ... there is no such relation between body and body, nor between one mind and another. No

[25] *Search After Truth*, p. 15.   [26] Ibid.
[27] *Dialogues on Metaphysics*, p. 179.

created being can, in short, act on any other by an efficacy which it has *of itself*.... Everything depends on God because all causes are able to act only through the efficacy of the divine power.[28]

The new criterion of true causality is: could we conceive of secondary causes acting on their own, or in virtue of their own power or force independently of God? The argument against this possibility is as follows:

Whatever effort I make in order to understand it, I cannot find in me any idea representing to me what might be the force of the power they [opponents] attribute to creatures. And I do not even think it a temerarious judgment to assert that those who maintain that creatures have force and power *in themselves* advance what they do not clearly conceive.[29]

This argument hardly depends on whether the force in question can be imagined or perceived; Malebranche is willing to grant the existence of many things which cannot be imagined or perceived, including the efficacy of God's causality! The argument relies, therefore, on whether or not the concept of an independent force in bodies, that is, one which does not presuppose any creative concurrence on God's part, is intelligible.

This kind of argument could be understood in two different ways. One interpretation is that we should examine the contents of our minds and see if we find there the concept of a secondary cause which acts by its own power. Introspection of the Berkeley variety is manifestly too weak to support the conclusion required, especially for a philosopher for whom knowledge ultimately depends on our access to ideas in the mind of God. The limited content of our own consciousness is therefore irrelevant to the possibility of constructing a theory of forces. A less weak interpretation of the argument would be: there are good reasons for claiming that all secondary causes presuppose the co-operation of God's causality. Therefore, the concept of an independent secondary cause—one which does not need God's support—is a pseudo-concept which corresponds to nothing in our understanding. It should be noted, however, that this argument is not concerned with what we can conceive, but rather with the kinds of concepts which Malebranche's theory will tolerate. It is necessarily a parasitic argument which depends on other independent reasons for support.

There is also an echo, in Elucidation XV of the *Search After*

---

[28] *Dialogues on Metaphysics*, pp. 89, 257.
[29] *Search After Truth*, p. 658.

Truth, of the arguments about substances and modes which have already been discussed above:

When I consult my reason I clearly see that since bodies cannot move themselves, and since their motor force is but the will of God that conserves them successively in different places, they cannot communicate a power they do not have and *could not communicate even if it were in their possession*. For the mind will never conceive that one body, *a purely passive substance*, can in any way whatsoever transmit to another body the power transporting it [emphasis added].[30]

This shows that Malebranche's rejection of the concept of force is not based merely on his failure to find the idea of force among those which were available through introspection. Instead he is assuming a position like that of La Forge and Cordemoy, in which the passivity of matter as an extended substance precludes the possibility of force being a distinct mode which could be transferred from one body to another: 'the moving force of a body in motion . . . is not a quality which belongs to the body. Nothing belongs to it other than its modalities; and modalities are inseparable from substances. Hence bodies cannot move one another . . .'[31] In fact, 'properties of extension can consist only in relations of distance',[32] and therefore the power of moving is not one of the modes which may be predicated correctly of material objects.

One of the difficulties in articulating Malebranche's objections to forces, or to efficacious secondary causes, derives from the complementary character of the many disparate arguments on which he relies to support what he presents as an almost self-evident thesis. Besides the arguments already mentioned, considerations of simplicity also play an important role in defending the occasionalist conclusion. The central idea, in this argument, is that forces are redundant explanatory entities. 'It should be noted that God always acts by the simplest means . . .'[33] The simplicity of God's actions is relevant even in explaining the regularities in nature which we observe and which we describe by laws of nature. Malebranche assumes that any explanation of natural regularities must involve at least two factors: (*a*) the efficacy of divine causality, which is required as a first cause in any viable mechanics; and (*b*), the laws of

---

[30] Ibid. 660.   [31] *Dialogues on Metaphysics*, p. 159.
[32] Ibid. 147.
[33] *Search After Truth*, p. 596. The same assumption is expressed as a principle in the *Traité de la nature et de la grace*, *Œuvres complètes*, v. 31.

nature which describe the regularities we observe. Once these two are in place, there is no need to postulate the existence of a third kind of entity called force in order to explain the efficacy of secondary causes. God causes the laws of nature to be as they are; in fact, the laws can be derived from a consideration of the simplicity of God's actions.[34] Therefore, forces or efficacious secondary causes are redundant. This argument effectively undermines the model of divine activity proposed by Descartes, in which the efficacy of God's actions is mediated through real secondary causes:

the nature or power of each thing is nothing but the will of God; that all natural causes are not *true* causes but only *occasional* causes. . . . A natural cause is therefore not a real and true but only an occasional cause, which determines the Author of nature to act in such and such a manner in such and such a situation.[35]

The inefficacy of secondary causes does not require a change in ordinary language; in fact, when we ask for the cause of some physical phenomenon it is the occasional cause, or what Malebranche often calls the *physical* cause, which is being sought. Thus 'one could say that this body is the physical or natural cause of the motion which it communicates, because it acts in accordance with natural laws'.[36] To provide an explanation of some event, therefore, is to describe how it results from occasional causes; and if anyone were to say that it is caused by God, that is both true and non-explanatory, since everything which happens is caused by God.[37] Nor do we know enough about the operation of secondary causes to be able to identify divine interventions which suspend the laws of nature.[38] Our approach to explanation should always be to attribute physical events to the general will of God and to the operation of occasional causes according to the laws of nature. This is consistent with Malebranche's own practice. He constantly talks about the physical causes of natural phenomena, as, for example, in suggesting subtle matter as the cause of refraction.[39] But there is no going back

[34] See *Dialogues on Metaphysics*, pp. 243, 321, and *Search After Truth*, p. 663.
[35] *Search After Truth*, p. 448.
[36] *Méditations chrétiennes et métaphysiques*, *Œuvres complètes*, x. 54. Cf. *Dialogues on Metaphysics*, p. 243: 'the impact of bodies is . . . the occasional or natural cause which determines the efficacy of the general laws.' Also p. 291.
[37] *Dialogues on Metaphysics*, p. 87, and *Conversations chrétiennes*, *Œuvres complètes*, iv. 77.
[38] *Traité de la nature et de la grace*, *Œuvres complètes*, v. 150–1.
[39] *Search After Truth*, p. 710.

on the fundamental thesis that all such occasional, physical, or natural causes are merely expressions of the general will of God and therefore have no need of forces to explain their operation.

All the reasons in favour of occasionalism which have been canvassed up to this point might have been given by any philosopher who shared the initial assumptions of Descartes about God's causality and the philosophy of substances and modes. However, the plausibility of the arguments, at least for their proponents, was supported by the Jansenist sympathies of the Oratory, and by the influence of Jansenist theories of grace on French thought in the second half of the seventeenth century. In Jansenist theology, God's grace (or the action by which God redeems sinful man) is both necessary and sufficient for salvation. Human effort cannot be understood as affecting God's completely free decision to grant salvation to those whom he elects. In fact, the opposite is the case. What may look like meritorious activity in human terms is an effect, rather than a cause, of God's freely conferred grace. There is an obvious parallel between our observation of collisions between moving bodies and our observation of morally good human behaviour. Our senses seem to identify one moving body as the cause of another body's motion; but only reason, which understands true causes, can correctly interpret the available evidence. This parallels the theological interpretation of good works. If we merely observe the good behaviour of our neighbours, we might imagine that these good works are meritorious, that is, that they are the cause of subsequent divine favours. However, only a well-founded theology of grace, such as Jansen's interpretation of St Augustine, can enable us to interpret the situation correctly. The 'good works' are caused by God's grace, not by the human agent. Thus human salvation is completely one-sided, in God's favour. The sufficiency of God's grace in explaining salvation makes human effort redundant. Transposed on to questions of physical causality, this gives us Malebranche's theory of causality. The necessity and sufficiency of God's creative power makes physical forces redundant.

The analogy between physical theory and Jansenist theology of grace might look like a purely gratuitous and speculative hypothesis; it is much less speculative, however, once the texts are examined in detail. Elucidation XV of the *Search After Truth*, which concerns 'the efficacy attributed to secondary causes', begins as follows:

Since the sin of the first man, the mind constantly spreads itself externally; it forgets itself and Him who enlightens and penetrates it . . . God, who alone is capable of acting on us, is now hidden to our eyes; . . . Some philosophers prefer to imagine a *nature* and certain *faculties* as the cause of the effects we call nature, than to render to God all the honour that is due his power; . . . we should see God in all things . . .[40]

The implication is clear. It is our sinful condition which makes us blind to the efficacy of God's power. In default of recognizing the truth, we invent powers and natures as a substitute. Our belief in forces is exactly analogous to Pelagian theories of grace. In our spiritual blindness we foolishly attribute powers to human agents (in respect of salvation) and to physical forces (in scientific explanation) when all the while we should have recognized that God's power *alone* adequately explains both theological salvation and the laws of nature. The adequacy of God's power makes all subsidiary powers redundant.

Malebranche's commitment to these metaphysical considerations about God's power is most evident in his repeated attempts to revise Descartes's collision rules. From the first edition of the *Search After Truth* (1674–5) to the final (sixth) edition in 1712, he adjusted the Cartesian rules partly in response to objections from Leibniz and partly as a result of the work of Huygens and Mariotte, both of whom had made their results known through the Académie royale des sciences. Through the various emendations, one basic assumption remained unaltered, namely, that a body at rest has no power to resist motion:

I conceive only that bodies in motion have a motor force, and that those at rest have no force for their state of rest, because the relation of moving bodies to those around them is always changing; and therefore there has to be a continuous force producing these continuous changes, for in effect it is these changes which cause everything new that happens in nature. But there need be no force to make nothing happen.[41]

This follows from Malebranche's understanding of God's causality. In respect of moving bodies, God has to cause both their existence and their motion; if he were to stop supporting their motion, everything would come to an abrupt halt. Physical objects would continue to exist without moving, and their lack of motion would not require any positive intervention on God's part. 'Thus, to give

---

[40] *Search after Truth*, p. 657.   [41] Ibid. 517.

bodies some force for remaining at rest would be to admit in God a positive will without reason or necessity.'[42] The lack of motion of a body at rest requires no explanation and no action on the part of God. Malebranche concludes that the non-motion of bodies has no force to resist motion, because any real force in bodies at rest would be an activity on the part of God which is unnecessary. 'It is therefore obvious that rest has no force for resisting motion . . . we should not compare the force of motion and of rest according to the proportion we find between the size of bodies in motion and those at rest, as did Descartes.'[43]

The non-existence of inertial forces, in Descartes's sense, conveniently provides Malebranche with an escape from the more counter-experiential implications of Descartes's collision rules. The most notorious of those rules, Rule IV, stipulated that a moving body cannot move a larger body at rest, no matter how fast it moves prior to impact with the larger body. If Malebranche is right, then of course the larger body has no force to resist motion, and it will be moved by the smaller body on impact. The only issue remaining is to calculate the redistribution of motion which results from these kinds of collisions in proportion to the size (*masse*) and the initial speeds of the two bodies.

The Challenge of Leibniz

Malebranche's theory of secondary causes and of the reducibility of force to quantity of motion was published over a period of approximately thirty-eight years between 1674 and 1712. During this time he was constantly challenged by developments in the mechanics of elastic collisions, especially by the contributions of Huygens and Mariotte, and by an intermittent correspondence with Leibniz concerning both the metaphysics and mechanics of causality through impact. Leibniz's objections eventually bore fruit in the modification, by Malebranche, of his method of calculating the quantity of motion of moving bodies, but they were unsuccessful in resolving the fundamental metaphysical issue which separated them concerning the efficacy of secondary causes.

---

[42] Ibid. 516.
[43] Ibid. 518. Cf. axiom iv of the 1712 edn., 'Rest has no force to resist motion'; *Œuvres complètes*, xvii, part i, 59.

Leibniz objected that the occasionalist theory makes the operation of secondary causes look like a miracle, and that the continual intervention of a *deus ex machina* is an unreasonable account of God's agency in nature.[44] The contrast between Leibnizian pre-established harmony and occasionalist causality was explained by analogy with two synchronized clocks.

Imagine two clocks or watches which are in perfect agreement. Now this can happen in *three* ways. . . . The *second* way of making two clocks, even poor ones, agree always is to assign a skilled craftsman to them who adjusts them and constantly sets them in agreement. The *third* way is to construct these two timepieces at the beginning with such skill and accuracy that one can be assured of their subsequent agreement. Now put the soul and body in the place of these two timepieces. Then their agreement or sympathy will also come about in one of these three ways. . . . The *way* of *assistance* [i.e. the second way] is that of the system of occasional causes. But I hold that this makes a *deus ex machina* intervene in a natural and ordinary matter where reason requires that God should help only in the way in which he concurs in all other natural things. Thus there remains only my hypothesis, that is, the *way of pre-established harmony*, according to which God has made each of the two substances from the beginning in such a way that though each follows only its own laws which it has received with its being, each agrees throughout with the other . . . as if God were always putting forth his hand, beyond his general concurrence.[45]

The choice in this analogy between occasional causality and pre-established harmony apparently depends on whether or not God constantly intervenes in nature to adjust the independent actions of causes. However, this way of characterizing the difference between the two theories involves an odd interpretation of occasional causes.

---

[44] See the *Specimen Dynamicum* (1695), in Leibniz, *Philosophical Papers and Letters*, ed. Loemker, p. 441; and *A New System of the Nature and Communication of Substances, as well as the Union between the Soul and the Body* (1695), ibid. 457.

[45] Leibniz's reply to Beauval's critique of his *New System*, Jan. 1696, *Philosophical Papers and Letters*, ed. Loemker, pp. 459–60. The contrast between Leibniz and Descartes on the way in which God's causality applies to natural phenomena is clarified in the *Mémoires de Trévoux* (1708), 489, in which Leibniz explains that his system of *Harmonie préétablie* cannot explain the union of body and soul more successfully that the Cartesian's theory, because 'je n'ai tâché de rendre raison que des phénomenes, c'est-à-dire du rapport dont on s'apperçoit entre l'Ame & le corps. Mais comme l'union métaphysique qu'on y ajoute, n'est pas un phénomene . . . je n'ai pas pris sur moi d'en chercher la raison.' In other words, his pre-established harmony was not a metaphysical theory of the interaction of divine and natural causes, but a mere statement of fact which does not purport to explain the harmony which apparently exists between the two.

In an occasionalist account, God does not interfere in nature at all and, despite the possible implications of the language of occasional causes, God's actions are not determined by physical events. In fact, Malebranche's emphasis on the simplicity of the divine agency and his manifest endorsement of Descartes's identification of creation and conservation suggest that God does nothing more than create/conserve both physical phenomena and the laws which determine their interactions. Creation and conservation is an atemporal, unique action on God's part which bears little comparison with the repeated interventions of the assiduous watchmaker. The analogy with the watchman is therefore completely misleading. Apart from the chronological connotations of *pre*-established harmony, there is no significant difference between the accounts of God's causal agency, in respect of nature, which are defended by Leibniz and his Cartesian correspondent.

Irenic considerations of a similar kind fail, however, to resolve the real differences between Leibniz and Malebranche concerning the reality and measurement of forces. The Oratorian defended the orthodox Cartesian view that extension is the defining property of matter. The conceptual argument which isolated extension as the identifying property of material substances determined the outcome of any counter-claims by Leibniz. As far as Malebranche was concerned, these claims would have to be decided by conceptual analysis rather than, for example, by the relative success of competing theories.

One of the dominant features of the Malebranche–Leibniz discussion of forces was the acceptability or otherwise of anything described in the language of scholastic forms or qualities. This point is taken up again below; for present purposes it is enough to notice that the Paris metaphysician classified forces among the occult qualities from which seventeenth-century natural philosophy needed to be emancipated: 'practically all books of science, and especially those dealing with physics, medicine, chemistry, and all the other specific areas of nature, are full of arguments based on elementary qualities and on secondary qualities such as *attractives*.'[46] Attractive forces were occult, not in the sense that they were invisible, but because they were unintelligible within the metaphysical categories

---

[46] *Search After Truth*, p. 242. See also p. 30, where the attraction of the moon, rather than the pressure of the surrounding air, is listed as another example of 'occult' explanatory entities.

of Cartesian philosophy. Any attempt to introduce forces into physics, especially if they were categorized as scholastic qualities, would therefore run contrary to the deepest reservations of Cartesians. And that is exactly what Leibniz tried to do.

In the *Discourse on Metaphysics* (1686), Leibniz rehearsed some of his standard objections to the Cartesian account of collisions. He proposed, instead, a dynamic account which presupposes the reality of force as an irreducible explanatory concept. Leibniz argues against the Cartesians that if motion is defined only in relation to some framework, then it is impossible to say that one body truly moves while another is at rest. Apart from the changing relations with other bodies, which are extrinsic relations, there must be some real quality which distinguishes moving bodies from bodies at rest:

But the force or the immediate cause of these changes is something more real, and there is a sufficient basis for ascribing it to one body rather than to another. This, therefore, is also the way to learn to which body the motion preferably belongs. Now this force is something different from size, figure, and motion, and from this we conclude that not everything which is conceived in a body consists solely in extension and its modifications, as our moderns have persuaded themselves. Thus we are compelled to restore also certain *beings* or *forces* which they have banished.[47]

The restoration of banished forms highlights the nub of the issue in dispute. Indeed, Leibniz almost seems to relish talk of forms as a way of taunting the ontological squeamishness of the Cartesians:

I perceived that the sole consideration of *extended mass* was not enough but that it was necessary, in addition, to use the concept of *force*, which is fully intelligible, although it falls within the sphere of metaphysics. . . . It was thus necessary to restore and, as it were, to rehabilitate the *substantial forms* which are in such disrepute today, but in a way which makes them intelligible and separates their proper use from their previous abuse.[48]

The candid admission by Leibniz that his dynamical theory involved a rehabilitation of something very much like scholastic forms was enough to provoke a Cartesian repudiation. The most obvious reason for rejecting these forms was the standard Cartesian objection that they are non-explanatory. However, another factor may also have been at work here, which deserves more detailed discussion, namely, the criteria which were implicitly invoked in

---

[47] *Philosophical Papers and Letters*, ed. Loemker, p. 315.
[48] *New System, Philosophical Papers and Letters*, ed. Loemker, p. 454.

deciding what kinds of theoretical entity could be clearly and distinctly conceived.

On the question of clear and distinct understanding, there is an interesting analogy between the Cartesians' response to forces and that of George Berkeley. Berkeley wrote in the *De Motu* (1721): 'Motion though it is clearly perceived by the senses has been rendered obscure rather by the learned comments of philosophers than by its own nature.'[49] He went on in the same paragraph to give two examples of those whom he thought had obscured our understanding of motion; Aristotle and the schoolmen, and 'a famous man of modern times' who is not identified by name. The famous man in question was Leibniz, for the obscure definition which is quoted in the text is taken from the *Specimen Dynamicum* (1695): 'There is nothing real in motion itself except that momentaneous state which must consist of a force striving towards change.'[50] Berkeley's criterion for accepting or rejecting concepts is explicit; he cannot understand anything which is not available in perception. The question arises whether a similar kind of consideration is implicitly at work among the French Cartesians.

Rohault, for example, introduced the discussion 'Of Motion and Rest' in the *Traité de physique* as follows: 'Because it is easier to understand what motion is, by experience, than to give a definition of it, or to find out the cause, I shall here make use of a familiar example, agreed upon by all, which may serve to explain to us the nature of motion.'[51] Rohault's clarification of motion—understood as the displacement of one object relative to another which is considered to be at rest—is repeated by all the Cartesians in this period, including Malebranche. Thus the *Search After Truth*, in Book I, chapter 8:

Ordinarily, this term [i.e. motion] signifies two things: the first is a certain force imagined to be in the body moved and that is the cause of its motion; the second is the continual transport of a body approaching or receding from another object taken to be at rest. . . . In short, the term *motion* signifies both the cause and the effect, which are nevertheless two quite different things.[52]

---

[49] *The Works of George Berkeley*, iv. 42.

[50] *Philosophical Papers and Letters*, ed. Loemker, p. 436. Berkeley's reference is in *Works of George Berkeley*, iv. 43. Roger Woolhouse has independently identified the 'famous man' in Woolhouse (1979).

[51] *Traité de physique*, i. 38.

[52] *Search After Truth*, p. 37.

The standard Cartesian account made motion in the second sense (relative transport) available to experience; it also suggested that the concept of relative motion could be understood more easily by reflecting on our perception of simple physical displacements than by consulting scholastic definitions or, perhaps, any theoretical account at all.

As far as motion in the first sense is concerned—i.e. the cause of particular physical displacements—Malebranche argued for reasons already considered that this was adequately accounted for by reference to God's agency, and that Leibnizian forces are therefore redundant. There was also a quite different type of objection raised against such physical (or metaphysical) forces, and it is here that the comparison with Berkeley is appropriate. There was a strong empiricist reluctance among Cartesians to endorse any concept in physical science which denoted an entity which could not be modelled mechanically. This ontological bashfulness was inherited from Descartes, who argued that the only difference between elementary particles and macroscopic bodies is a difference in size.[53] Therefore, anything we predicate of physical bodies must be the kind of quality which we can experience in macroscopic physical objects. This is precisely what is lacking in the case of concepts such as 'attractive force' or 'repulsive force'. The unintelligibility of these concepts for the Cartesian is partly explained, therefore, by a lack of acquaintance with similar features in regular-size physical bodies. This kind of empiricism with respect to the origin or viability of certain concepts may be presented in most cases under the rubric of 'clear and distinct ideas'; however, the operative criterion of clarity and distinctness is often a less explicit version of Berkeley's test: is this is the kind of entity which I can perceive (and subsequently imagine)?

In short, Malebranche's objections to forces ramified in a variety of directions and were based on a cluster of interdependent reasons. Occasionalism was an important part of the thesis, and this in turn depended as much on a Cartesian theory of substances and modes as on the Oratorian's analysis of the simplicity of God's agency. The ongoing debate with his correspondent in Hanover brought to light a less obvious reservation about forces, namely, the objection to any concept which purported to denote something which was not available to perception in mechanical models.

[53] Descartes, *Œuvres*, ii. 367–8.

Malebranche's critique of forces had a lasting effect on the Cartesian tradition in France. It provided a coherently articulated position from which it was almost impossible to break without also challenging some central assumptions of Cartesian philosophy. Pierre-Sylvain Régis provides a good example, as usual, of someone who attempts to salvage the orthodoxy of Descartes without many of the conclusions which the Oratorian had generated from his system. Régis rejects the radical implications of Malebranche's stark understanding of God's role. He is willing to identify God as the primary cause of motion in conjunction with purely occasional, physical causes. 'God alone is the primary and total cause of all the motion in the world.'[54] At the same time, Régis claims that we may continue to speak of secondary causes as true causes: 'Therefore, we retain this way of speaking [about secondary causes], but only on condition that when we say that one body moves another, we only mean that God avails himself of the contact [between the bodies] and of the impenetrability of a body to move another one which is at rest.'[55] In other words, a body in motion A does not produce a new force in B, but is merely the occasion on which 'God, who moved body A, begins to move body B'.[56]

The assignment of metaphysical roles to God and physical bodies in the causation of motion has no direct implications for Régis's physical analysis. In contrast with Malebranche, he claims that motion and rest both involve the operation of forces, and he even goes so far as to borrow the Leibnizian language of active forces to describe the reality of motion. However, this attempt to introduce forces within the Cartesian framework required much more than a transposition of terminology, and it eventually failed to resist Malebranche's arguments.

Régis suggested that the nature of motion cannot be understood properly by those 'who are accustomed to judge things by the senses rather than by reason'.[57] He decided to rely on reason; his 'reason', however, is nothing more than an analysis of what is known by observation: 'l'expérience fait voir que . . .'[58] The rational analysis which was proposed involved examining various situations in which something is said to be in motion and attempting to construct a definition of motion which identifies some property which is common to all the cases considered. The resulting

[54] *Système*, i. 305.   [55] Ibid. i. 311–12.   [56] Ibid. i. 310.
[57] Ibid. i. 301.   [58] Ibid. i. 302.

definition is as follows: 'motion is the successive, active application of a body, by all of its exterior surface, to different parts of bodies which immediately touch it.'[59]

This definition was generated by considering the motion of any physical body in relation to others in its vicinity; the implications of the various parts of the definition are made explicit as follows:

1. Application, rather than an applied thing, to suggest that motion is a mode of a body rather than a substance.

2. Successive, in order to distinguish it from a form of rest where a body is constantly applied to some surroundings, as a stone in a wall.

3. Active, to distinguish it from another kind of rest, which is a form of passive successive application; e.g. a vessel at rest in water, which tends to be moved in one direction by the motion of the water and in the opposite direction by an opposing wind. No part of the ship is constantly in touch with the same surrounding medium, since the air above and the water below are both constantly changing. Yet the ship itself is said to be at rest.

4. By its whole exterior surface, to distinguish a body in motion from one which only moves part of itself while remaining in the same place.

5. Finally, the motion of a body is defined by reference to its immediate environment rather than to some distinct body or framework, such as the stars. Thus Régis openly rejects Descartes's definition of motion. The relationship between a body and the stars 'considered at rest' is merely an 'external relation' (*dénomination extérieure*) which changes nothing in the subject of which it is predicated.[60] Régis, by contrast, is interested in defining motion as a 'real and true change which occurred in a body in motion from the time it was at rest'.[61]

This definition, according to Régis, includes everything which is relevant to the definition of motion. It can be further analysed into two components: (*a*) 'formal motion', which is the successive application of a body to different surrounding bodies; and (*b*) the 'moving force' which causes the change of application. The first type of motion is a mode of the moved body, and therefore cannot be transferred from one body to another; by contrast, the moving force is not a mode of a body and 'experience shows that it passes

---

[59] *Système*, i. 296.   [60] Ibid. i. 302.   [61] Ibid. i. 297.

from one body to another'.[62] Therefore the moving force is really distinct, and not merely modally distinct, from the moved body.[63] The real distinction involved here is compatible with the view that 'the moving force is nothing other than the will which God has to move matter'.[64] Considered as God's will, there is no difficulty in seeing a real distinction between a moving force and a body in motion. However, this seems to collapse Régis's position into that of Malebranche, for whom force is not a real entity of some kind in moving objects. How can one have a real force in bodies which is really distinct both from God and from the bodies in motion?

Régis partly broaches this question in Book I, chapter 5 of the *Physique*, which is entitled 'That motive force produces rest as well as motion'. The opinion being rejected is clearly that of Malebranche.

One is easily convinced that . . . motion depends on some efficient cause to produce it, whereas one has great difficulty in believing that . . . rest also depends on an efficient cause. The reason for this is that we are naturally led to think of motion as a very positive thing, which we experience in ourselves whenever we move ourselves; whereas we are accustomed to think of rest as a simple cessation of motion. We believe that a body remains at rest from the mere fact that no one touches it and we do not perceive anything which pushes it or which gives it some of its own motion. We conclude from this that, although it is necessary to have a cause to produce motion, it appears as if we do not need a cause to produce rest.[65]

Régis wanted to argue instead that there 'is a force and positive action in rest just as much as in motion'.[66] In fact, it is 'the *same* force which produces motion and rest'.[67]

This can be demonstrated by consulting our experience of falling bodies. The force of gravity causes an object to descend until it is prevented from further downward motion by contact with the ground.

It is easy to conclude from this that it is the same force which makes a body descend and which holds it at rest against the earth, with this one difference, however, that it [i.e. the force] makes it descend through the air . . . *of itself* because nothing resists it, whereas it only keeps it at rest against the earth *by accident*, because the earth resists it.[68]

In other words, the force of gravity explains both the downward

[62] Ibid. i. 303–4.   [63] Ibid. i. 304.   [64] Ibid. i. 306.
[65] Ibid. i. 306–7.   [66] Ibid. i. 307.   [67] Ibid.
[68] Ibid.

motion of falling bodies and the state of rest of bodies on the surface of the earth. The only difference between the two cases is that 'the first one is always thought to be in the body which moves, whereas the second one is always considered as external to the body which is at rest'.[69]

Régis returns at this point in the discussion to an obvious type of objection from Malebranche: since God is the cause of both motion and rest and is equally external to all bodies whatever their condition, it follows that 'motive force' is also external to bodies in motion or at rest. The reply surprisingly concedes the main point of this objection, that motive force is not really distinct from the will of God, and hence that it is equally external to both motion and rest. However, Régis still maintains that the following distinction can be made:

God wills directly and as we say *par soy* that bodies in motion are applied successively to different parts of bodies which touch them immediately; he only wills indirectly, or *par accident*, that the other bodies are applied to bodies in motion. That is why, in order to distinguish these two kinds of applications, we have called those which God wills directly 'active' (*actives*) . . . whereas we have used the word 'passive' (*passives*) to describe those which he wills only indirectly.[70]

This distinction in the modalities of God's willing only postpones the difficulty raised by Malebranche. The various ways in which God wills things are, in the Cartesian perspective, identical in God; more accurately, the various ways in which we describe God's will do not denote any real distinctions in God. Besides, there is no hope of basing any other real distinctions on such considerations. The only way out of the problem is to recognize forces as distinct, in some sense, from God's will. Once that is rejected, it is hard to see how Régis might have endorsed the occasionalism of Malebranche and still maintained the independent reality of force. Even in his efforts to attribute force to bodies at rest, he explains the state of rest along Malebranchian lines, where the condition of the body at rest is a function of its being pushed or impeded by other bodies in motion or at rest. So that ultimately the condition of rest or motion of every body is explained by the extrinsic forces of other bodies in motion. There is hardly room here for a viable reversion to Descartes.

---

[69] *Système*, i. 308.   [70] Ibid. i. 309.

Besides, Régis has explicitly rejected Descartes's attempt to define motion in purely relative terms. He apparently wanted to characterize the condition of a body in motion in terms of some real, intrinsic property of that body, in contrast with its changing relations with other bodies which are mere 'extrinsic denominations'. This was accomplished by making force a condition which is really distinct, and not merely modally distinct, from a body in motion. However, the reality of force, together with the constraints of occasionalism, conspired to collapse any distinction which he might have forged between force and God's will. The language of active and passive forces is idle in this context, as long as force has not been recognized as something distinct from God and the motion of moved bodies.

The failure on the part of Régis to incorporate forces into Cartesian physics underlines the success of Malebranche's critique, and it also shows the extent to which the Oratorian's analysis was a natural development of fundamental assumptions which are at least implicit in Descartes's system. The exclusion of forces has implications for the Cartesian concept of explanation, and these are taken up again below. Perhaps the most surprising feature of the Cartesian discussion of force is the almost implicit epistemological criterion which only emerged in the correspondence with Leibniz; according to this criterion of acceptability, forces were suspect because they denoted entities which are not perceived in mechanical models. This kind of conceptual empiricism, together with the short-circuiting of divine agency in the interests of simplicity and the consequent redundancy of secondary causes, creates a context in which Berkeley is the non-paradoxical successor of the French Cartesians of the seventeenth century.

The net result of Cartesian analyses of matter in motion was a radical separation between the powerless, inert, and almost propertyless stuff called matter, the defining feature of which is its extension, and spiritual substances which are exclusively the cause of motion and to which properly the power to cause motion should be attributed. In this sharp division between the roles of matter and spirit, Cartesians were persuaded by a wide range of interlocking arguments to defend their attenuated concept of matter against the apparent demands of empirical evidence. The characteristic concepts of substance and modes which was inherited from Descartes, the unrelenting allegiance to extension as the defining property of matter, the penchant for uncompromising reductions even when they seemed initially to be implausible, the unequivocal rejection of so-called occult properties in the guise of scholastic qualities, and the acceptance of God's dominant role as the universal and first cause of everything which occurs in nature; all these considerations conspired to divest Cartesian matter of most of the properties which natural philosophers in the seventeenth century were willing to entertain as fundamental qualities of natural phenomena. As a result of the efforts of those who were committed to a strictly Cartesian natural philosophy, the explanation of motion was confined to the efficacy of divine concurrence and the regularities, in the form of laws, in which that divine causality was expressed. The matter which God moves was in turn described by reference to a very limited list of fundamental or primary qualities which excluded, not only the suspect qualities of the scholastic tradition, but also many other properties such as elasticity or gravity. The metaphysical economy of the Cartesians was sustained, as might be expected, by an almost prodigal attitude towards the construction of mechanical hypotheses. The limited range of theoretical entities at their disposal demanded a corresponding ingenuity and lack of restraint in imagining ways in which matter in motion might explain the diversity of natural phenomena.

5

Hypotheses Fingo

W H E N Newton penned his famous phrase, *hypotheses non fingo*, in the General Scholium to the second edition of the *Principia* (1713), there can be little doubt that he was contrasting his discussion of gravity with his perception of the Cartesians' procedure in discussing the same phenomenon.[1] It is equally clear that Newton's perception of the Cartesians' penchant for constructing hypotheses was reasonably accurate; by the end of the seventeenth century, there was general agreement among natural philosophers that the followers of Descartes were leading proponents of an apparently unrestricted use of hypotheses in scientific explanation. In stark contrast with Newton's reluctance to endorse hypotheses—at least in his official or explicit methodology—the Cartesians were strongly urging a policy which might be summarized in the slogan: *hypotheses fingo*.

The endorsement of hypotheses should have been accompanied by a corresponding recognition, by the Cartesians, that natural philosophy cannot emulate the certainty or demonstrative character of mathematics. However, there was less agreement about this conclusion than one might expect, and there were significant variations from one author to another in recognizing the extent to which uncertainty might follow the adoption of a hypothetical method. Malebranche provides a good example of the ambivalence of Cartesianism in this respect. He concedes, through his spokesman

---

[1] Sir Isaac Newton's *Mathematical Principles of Natural Philosophy and his System of the World*, p. 547. Cf. the notes by F. Cajori, pp. 671–6, on the possible interpretations of this famous disclaimer by Newton. The original Latin was: 'Rationem vero harum gravitatis proprietatum ex phaenomenis nondum potui deducere, & hypotheses non fingo.' Cf. *Opticks*, Bk. I, part 1: 'My Design in this Book is not to explain the Properties of Light by Hypotheses, but to propose and prove them by Reason and Experiments', p. 1. There is an extensive literature on Newton's use of hypotheses and alternative interpretations of his attitude towards their use in natural philosophy. For an analysis of Newton's various hypotheses about the cause of gravitational phenomena, see McMullin (1978a).

in the *Dialogues on Metaphysics*, that hypotheses are uncertain.[2] At the same time he quite explicitly relies on hypotheses to explain magnetism, for example, or to account for Newton's experiments on light.[3] The Oratorian's ambivalence about hypotheses is not surprising. He argues against accepting merely probable opinions in science, unless they are entertained only provisionally with a view to subsequent conversion to demonstrated truths.[4] Malebranche also recognized that some hypotheses cannot be redeemed as demonstrated knowledge, especially the 'particular laws of nature' which physicists use to explain individual phenomena, 'because the experiences which are the most reliable way of discovering them are very deceptive'.[5] For this reason 'there are few truths concerning natural things that are fully demonstrated, [although] it is certain that there are some indubitable general ones'.[6] In a word, natural philosophy ought ideally to approximate the certainty which is available in mathematics; at the same time, hypotheses are unavoidable in physical explanations, and many physical hypotheses are doomed to remain uncertain.

Malebranche's evident reluctance about the implications of accepting a hypothetical method was not felt as keenly by other Cartesians. For example, Gadroys introduced his *Système du monde* with an open admission that he was choosing between alternative plausible hypotheses.[7] One of the consequences of this approach was that one had to be satisfied with a science which was not demonstrated. This point is developed at length by Gadroys in his examination of astrology, the *Discours sur les influences des astres, selon les principes de M. Descartes* (1671):

I think that I will have made great progress if I only approach plausibility. These kinds of things are at the same time so deep and so obscure that, in order to know them to the extent to which the human mind is capable, it is sufficient to know that they may be as we describe them, and that one finds no contradiction nor absurdity in the explanation which one gives of them. One should not look for absolutely necessary propositions in all the sciences. There are some disciplines which enjoy the name of a science and which do not have the certainty of geometry. One should distinguish between different matters; and it is a mistake to demand mathematical

---

[2] *Dialogues on Metaphysics*, pp. 127, 129.
[3] *Search After Truth*, pp. 93, 696, 717.   [4] Ibid. 10–11.
[5] *Conversations chrétiennes*, in *Œuvres complètes*, v. 198–9.
[6] *Search After Truth*, pp. 484–5.   [7] *Système du monde*, p. 3.

demonstrations everywhere. A great man said that there are different degrees of proof. There is one which shows that something is certain; there are others which show that it is probable. Besides, one can sometimes derive a conclusion which all reasonable minds should recognize as certain from many probabilities. It is true that in the science of the influences [of the stars] there are only conjectures; but these conjectures should not be rejected, because they cohere together very well.[8]

In this text, Gadroys is willing to confront some of the most contentious implications of adopting a hypothetical method in science. In fact, this tolerant attitude towards conjectures is as much a reflection of the general approach of Cartesians during this period as the scrupulous ambivalence of Malebranche.

The contrast between Malebranche and Gadroys underlines a central issue, therefore, for the Cartesians, namely, the extent to which they can introduce hypotheses into science and at the same time realize an ideal of demonstrated or deductively warranted knowledge.

Cartesians were obviously not the only proponents of a hypothetical method in the latter part of the seventeenth century; indeed, it would be difficult to identify any natural philosopher of the period who failed to use hypotheses as an explicit part of his scientific method. Claude Perrault, for example, discourses at length on the inevitability of accepting plausible hypotheses in physics because nothing more certain is available: 'physics can hardly be done except in this way, that is, by problems; that which is of a different nature [i.e. more strictly deductive] does not belong to it. By contrast with those sciences in which one only admits what is certain and demonstrated, physics should accept everything which is probable.'[9] One of the consequences of understanding physics in this way is that new hypotheses will replace older ones 'as long as reflection on different phenomena provides an occasion for inventing new hypotheses, without any hope of ever being able to discover the truth'.[10] Similar sentiments were expressed by Mariotte and Huygens and, with the exception of the scholastic philosophers of nature, by most other scientists who recognized the necessity of using hypotheses to identify the causes of natural phenomena.[11]

---

[8] *Influences*, pp. 217–18.   [9] *Essais de physique*, iii. 5.
[10] Ibid. 6.
[11] Mariotte, *Essai de logique*, in *Œuvres*, ii. 609–701, esp. principle 53 on p. 624; C. Huygens, *Treatise on Light*, preface, pp. vi–vii.

Although there was a widespread recognition of the necessity of hypotheses in natural philosophy, Cartesians were more publicly associated with a hypothetical method than many of their contemporaries in the seventeenth century and they seemed, to some of their opponents at least, to be lacking in due restraint in exploiting hypotheses. This raises two sets of issues about their scientific method: (a) their understanding of the term 'hypothesis', and of the role of hypotheses in scientific explanation; (b) their criteria for choosing between competing hypotheses, and their account of how those chosen might eventually be confirmed or disqualified. One of the questions which straddles the two issues distinguished here and which was peculiar to the Cartesians, was the extent to which metaphysical insights or principles could function as a foundation from which, in Régis's words, the principles of physics might be deduced and thereby confirmed. Chapter 7 below is devoted to discussing the Cartesian theory of confirmation. This chapter offers a preliminary account of (a), and of the proposed deduction of scientific hypotheses from metaphysical foundations.

The Concept of a Hypothesis

The conceptual restrictions discussed in the previous chapters suggest that, whatever its precise structure or logical form, a scientific explanation of any physical phenomenon in Cartesian science can be expressed only within the scope of a very restricted range of concepts. Cartesian theoretical entities were limited to small parts of matter and their primary qualities, including motion. Both the particles and their motions are invisible and were assumed to be invisible even with the help of magnifying instruments. Therefore, nothing which Cartesians might say about matter in motion can be learned directly from observation or experience of any kind; the motions and interactions of unobservable corpuscles can only be described if we deduce a description of them from some other principles, or if we are willing to construct hypotheses. There is a suggestion in Descartes that the first of these options is the correct one; this suggestion continues to recur in various forms in later Cartesians. The precise extent of its role will be examined in more detail below. Descartes had also acknowledged that we cannot discover, by reason alone, what kinds of elements were created by

God in nature, and that we must be willing to make hypotheses about their size and motion. This suggests that we are working with invisible particles, the size and shape of which can only be determined, initially, by hypothesis. It is a very short step to conclude that anything we say about these particles of matter in motion will be equally hypothetical. Both Rohault and Régis argued along these lines in favour of the essentially hypothetical character of scientific explanations.

Rohault situates his discussion of astronomical phenomena, in Part II of the *Traité de physique*, within the framework of a God who has options in creating the universe:

Since the world is the work, or rather the diversion of the hand of God, who could divide it into as many parts as he pleased, and dispose them in an infinite variety of ways; it is impossible for us to know the number or order of them, by any reason drawn from the nature of the things themselves; and we can know only by experience, which God was pleased to choose, out of those many ways in which they might have been disposed. We ought therefore to consider every particular, as far as the weakness of human nature, assisted by all the helps of art and industry, will permit, that we may go back, as far as we are able, from the effects to the causes; and first take notice, how things appear to us, before we make a judgement of the nature and disposition of them.[12]

The accurate observations we make are the basis on which we hypothesize possible causes. The most we can hope for in this context is to imagine a plausible cause, without being able to know for certain if it is the true cause by which God actually creates the phenomena we observe. 'Thus we must content ourselves for the most part, to find out how things may be; without pretending to come to a certain knowledge and determination of what they really are; for there may possibly be different causes capable of producing the same effect, which we have no means of explaining.'[13]

The connection between invisible particles and hypothetical causes is even more explicit in Régis. In the Preface to *La Physique*, he distinguished between what he calls a 'physical body' and a 'mechanical body'.

By the term *physical body* we understand a body which is composed of many insensible parts which are shaped and arranged in such a way that one can explain all the properties of this body by the configuration and

---

[12] *Traité de physique*, part II, 4.   [13] Ibid., part I, 14.

arrangement of the parts. By the term *mechanical body* we understand a body which is composed of sensible parts which are large and palpable; when they are connected together they are able, because of their shape and situation, to augment or diminish the motion of bodies to which the mechanical body is applied.[14]

A watch is an example of a mechanical body; its parts are visible and the interactions of the parts can be observed easily. A magnetic stone, however, is a physical body because 'it is composed of insensible parts which are shaped and arranged in such a way that, if they were otherwise shaped and arranged, the magnetic stone would not produce the same effects as it does'.[15] The common feature in both types of body is the interaction of constituent parts to cause the results which we can observe, the motion of the hands on a watch or the motion, for example, of iron fillings which lie close to a magnet. The characteristic feature of a 'physical body' is that some of its properties can be explained only by reference to its unobservable constituent parts.

Régis contends that one can easily explain the effects of a mechanical body because the connections between the parts are visible and their effects predictable. By contrast, the interactions between insensible parts of physical bodies can only be hypothesized:

It is quite different for physical bodies; because their parts are insensible, one cannot perceive their order or arrangement, and the most one could hope to do would be to guess (*deviner*) at it from the effects. There are therefore two parts in physics; one concerns the knowledge of the effects, and the other which consists in the knowledge of causes. The first may be called practical physics, and the other speculative physics. . . . the speculative part consists in the reasonings which one can make to discover the causes of effects.[16]

It is quite clear from this policy statement on method that the hypothetical character of physics follows necessarily from the invisibility of the particles which are ultimately assumed to be the causes of mechanical effects. Lest the reader be dissatisfied with the resulting uncertainty of speculative physics, Régis reminds us that we should

---

[14] *Système*, i. 273.   [15] Ibid. i. 274.

[16] Ibid. i. 274. Cf. ibid. ii. 504, where Régis explains that the bodies of animals may be classified as both mechanical and physical in the senses defined here; they are mechanical in so far as we can see the interconnection of different parts of the body, and they are physical in so far as the explanation of all the properties of animals ultimately depends on the interactions of invisible particles of matter.

not expect mathematical certainty in physics, just as we should not be satisfied with mere probability in mathematics.

Even though speculative physics can only be conducted in a problematic manner and contains no demonstrations, it should be recognized nevertheless that this part of physics, no matter how uncertain it is, still holds one of the highest ranks within human knowledge. For although one cannot be entirely certain of what it teaches, one can however believe that one has learned everything which the human mind is able to discover about a physical body if one has been able to conceive distinctly of such a disposition, shape and arrangement of its parts that one can deduce easily all the effects which result from that body. It follows from this that it would be equally unreasonable to demand demonstrations in physics, as it would be to be content with probabilities in mathematics; just as the latter should only include what is certain and demonstrated, the former has to accept everything which is probable, on condition that it is deduced from one unique system founded on the first truths of nature.[17]

The last phrase in this defence of a hypothetical method introduces a significant restriction on the kinds of hypotheses which are acceptable, and this is discussed below in the context of 'deducing' physics from a metaphysical foundation. In the meantime, the main point at issue is established clearly by Régis: if we explain phenomena by reference to *invisible* particles, then we must accept hypotheses. It is the same point which was made by Fontenelle, in *The Plurality of Worlds*: 'All philosophy is founded upon these two propositions: 1. That our minds are curious; and 2. That our eyes are poor; . . . So that true philosophers will not

---

[17] Ibid. i. 275. Huet objected to precisely this procedure in Cartesian science, of assuming a possible cause and subsequently claiming that one had identified the true cause of some natural phenomenon: 'even if we concede that all corporeal things and the whole world may have developed from those principles which he proposed . . . it does not follow that the world developed from these principles', *Censura Philosophiae Cartesianae* (1690), p. 96. Régis replied that Huet was demanding too much in physical science by failing to recognize that science cannot but be hypothetical. 'M. Huet obviously did not note that speculative physics can only be done in a problematic way, and that there are no demonstrations in it. If he had paid attention, he would have been persuaded . . . that one knows everything which the human mind is capable of knowing about physical things, if one can distinctly conceive of a disposition or arrangement of their parts such that all the effects which one observes in these bodies can follow absolutely from this arrangement or disposition', *Réponse à Huet* (1691), p. 304. Cf. Descartes to Mersenne, *Œuvres*, iii. 141–4, where he defends the necessity of using hypotheses in optics because no other method is possible in physical science.

believe what they see, and are always guessing about (*deviner*) what they do not [see].'[18]

These endorsements of hypothetical reasoning raise a number of issues about the sense in which the term 'hypothesis' is being used. For example, are the Cartesians joining the 'saving the phenomena' tradition of Osiander or, if not, what level of uncertainty are they willing to tolerate in hypotheses?

The acceptability of false hypotheses arose as an explicit issue in Cartesian cosmogony.[19] It developed from the apparent conflict between the account of the earth's origin given in Genesis and the Cartesian account of a structured universe evolving from an initial chaos. The Cartesian account implied that the present condition of the earth can be understood scientifically only if one can show how it might have evolved according to the laws of nature. However, a literal reading of Genesis suggests that the earth was created in six days by God; hence the Cartesian explanation of its origins is not historically true. In order to reconcile the demands of scientific explanation and of fidelity to a religious tradition, the concept of a model was introduced to characterize Descartes's cosmogony. Despite that, there is no suggestion here or anywhere else that it is a 'mere' hypothesis, because the earth could have evolved in exactly that way had God not intervened to quicken the process. Thus, in contrast with the instrumentalist or mathematical-fiction tradition, there is a robust realism in Cartesian science which is apparently not compromised by the acknowledged insensibility of the theoretical entities on which explanations ultimately rest.

In their attempts to define explicitly what they meant by the term hypothesis, Cartesians focused on the role of certain propositions which are assumed in a given context, rather than on the certainty or otherwise of what is being assumed. Régis confronted this issue in the glossary to *L'Usage de la raison et de la foy* (1704), and proposed the following: 'Hypothesis: this is a Greek word, which means *supposition*; it is what is established as the foundation of some truth and it serves to make it understood, whether the thing which one assumes is true, certain and known, or whether it is only

[18] *Plurality of Worlds*, pp. 19–20. Fontenelle compares the philosopher's practice with the opera-goer who has to guess at what is happening behind the scenes in changes of set on the stage. The argument from the invisibility of parts of matter to the necessity of hypotheses is also used by La Forge, in his commentary on Descartes's *L'Homme* (1664), p. 177.

[19] Cf. Roger (1982).

used to explain some truth with which it is related.'[20] This definition implies that even self-evident axioms could function as hypotheses, depending on the role assigned to them in a particular context. Likewise, assumptions which are not known to be true may be hypotheses in this sense if they serve an explanatory function.

The Oratorian, Père Nicolas Poisson, undertook a systematic review of the different types of hypotheses used by Cartesians, in his *Remarques sur la méthode de Mr Descartes*.[21] Poisson distinguished five kinds of hypothesis: the hypothesis of revealed truths; the hypothesis of natural things; the hypothesis of possible natural things; the hypothesis of analogous things; and finally, the hypothesis of existent natural things. The first of these, the hypothesis of revealed truths, is not directly relevant to science; it involves an assumption that some religious belief is true even though it is not known by reason. Once this assumption is made, one may argue to further conclusions which are based on the initial assumption. For example, the 'revealed truth' that the soul is immortal may provide the starting-point for a philosophical discussion of the status of the separated soul.

The 'hypothesis of natural things' applies to any assumption about a natural phenomenon from which an inference is drawn. For example, 'assuming that the sun is elevated above the horizon, there is no doubt that it is day'.[22] This type of hypothesis seems to be a general category of which the third and fifth types are subclasses, although Poisson does not present it in this way. The 'hypothesis of possible natural things' is Poisson's terminology for idealization in physical explanations. To assume that a body is perfectly hard, that it travels in a straight line, or that it is not impeded by friction is to assume a series of conditions which are possible, but not actually true. In spite of the fact that they are false, Poisson claims that Descartes was able to use this type of hypothesis to discover laws of motion which made a major breakthrough in explaining naturally occurring phenomena. 'Once one has incontestable laws and rules, such as those which he established in that place [the *Principles*], all one needs to do is to subtract more or less of the hardness of those bodies which collide together, or more or less of the resistance of the parts of the medium in which they move, to make an exact

---

[20] Unpaginated glossary, at the end of *L'Usage de la raison*.
[21] *Remarques* (1671), pp. 175–80.
[22] Ibid. 176.

calculation of their motion.'[23] In this way, the temporary assumption of counterfactuals is a necessary part of constructing scientific explanations.

The 'hypothesis of existent natural things' is Poisson's way of describing the assumption of causes for actually occurring phenomena. The basis of this type of assumption is 'many observations which one has made on some particular phenomenon'.[24] For example, one might list all those reliable observational facts which are available about the apparent motion of the sun. To explain these apparent motions, one assumes either that the sun moves in certain ways, or that the earth moves, or some combination of these. Whatever option one prefers, Poisson suggests that the cause of the apparent motion of the sun cannot be identified either by observation or by engaging in philosophical discussion about 'being in general'. There is no other way of making progress in identifying physical causes except by hypothesis. This argument is similar to those already cited from Régis and Rohault; the invisible causes of observable effects can only be discovered by hypothesis. 'Since the particular causes of so many effects which he [Descartes] observes in nature are not revealed to him, it seems to me that, after the exact knowledge of these effects, he had to assume certain causes which he was not able to verify except by showing that these effects which he had observed follow naturally from those causes which he had assumed.'[25] There are definite limits on the kinds of assumptions which may be introduced in guessing the causes of natural phenomena. Poisson discusses this problem under the rubric of arbitrary hypotheses; this is examined in more detail below.

The final category of hypotheses is what Poisson calls *hypothèse des choses comparées*, by which he means 'using our knowledge of known things to raise ourselves to a knowledge of things which are unknown, by comparing one with the other'.[26] As examples of this method, he cites the analogies used by Descartes in the first discourse of the *Dioptrics* in order to explain the nature of light.[27] These were explicitly recognized by Descartes as assumptions; Poisson's discussion helps focus attention on where exactly an assumption was being made. The behaviour of the blind man and his stick is accepted as factual, as is the motion of a tennis ball or the squeezing of wine through apertures in a vat. The hypothesis

[23] *Remarques*, p. 177.   [24] Ibid. 180.   [25] Ibid. 182.
[26] Ibid. 178.   [74] Descartes, *Œuvres*, vi. 83 ff.

consists in the assumption that the motion of light resembles one or more of these known phenomena. For this reason Poisson appropriately names this procedure an hypothesis of comparison or an analogical hypothesis.

These distinctions in the Cartesian use of the term 'hypothesis', together with the definition already cited from Régis, suggest that the common feature of all hypotheses was the fact that they are premisses from which something else may be inferred. In other words, it is the role of an assumption in a given context, rather than its epistemic status, which makes it function as an hypothesis. Poisson presumably thinks that revealed religious beliefs are true, and yet he characterizes them as hypotheses. In a similar way, Régis explicitly includes beliefs which are known to be true among his hypotheses. However, there are also connotations of non-standard knowledge in Poisson's account; religious beliefs cannot be known by reason, just as the causes of physical phenomena cannot be discovered by observation. In each case we are assuming the truth of something which may eventually be known with certainty, but at least it is not initially known by either reason or direct experience. Of course it remains to be seen what kind of certainty or knowledge may be claimed for the hypotheses on which scientific explanations rely.

Once it was clearly acknowledged that speculative physics must operate by postulating unobservable causes for observable effects, it became equally clear that a resourceful physicist could always imagine some hypothetical cause which is tailor made to explain any conceivable effect. The apparent latitude allowed here was restricted by the exclusion of what were called 'arbitrary' hypotheses.

Poisson distinguishes between 'reasonable hypotheses' and those which are 'completely arbitrary':

It is necessary to distinguish well between completely arbitrary hypotheses which have no basis except in the brain of some constructors of chimeras, and reasonable hypotheses which cannot always be arranged so as to deduce anything one wishes from them. The latter [reasonable hypotheses] present themselves to us already made and need only be applied to their subject; they are not works which the human mind constructs wantonly from bits and pieces which have no relation or correspondence one with another. A truly natural hypothesis is a machine in which the wheels turn of themselves without any need for men to make each of its parts work by hand; the interplay of the parts, however, makes it clear to see, without difficulty, thousands of things which could not be understood from a simple description.[28]

Gadroys repeats almost verbatim, four years later, the same analysis of arbitrary hypothesis in his *Système du monde*. He argues that 'if it were only a matter of making assumptions, it seems to me that there would be nothing which could not be proved; however, since the consequences always depend on their principles, if these assumptions are themselves arbitrary, then whatever follows from them cannot be very reasonable.'[29] For example, the assumption that there is a fire at the centre of the earth falls into the category of arbitrary hypotheses:

But what proof have I of what I say; this would be a purely arbitrary hypothesis and it would have no other foundation except my imagination. One should accept as hypotheses only those which represent machines all the wheels of which run of their own accord, without having any need, one might say, for men to turn each of the parts of the machine by hand; in other words, only those the operation of which shows without difficulty each of the individual parts which we have been able to observe. . . . The hypothesis which I have adopted is of this kind, for it seems to me that all the phenomena follow from it, without forcing nature, one might say, to come to its aid.[30]

The interconnection of parts of a machine gives some idea of what Cartesians meant by a reasonable hypothesis. Each moving part of a machine functions as a direct result of its connection with other parts rather than as a result of some extrinsic cause; likewise reasonable hypotheses are appropriately connected with other parts of one's physical theory and are not devised independently to explain a particular phenomenon. There is a revealing indication of how Gadroys understands the connection between individual hypotheses and a background theory when he compares arbitrary hypotheses with assumptions whose truth has not been established. The implicitly assumed model of logical inference suggests that all the consequences which are deduced from a proposition are

---

[28] *Remarques*, p. 175.   [29] *Système du monde*, p. 177.

[30] Ibid. 178–9. Cf. also the unpaginated preface: 'The mind is not satisfied if a hypothesis explains the appearances well; it also expects it to have some plausibility, and since the world is a great machine, and since it is made by such an excellent workman, its movements should be simple and its wheels never forced. Those who have suggested hypotheses about it should keep this rule in mind; but it surely seems as if Ptolemy and Tycho did not consider this point.'

arbitrary as long as the original assumption is not known to be true. Indeed, it suggests that the basic assumptions of scientific explanations are much more solidly established than the term 'hypothesis' usually implies. Before pursuing this question, it may consolidate one connotation of the phrase 'arbitrary hypothesis' if we take account of Régis's use of the same term.

Régis emphasizes the systemic unity of hypotheses as a criterion for distinguishing between 'arbitrary' and plausible assumptions. For example, in Book IV, Part III, of *La Physique* he lists many of the properties which a theory of magnets must account for, and then distinguishes between arbitrary and plausible hypotheses:

Many hypotheses have been proposed to explain these properties of the magnet, but since they are all arbitrary—that is to say, they are such that they do not relate to any general system—we will try to establish one which is more exact, that is to say, which is such that it depends necessarily on the general laws of nature which were explained in the first Book and on the particular construction of the universe which was demonstrated in the second [Book].[31]

The demand for systematic unity is equivalent to the requirement of Gadroys or Poisson that hypotheses should fit into a coherent account of nature which is ultimately based on laws of nature. Régis constantly relied on the contrast between 'arbitrary' and plausible to characterize hypotheses which merely save the phenomena, without being appropriately related to the general laws of physics. For example, Copernicus is included among those who were merely saving the phenomena because his theory of planetary motions was not deduced from laws of nature:

Copernicus assumed before us that the sun does not have the daily motion which it seems to have; however, there is this difference between him and us, that his assumption is purely arbitrary, and that ours should pass as truly demonstrated, because it is nothing more than an accumulation of many physical conclusions which have been deduced in the previous Book from the knowledge of matter and from the general laws of nature alone.[32]

[31] *Système*, ii. 222.

[32] Ibid. ii. 48; see also ii. 93, 297. In the introd. to his explanation of meteorological phenomena, in Bk. V of *La Physique*, Régis outlines a similar policy: 'We hope nevertheless to explain these phenomena by reasons which will seem so much more natural because they do not depend on any new hypothesis, and because they are nothing but the necessary consequences of the general laws of motion and of the particular construction of the elementary mass, both of which have been established earlier', ibid. ii. 338.

There are no objections in principle to astronomers using hypotheses which only save the phenomena, as long as we remember the more rigorous standards which apply to physicists, standards which are satisfied by Cartesian hypotheses!

Thus we heartily agree that the astronomers may use the hypotheses of Tycho as much as they wish; since they only intend to make calculations, they are allowed to use any hypotheses they wish without bothering to know if they conform with, or contradict, the laws of nature. But we could not approve of physicists wishing to accept this hypothesis as if it were true, because they must only admit as true those hypotheses which accord with the rules of motion; to which that of Tycho is absolutely contrary.[33]

There are two different suggestions being made here, as in the texts cited above from Gadroys. One general point is that hypotheses are *ad hoc* or arbitrary if they do not cohere with a general theory of the universe. Such assumptions may be tolerated in astronomy in order to make calculations, but they have no part in physics if one claims to explain why phenomena are as we observe them to be. A second point with a more traditional Cartesian flavour is that the coherence demanded of hypotheses is ultimately explained by reference to general laws of nature from which all other scientific explanations are 'deduced'. The explicit discussion of this point cannot be deferred any longer.

Demonstration from Metaphysical Foundations

Despite the frequency of references to hypotheses and probability, Régis retained the scholastic definition of science which so confused the debate, almost seventy years earlier, between Galileo and Bellarmine.[34] Régis distinguishes, in his *Logic*, between scientific

[33] *Système*, ii. 102.

[34] For the discussion of demonstrated science in Galileo and Bellarmine, see Drake (1957) and McMullin (1978*b*). Cf. also Antoine le Grand, *Institution of Philosophy*, part 1: 'Science is the certain and evident knowledge we have of any thing: For whatsoever is so evident to us, that we are certain of it, that we are said to know, or have the science of. Accordingly the knowledge of a conclusion is certain and evident, when the premisses, whereon as principles it doth depend, are so' (*Entire Body of Philosophy*, 39–40). In the fourth part of the same book he defends the demonstrative character of natural philosophy: 'Nevertheless, we must say that natural philosophy is indeed a science, because the nature of a science is not consider'd with respect to the things it treats of, but according to its axioms of an undoubted eternal truth. . . . we may have as well demonstrations of natural things, as of mathematical', p. 92.

knowledge and probable opinion: 'science is a certain and evident knowledge which is acquired by demonstration. . . . opinion is an uncertain knowledge which is based on a reason which is only probable.'[35] This typically scholastic distinction was a source of ambiguity in Cartesian philosophy as long as the term 'demonstration' retained the Aristotelian connotations of a type of knowledge which had nothing in common with uncertain opinions. There was as little in common between demonstration and probable opinions, in the Peripatetic tradition, as there was between celestial and terrestrial mechanics. Thus, in the course of debates during the seventeenth century concerning the epistemic status of mechanical hypotheses, scholastic philosophers continued to repeat the stark options which had been offered to Galileo by Bellarmine: that every proposed explanation must be a strict demonstration in the sense demanded by Aristotle's *Posterior Analytics*; otherwise, it is a mere hypothesis in the sense in which Ptolemaic epicycles are only mathematical fictions which do not purport to describe the actual orbits of planets. As long as this traditional concept of demonstration was standardly accepted in the schools, any attempt to describe one's scientific advances as 'demonstrations' invited the rebuke from school philosophers that one had misappropriated the language of the schools to describe mere hypotheses as genuine demonstrations.

At the same time, the term 'demonstration' had been adapted to new linguistic demands in the course of the seventeenth century so that, by the 1670s and 1680s, it was difficult to decide if it was being used by Cartesians to exaggerate the rigour of their hypothetical conclusions or to acknowledge the characteristic uncertainty of hypothetical reasoning. Descartes seems to have stumbled into this problem, in the Sixth Part of the *Discourse on Method*, when he used the word *démonstrées* to denote both the relation between hypothetical causes and their effects and, in the opposite direction, between our knowledge of effects and the suppositions which we invent to identify their unknown causes.

Should anyone be shocked at first by some of the statements I make at the beginning of the *Optics* and the *Meteorology* because I call them 'suppositions' . . . let him have patience to read the whole book . . . For I take my reasonings to be so closely interconnected that just as the last are

[35] *Système*, i. 58.

proved (*démonstrées*) by the first, which are their causes, so the first are proved by the last, which are their effects.[36]

In response to one of the many queries which this discussion provoked, Descartes wrote unambiguously to Father Morin in 1638: 'There is a big difference between proving and explaining. I should add that the word *démontrer* can be used to mean either, at least if it is used according to common usage and not in the technical philosophical sense.'[37] Thus hypothetical causes demonstrate effects by *explaining* them, while our knowledge of effects demonstrates the assumed causes by confirming or proving them.

This new, non-technical or non-scholastic usage became more common during the course of the century in parallel with the traditional usage of the term. Demonstration came to mean, as Descartes had suggested in the *Discourse*, any type of 'certain and evident reasoning'.[38] Samuel Sorbière illustrates this semantic development in a lengthy letter to Mazarin, in 1659, in which he tries to show that 'politics has its demonstrations just as much as geometry'.[39] Sorbière argues that the term 'demonstration' is used in two ways. There are demonstrations which begin with causes and then reason towards a description of their effects; and there are demonstrations which go in the opposite direction, beginning with effects and reasoning towards their likely causes. 'One can strive for demonstration by either one of these two methods.'[40] The former is called a priori demonstration, and the latter a posteriori. The paradigm of an a priori demonstration is when we construct the axioms from which our reasoning begins, because in that case the causes (i.e. the axioms) are within our own control. Evidently, explanation in the physical sciences can only be a posteriori:

With regard to the causes of natural things—which are not within our power but depend rather on the will of God who created them, and which remain invisible for the most part—we cannot deduce the properties of natural things from their causes, since we do not see the causes. Therefore what we do in drawing consequences from those of their properties which we do know is to go back as far as we can [in identifying their causes] and show that it is not impossible that these or those things may have been their

---

[36] *Œuvres*, vi. 76; Eng. trans. in *The Philosophical Writings of Descartes*, i. 150.
[37] Descartes to Morin, 13 July 1638, *Œuvres*, ii. 198. For a discussion of Descartes's use of the terms *démontrer* and *déduire*, see Clarke (1982), 65–70, 207–10.
[38] *Discourse on Method*, in *Œuvres*, vi. 19; Eng. trans., i. 120.
[39] Sorbière, *Lettres et discours*, pp. 712–17.   [40] Ibid. 714.

causes. This type of demonstration is a posteriori, and the science which it generates is called physics.[41]

Sorbière's analysis is typical of the less restrictive use of the term 'demonstration' in mid-century; however, even in the case of physical hypotheses he continues to demand that 'demonstrations should be supported by unshakeable foundations'.[42]

The extension of the term beyond the limits set by the scholastic tradition leaves open the question of the degree of certainty which Cartesians hoped to realize in their so-called a posteriori demonstrations. Are hypothetical explanations as logically rigorous as mathematical demonstrations, or are there varying degrees of certainty associated with the different types of demonstration which had become acceptable? This question is taken up in Chapter 7 below.

The ambiguity which resulted from parallel, overlapping uses of the term 'demonstration' both inside and outside the scholastic tradition was exacerbated by the repeated suggestion by both sides that any worthwhile scientific explanation must begin with metaphysical axioms from which one's hypothetical explanation is 'deduced'. The type of deduction which was envisaged by Cartesian philosophers in this context was such that it did not compromise the essentially hypothetical character of explanations in 'physics'.

The term 'axiom' usually meant, for Cartesians, a self-evident truth which is warranted exclusively by conceptual analysis. Régis is more explicit here than others: 'The rule for axioms is: if it is only necessary to consider the two concepts of the subject and the predicate with a mediocre attention in order to see clearly that an attribute belongs to a subject, then one can take the proposition to be an axiom which has no need of being demonstrated.'[43] An axiom

---

[41] Ibid. 715–16.

[42] Ibid. 714. The idea that political philosophy is capable of demonstration was also suggested by many authors as diverse as Grotius, Pufendorf, or Locke. Cf. the distinction between a priori and a posteriori demonstrations of natural law in Grotius, *On the Law of War and Peace*, pp. 42, 507. The analogy between axiomatic reasoning in mathematics and in legal theory is even more evident in Grotius's *On the Law of Prize and Booty*, p. 4. Pufendorf makes similar claims for 'genuine demonstrations which are capable of producing a solid science' in moral theory, in *On the Law of Nature and Nations*, p. 25. Finally, Locke argues for reasons similar to those of Sorbière that 'moral knowledge is as capable of real certainty as mathematics', in *An Essay Concerning Human Understanding*, iv. 7. iv.

[43] *Système*, i. 21.

of this kind or a first principle is known by what Régis calls 'understanding' (*intelligence*).[44]

Cartesian physics is supposed to be based on, or derived from, metaphysical axioms: 'all the truths of nature can be reduced to the principles which we have proposed in the reflections on metaphysics.'[45] 'Physics is based on (*fondée*) . . . its principles [i.e. those of metaphysics]; . . . if physicists are assured that extended substance exists and that it is divided into many bodies, that is something which they know from metaphysics . . .'[46] What are those metaphysical axioms on which the whole of physics is said to depend? Régis introduced four basic axioms in Book I of the *Metaphysics*: (*a*) 'Nothingness, or that which does not exist, has no properties'; (*b*) 'Every effect presupposes a cause'; (*c*) 'An effect cannot have more perfection than it has received from its total cause'; (*d*) 'Every change which occurs in a subject proceeds from some external cause'.[47] The third axiom is said to imply that every body remains in whatever condition it is in; otherwise, any new condition it might acquire would be caused by nothingness. Likewise, the fourth axiom implies that 'a body which is at rest will never move on its own', that is, without being caused to move by some external cause.[48]

Malebranche uses the term 'axiom' in a similar way to describe the principal conclusions of his conceptual analysis. Thus, in the *Search After Truth*, he reproaches those who neglect metaphysics which is the only reliable foundation for any kind of knowledge, including physics:

Metaphysics is a similarly abstract science that does not flatter the senses . . . There are even some who deny that we can and should assert of a thing what is included in the clear and distinct idea we have of it; that nothingness has no properties; that a thing cannot be reduced to nothing without a miracle; that no body can move itself by its own forces; that an agitated body cannot communicate to bodies with which it collides more motion that it possesses, and other such things. They have never considered these axioms from a viewpoint clear and focussed enough to discover their truth clearly. And they have sometimes performed experiments that convinced them falsely that some of these axioms were not true.[49]

This is a representative sample of Cartesian metaphysical axioms on which physics is said to depend. By 'metaphysics' Malebranche

---

[44] *Système*, i. 58. [45] Ibid. i. 290. [46] Ibid. i. 64.
[47] Ibid. i. 69–70. [48] Ibid. i. 70. [49] *Search After Truth*, p. 315.

means 'the general truths which can serve as principles for the particular sciences'.[50]

The Cartesian discussion of principles is complicated by the standard ambiguity between 'principles' understood as propositions and principles which are causes. This is especially clear in Rohault's search for foundations for his physics:

By the *first principles* of natural things, we understand, that which is first, and most simple in them, or that of which they are originally composed, and beyond which they cannot be reduced. Thus, the first principle of a chicken, are those things which are united together to compose a chicken, and which are so simple, that they themselves are void of all composition.[51]

There is no ambiguity in this text; the phrase 'first principle' denotes the basic particles into which a physical object can be analysed. Rohault had agreed with Descartes and with the whole tradition which followed his lead that this kind of first principle was necessarily hypothetical. One cannot hope to do any better than to guess at the size, shape, and number of the small particles out of which physical objects are constructed, and to use those guesses as the basis from which an explanation is developed. There is no claim to metaphysical certainty or axiomatic insight on this question; first principles in this sense are known only by hypothesis.

The two senses of the term 'principle' are relevant to Rohault's choice of first principles. Any hypothetical description of the qualities of first causes is constrained by the metaphysical or conceptual considerations about matter and motion which have been discussed in Chapters 3 and 4 above. More generally, the Cartesian tradition continued to defend the foundationalist strategy adopted by Descartes in respect of problems about knowledge and certainty. Metaphysical theses provided a basis for thinking that we could know anything with scientific certainty, and for distinguishing scientific knowledge from non-scientific opinion. Hence metaphysics is a necessary preliminary for any science in at least two senses: it supports its claim to being scientific, and it provides the conceptual clarifications which delimit the scope of the explanatory concepts which are acceptable in science. Scientific theories depend on, or are derived from, metaphysics in this sense.

There are also suggestions that the conceptual analyses of matter, motion, or force, which have been discussed above in Chapters 3

---

[50] *Dialogues on Metaphysics*, p. 129.   [51] *Traité de physique*, p. 17.

and 4, can deductively imply the truth of various general laws of nature; for that reason, the warrant for these laws would derive completely from what might be called metaphysical axioms. These suggestions invite a closer look at what the Cartesians claimed to have done when confirming the general laws of nature, because there is a possibility that the rhetoric of demonstrative certainty is more easily explained by the methodological demands of their scholastic opponents rather than their own estimate of how one can realistically warrant a law of nature.

Gadroys, in the *Système du monde*, gives three basic laws of nature: (*a*) everything remains in whatever condition it is in, unless some cause intervenes to change its condition; (*b*) the law of rectilinear motion; and (*c*) a body moving in a circle tends to move outwards from the centre of motion. After listing the three laws, Gadroys claims that the second and third follow from the first, and that 'the first one depends on the immutability of God', thereby implying that all three laws depend on a metaphysical principle about God's immutability.[52] The dependence on God is not so secure that experiential arguments are redundant for confirming the laws; thus we find that *expérience confirme* the second law, and that one can prove (*prouver*) the third law 'by another experiment'.[53]

There is a more explicit version of deducing physical laws from metaphysical axioms in Régis's *Système de philosophie*. He introduces the physics of collisions by distinguishing two different cases which require separate treatment; one is concerned with collisions between idealized bodies which have no weight, hardness, flexibility, elasticity, etc.—in fact, none of the qualities which normally characterize physical bodies. The second type of collisions involves physical bodies which possess the qualities excluded from consideration in the first approach.[54] The collisions of idealized bodies are described by *laws* which are deducible from the fourth axiom of metaphysics; by contrast, the interactions of real physical bodies are described by *rules* which involve a significant experimental input.

'As regards bodies considered in the first way, it is evident that the communication of their motion is in proportion to their size (*grandeur*). This is deduced necessarily from the fourth axiom of the first metaphysical reflections, according to which every body tends to remain, in so far as it can, in whatever condition it is in.'[55]

---

[52] *Système du monde*, p. 144.   [53] Ibid. 150, 151.

[54] *La Physique*, Bk. I, in *Système*, i. 332.   [55] Ibid. 332.

The inference from the fourth axiom to the principle defining the communication of motion in proportion to size presupposes a principle of least modal change, which Régis borrows from Descartes and expresses as follows:

It is therefore something constant that the laws, according to which the motions of colliding bodies change, depend on this one principle which is: that when two bodies meet which have two incompatible modes (of motion), there must occur some real change in these modes to make them compatible, but that this change is always the least possible. In other words, if they can become compatible by a change in a given quantity of these modes, then they will not change by a greater quantity than that.[56]

Régis followed Descartes in distinguishing two modes of motion, speed and determination, where 'determination' is defined as 'the relation which they [bodies] have with the direction in which they are moved'.[57] The argument supporting the proportionality between transfer of motion and size is as follows. If a body in motion strikes another body of equal size at rest, then it may either rebound or it may transfer some of its motion to the stationary body. Given the equality in size of the two bodies, the moving body would have to transfer half of its original motion to the body at rest in order to move it along at an equal speed in front of itself. Régis claims, without offering any reason, that a greater modal change would be involved if the moving body were to rebound than if it transferred half of its motion to the body at rest. Therefore, the fourth axiom of metaphysics (together with the analysis of motion into two distinct modes, and the principle of least modal change) implies the following law of physics: that the transfer of motion from one body to another, on collision, is proportional to the size of the colliding bodies.

The law of rectilinear motion is established by similar considerations. 'Since bodies in motion tend of themselves to continue in their motion according to the 4th axiom of the first metaphysical reflections, we should recognize that, for the same reason, bodies which are determined to move in one direction, continue of themselves to move with the same determination as long as nothing impedes them.'[58] This is nothing more than the application of the

---

[56] Ibid. 333–4. For Descartes's version of the same rule, see Descartes to Clerselier, 17 Feb. 1645 (*Œuvres*, iv. 183–5).
[57] Ibid. i. 317.   [58] Ibid. i. 337.

principle of sufficient reason to possible changes in one mode of a body's motion, namely its determination.

The kind of abstract considerations which feature in the formulation of the laws of nature is part of what Cartesians meant by deducing physics from metaphysics. It involved at least this much: various concepts which originally derived from reflection on ordinary experience were refined by further analysis, as in the distinction between the various modes of a body's motion. Secondly, Descartes assumed as self-evident a number of principles which were universally classified, in the seventeenth century, as metaphysical—for example, a principle of sufficient reason. Given the kind of conceptual analysis which is summarized in Chapters 3 and 4 above, and the resourcefulness of simplicity considerations in helping choose between alternative possible explanations (for example, in warranting the principle of least modal change), it is relatively easy to appreciate how laws of nature could be formulated and warranted, to Descartes's satisfaction, metaphysically. In this loose sense of the term 'deduce', the laws of nature were deduced from a metaphysical foundation.

Once in place, the laws of nature function as limits within which any hypothetical explanation of a particular phenomenon must be developed. To decide if Cartesians also hoped to deduce explanations of particular phenomena from the laws of nature, it is necessary to review some of their proposed explanations of various phenomena in physics, physiology, and astronomy.

Physics, Physiology, and Astronomy

There is almost an aura of evangelical fervour in the way in which Cartesians promised to implement their programme of gradually building up a complete physics and physiology from the three laws of nature. The texts communicate to the reader an expectation of rigorous and careful argument, even if it is not always deductive in the modern sense.

The first step in implementing this research programme was, as already indicated, an application of the laws of nature to collisions between idealized, 'perfectly hard' bodies. This step was taken by French Cartesians in exactly the same way as Descartes had made the same transition, namely in a series of completely abstract, a priori considerations about idealized bodies which could not apply to the physical bodies that we might encounter in the natural world. In order to describe the collisions of real bodies, Régis introduced a second set of collision rules which are conceived and warranted in a much less a priori fashion. He prefaces the new rules with the suggestion that no progress can be made at this point without a machine for doing experiments which is modelled after the one introduced by Mariotte to the Academy of Sciences.

Before all else it is necessary to describe a machine which is suitable for arranging that two bodies collide directly, with whatever quantity of motion one chooses in each; this is absolutely necessary to understand the rules of motion, without which one could make little progress in physics. . . . This machine was presented to the public by M. Mariotte of the Royal Academy of Sciences.[59]

He proceeds to introduce twenty rules which are partly derived from prior definitions and 'reflections', but which depend just as much on the experimental work which had been done by Mariotte and Huygens. This fundamental part of physics or of any science which depends on physics is presented without any reference to hypotheses.

Thus the zeal for mathematical demonstration and the anticipated strings of deductions conclude with the first set of impact rules; the experimental compromises required to formulate collision rules which correspond with our experience of real physical bodies still allowed Cartesians the apparent rigour of quantitative calculations and a mathematical notation. This remnant of a mathematical model of science should be compared with the following proposed explanation in physiology. Descartes and subsequent Cartesians relied on the concept of 'animal spirits' as a basic theoretical entity in physiology. Animal spirits were a species of very rarefied fluid, composed of invisible particles, which explained a wide range of phenomena including such things as the contraction of muscles to move parts of the body when appropriately stimulated by the brain. Descartes suggested in his *Treatise on Man* that the more forceful and lively animal spirits go from the heart to the brain, while those which are less forceful or lively descend to the sexual organs.[60] This was obviously a mere speculation, with none of the redeeming qualities required to save it from being 'purely arbitrary'. Despite

[59] Ibid. i. 366, 367.   [60] *Œuvres*, xi. 128.

that, La Forge endorses it in his footnotes to the 1664 edition of *L'Homme*, and Gadroys repeats the very same 'hypothesis' in his discussion of astrology seven years later. La Forge even spells out some of the unpalatable implications of the hypothesis for male researchers or students:

In my opinion one can confirm this dependence and communication which obtains between the spirits of the brain and those of the testicles by experience, which shows that those who are dedicated to study and who exercise their imaginations and their brains a lot, are not ordinarily very suitable for procreative functions. It follows from this that if they engage in procreation, it often happens that their children fail to resemble them in the strength and ability of their minds; since most of those parts of the blood which have greater strength and motion have gone to their brains, there are hardly any of them left for procreation. By contrast, those who are given to debauching women are not very suitable for serious application to study.[61]

La Forge adds that he knew of one person who was especially dedicated to debauchery and was found, after his death, to have hardly any brain at all! By the time Gadroys published his book on astrology in 1671, it almost seems as if this hypothesis of a link between study and decreased male fertility is an established fact. Gadroys claimed that there was 'an infinity of examples which prove this communication [about which Descartes spoke]. Those who weary their imaginations by study are less suitable for procreation; while those who, on the contrary, dissipate their minds in debauching women are not as suitable for study . . .'[62]

The co-ordinated effects of animal spirits on the functioning of the brain and on male fertility is not a complete methodological aberration in the hypothetical account of nature proposed by Cartesians. It suggests a very different interpretation of the Cartesian programme of deducing hypotheses from the laws of nature to the one which might be implied by the language of mathematical demonstration. This much weaker link between axioms and hypotheses amounts to something like this: that the conceptual framework specified by the basic concepts and axioms of Cartesian physics provides the context within which all explanatory hypotheses must be articulated. In this sense, the axioms provide only a negative criterion for what is unacceptable in scientific explanation, rather than a positive contribution to the content of

[61] *L'Homme* (1664), p. 210.   [62] *Influences des astres*, p. 159.

any given hypothesis. The axioms or laws only imply that one may not use concepts which have been debarred by the metaphysical propaedeutic to science, nor may one assume anything which contradicts the basic laws of nature. Apart from these restrictions, one may hypothesize anything one wishes. Descartes had written, in a passage cited above, that 'we are at liberty to assume anything we please, provided that everything we shall deduce from it is entirely in conformity with experience'.[63] His followers in France in the seventeenth century took him literally at his word; they constructed imaginative mechanical models which were hypothetically proposed as explanations of every kind of natural phenomenon.

In physiology, La Forge led the field with extensive explanatory notes on Descartes's *L'Homme*. His understanding of the brain and its functioning was acknowledged to be hypothetical. When the Danish anatomist, Thomas Bartholin (1616–80),[64] objected to many of the details of the Cartesian account because they involved imperceptible parts of the brain, La Forge replied: 'We are much obliged to the frankness of Bartholin, who candidly acknowledges that our hypothesis explains clearly the functions of the senses, and we are indeed very glad that this author . . . has not found the least objection to show that our hypothesis was false.'[65] Within this hypothetical account, even Descartes's famous suggestion about the pituitary gland is described merely as the most reasonable explanation available: 'it is the only thing which we can reasonably believe to be the principal seat of the soul, to which its perceptions and its choices are immediately joined and united and which, as a result, can be the organ of common sense and of the imagination.'[66] Descartes's account of the nerves and of the role of animal spirits is similarly hypothetical; the assumptions involved should not be rejected 'because they are not seen; otherwise it would be equally necessary to deny that there are animal spirits, that the nerves are bored like

---

[63] *Principles*, iii. 106, art. 46. See Ch. 3, p. 76.

[64] Thomas Bartholin was professor of medicine at Copehnagen, and had been familiar with Cartesian discussions of blood circulation since his student days at Leiden between 1637 and 1640. See the note in the Supplement to vol. v of Descartes's *Œuvres*, pp. 567–71 (also paginated pp. 25–9).

[65] *L'Homme*, p. 307. Cf. ibid. 296, where he talks about the theory of the brain as *nostre hypothèse*.

[66] Ibid. 318.

tubes, and a thousand other things which the most scrupulous anatomists find no difficulty in admitting.'[67]

The use of invisible animal spirits is endorsed with equal equanimity by Rohault: 'Besides those sensible parts of our body which we have taken notice of, there is yet another sort of matter not to be perceived by the senses, which is like very fine and much agitated air, and which physicians call *Animal Spirits*. That there are such cannot be doubted . . .',[68] because, in a word, we need them for explanations! The precise nature of animal spirits is assumed to be a very fine vapour which comes from the heart:

That we may make this matter [i.e. animal spirits] more intelligible, let us consider, that the blood being heated and dilated in the left cavity of the heart, some of its parts, by dashing against each other, must be made subtler in such a manner, and acquire such sort of figures, as will enable them to move more easily than others, and to pass through such pores as the other will not pass through. These most subtle and most agitated parts come out of the heart along with those which are not so subtle nor so much agitated. And the disposition of the aorta is such, that whatever goes out of the left cavity of the heart, tends directly to the brain; but because there is a very great quantity of those particles, and because the passages of the brain are too strait to receive them, therefore the greatest part of them are forced to turn and go another way, and the finest and most agitated particles only can enter into the brain . . . Now it is these particles . . . that they call *Animal Spirits*.[69]

It must have been evident even to the most committed Cartesian that this account of animal spirits involved making assumptions which they were not in a position to test by experiment or observation. The acceptability or otherwise of this type of assumption would have to be determined by its success within a comprehensive physiology.

In astronomy, all Cartesian explanations involved an even more candid recognition that one can only proceed hypothetically. Thus Rohault suggests, in Part II, chapter 3, of his *Traité de physique*, that there are two principal hypotheses, suppositions, or conjectures available in astronomy, namely those of Ptolemy and Copernicus. In subsequent chapters he explains Ptolemy's theory, and then the alternative suggested by Copernicus. There is a brief discussion of Tycho Brahe in chapter 23, and the whole discussion is concluded,

---

[67] *L'Homme*, p. 217.
[68] *Traité de physique*, ii. 271.   [69] Ibid. ii. 272.

in chapter 24, with 'Reflections upon the Hypotheses of Ptolemy, Copernicus, and Tycho'.[70] All three hypotheses are taken in a realistic way, with the assumption that one of them must be the most accurate account of reality.

We have no reason to think, that the structure of the world is such, as we have no idea of; because in things merely natural, we can always judge of them according to the ideas and notions which we have of them. But because we have here proposed three notions of the same thing, one of which only can be the true one, we must necessarily reject two of them as false, and retain the other as the only true one.[71]

The hypothesis of Copernicus is adopted as the 'more probable' of the three available.[72]

There is a correspondingly clear reliance on *conjectures* and *hipothèses* in Gadroys's astronomy. He considers 'diverse hypotheses for explaining the motion of the stars' and comets.[73] Comets are so distant from us, he claims, that one could invent almost any hypothesis one wishes to explain them; 'however one ought not for that reason to invent capriciously. One must accommodate oneself to the phenomena; by accepting as a rule of our reasoning all that we have been able to observe, the hypotheses will be at least probable, even if they are not true.'[74] This coincides exactly with Rohault's reflections on the status of the hypotheses used to explain comets: 'I think I ought not so far to lay aside this matter, as not to say at least what is most certainly known about it; leaving it to them who shall come after, to philosophize in a different manner; if any new observations that shall at any time be made, oblige them to alter our hypothesis, or to mend our opinion.'[75] Gadroys shows a similar reluctance about dogmatic astrology, when he assumes that the stars are spheres of matter of the first element which are very agitated. This is quickly qualified as a conjecture: 'I wish that this should be taken only as a simple conjecture, and I would even like people to suspend judgment until I have drawn, from this supposition, all the consequences which experience shows us.'[76] Among the other assumptions (*conjectures*) which he makes about the influence of the stars on our lives, he suggests that the stars partly explain,

---

[70] Ibid. ii. 59.
[72] Ibid. ii. 61.
[74] Ibid. 296.
[76] *Influences des astres*, p. 23.

[71] Ibid.
[73] *Système du monde*, p. 61.
[75] *Traité de physique*, ii. 80.

together with the sun, variations in temperature in summer and winter.[77]

The adoption of a Copernican theory by the Cartesians still left open the task of explaining how the planets move in circular or elliptical orbits around the sun. Descartes had proposed a vortex theory of matter in the *Principles* to explain the planets' motions, and all the French Cartesians followed his lead.[78] In fact, the acceptance of vortices became so natural that it almost seemed as if they were the obvious way of explaining astronomical phenomena, especially since some kind of contact action was required, in a Cartesian universe, to push the planets along their paths. Thus Régis suggests, in 1690, that vortices are the simplest and most fundamental hypotheses available in this context. 'It is evident that the forms of vortices are the first and simplest which have been introduced into nature; they are the first, because they are the immediate consequences of the laws of motion; and the most simple, because they do not presuppose any other forms, while all other forms depend on them as their principles.'[79] The vortices can be adapted to elliptical shapes, as they are squeezed by neighbouring vortices;[80] they accommodate all the available astronomical data, including the precession of Mercury and Venus;[81] and they can even be pressed into service to explain the correlation of the tides with the position of the moon.[82] Finally, the phenomenon of gravitational motion can be explained by using the vortex theory, without assuming any of the mysterious attractive forces which were exploited, in this context, by scholastic philosophers.

The contrast with scholastic explanations which was to a greater or less extent implicit in all Cartesian explanations helps to identify what were considered to be the redeeming features of the new theories. In the case of gravity, Cartesians argued for what they saw as the obvious advantages of vortices over any theory which assumed the possibility of action at a distance; if this mysterious action were further compromised by being described in terms which only named what required to be explained, then Cartesians assumed that there

---

[77] *Influences*, p. 81: 'ce qui semble encore fortement établir ma conjecture . . .'
[78] For the details of this theory and its subsequent history in the 18th cent., see Aiton (1972).
[79] *Système*, i. 400.
[80] Ibid. i. 429.   [81] Ibid. ii. 65–71.
[82] Rohault, *Traité de physique*, ii. 114–21; Régis, *Système*, ii. 412–23.

was no real contest between the two rival accounts. La Grange's account of gravity is typical of the type of explanation which Cartesians rejected. In his *Principes de la philosophie* (1675), La Grange describes weight as a 'quality the nature of which is to push any subject in which it is found towards the centre of the earth'.[83] This quality corresponds to a *vertu attractive* in the centre of the earth: 'That is why I conclude that the attractive power of the earth is nothing other than its weight, and that weight is a sympathetic power (*vertu sympathétique*) which pushes the subject in which it inheres towards a body which possesses the same quality.'[84] In discussing *la sympathie* seven chapters later, La Grange claims that Descartes and others have contributed nothing to our understanding of gravity or magnetism; for want of anything better, therefore, 'the word *sympathie* is a very convenient word for those who do not know much about nature's secrets'.[85]

The standard contrasting account of gravity proposed by Cartesians is found in Rohault and Régis. Rohault explains gravity as less levity: 'By this experiment we see clearly that gravity is, properly speaking, nothing else but less levity.'[86] On first reading, this gives the reader the impression that Rohault is mimicking exactly the kind of scholastic explanation which he claims to avoid. The apparently enigmatic suggestion is based on an experiment which had been done by Huygens and which was eventually reported in his *Discours sur la cause de la pesanteur* (1690).[87] The experiment involved spinning a vessel containing water and pieces of wax and finding that the heavier pieces of wax tended to move towards the centre of the whirlpool which forms in the revolving vessel. By analogy with the wax in the spinning vessel, some lighter bodies are forced, by the swirling action of the earth's vortex, to move from the centre of motion; this displacement, in turn, forces other (heavier) bodies to move towards the centre. The motion of some bodies towards the centre is therefore explained by their having less of whatever property causes light bodies to move centrifugally.

---

[83] La Grange, *Les principes de la philosophie*, p. 209.   [84] Ibid. 213.

[85] Ibid. 305. Cf. discussions of gravity by other contemporary scholastics, such as Honoré Fabri, *Tractatus Physicus de motu* (1666), Bk. i, ch. 2; or Gabriel Daniel, *Traité métaphysique de la nature du mouvement*, which was published for the first time in the *Recueil de divers ouvrages* (1724), i. 280–304.

[86] *Traité de physique*, ii. 94.

[87] Huygens, *Discours sur la cause de la pesanteur* (1690), p. 136. See the discussion of this topic in Dugas (1958), 308–11, 439–50.

Régis, as often happens, provides a clear summary of Cartesian explanations of gravity in his *Système de philosophie*; his explanation of gravity coincides with that of Rohault and helps to clarify it.

Among all the effects of circular motion, one of the most considerable is, without doubt, to make it happen that while the most agitated and most solid parts of matter move towards the circumference of the circle which they describe, there are others which, at the same time, are forced from the circumference towards the centre. The parts of matter which move from the centre of motion as if by their own power are called *light*, and those which are pushed towards the centre are called *heavy*. Thus by the word 'lightness' we do not mean anything except the effort with which bodies moving in a circle tend to move from the centre of motion, nor by the word 'heaviness' anything other than the effort with which the less agitated or less solid bodies are pushed toward the centre of motion by those which have more force than them to move away.[88]

There is no intrinsic difference between heavy bodies and light ones, apart from their relative solidity or speed, since they all tend to move away from the centre of a vortex motion according to the law of rectilinear motion. One needs to distinguish, therefore, between absolute and relative lightness.[89] All bodies are light; only those which are lighter than others, however, move away from the centre of motion and this forces others to replace them at the centre. In this sense, heaviness is explained in terms of relative lightness!

It is not surprising if the most sustained attempts at explanation among Cartesian natural philosophers concentrate on those phenomena which had been discussed initially by Descartes. For example, there is a clear case of fidelity to tradition in Cartesian writing on magnetism, both in the kind of explanation suggested and in the explicitness of its hypothetical character. Rohault introduces his discussion as follows, in Part III, chapter 8 of his *Traité de physique*: 'Of the Load-stone. . . . in the first place I shall reckon up some of its properties, which I shall content myself, with only assigning a *probable* reason for; and after that, I shall endeavour to establish the truth of my conjecture, by showing that all the consequences that can be drawn from it, agree with experience.'[90] The subsequent discussion involves a consistent effort to explain all

---

[88] *Système*, ii. 436. He also summarizes the theories of Rohault, Gadroys, and Perrault, in Bk. II, ch. 18 of his *Physique* (ii. 442–9).

[89] Ibid. i. 437.

[90] *Traité de physique*, i. 163.

the known properties of magnets in terms of the screw-shaped particles which had been originally introduced by Descartes.

Although this kind of theorizing is unexceptional in the case of Rohault, it is somewhat surprising to find Malebranche equally dedicated to speculating about the cause of vision and the properties of light which make vision possible. Malebranche suggested a longitudinal wave theory in the *Dialogues on Metaphysics* (1687),[91] and he developed this theory in more detail in Elucidation XVI to the *Search After Truth* in response to his reading of Newton's *Opticks* (1704): 'in several of my books I propose that light and colors consisted only in different disturbances or vibrations of ethereal matter, or in *more or less frequent pressure vibrations* that subtle matter produces on the retina.'[92] Malebranche's theory of light assumes that the transmission of light is analogous to the transmission of sound, and that the wave pulses of light are transmitted through infinitesimal vortices which are similar to those used in astronomy by Descartes. 'The assumption I made that subtle or ethereal matter is composed only of an infinity of small vortexes that turn on their center with extreme rapidity, and that counterbalance each other like the large vortexes Descartes explained in his *Principles of Philosophy*, this supposition, I say, is not arbitrary.'[93] The reason why it is not arbitrary is not that there is any direct evidence to support it, because the size of the theoretical vortices precludes that possibility; rather, it is because the explanation he offers is proved by its success.

I think I have clearly proved that *different colors* consist only in the different *frequency* of the pressure vibrations of subtle matter, as *different tones* of music result only from the different *frequency* of the vibration of gross air (as experiment teaches), which vibrations also intersect without destroying each other. And I do not think that the way all these vibrations are communicated can be physically explained unless the principles I have just set out are followed.[94]

These examples suggest that the types of hypotheses used by Cartesians during the second half of the seventeenth century range from bizarre suggestions with no evidence at all to support them, such as the theory about animal spirits and male infertility, to

---

[91] Dialogue XII, p. 281.　　[92] *Search After Truth*, p. 689.
[93] Ibid. 695–6. The analogy with sound waves is on pp. 689–90.
[94] Ibid. 693.

reasonably well-developed theories with mathematically expressed predictions which were tested experimentally, such as the Cartesian theory of the rainbow.[95] From the various suggestions about hypotheses and their role in science which were proposed by their Cartesian defenders, the following points emerge as generally accepted by the French school.

1. The primary meaning of the term 'hypothesis' is some claim which is put forward in order to deduce other propositions from it. In this general sense, hypotheses are not necessarily uncertain; in fact, both revealed religious truths and metaphysical axioms may function as hypotheses in certain contexts. It is the role of a proposition in a given context, rather than its certainty or otherwise, which makes it a hypothesis.

2. When applied to the explanation of natural phenomena, the term 'hypothesis' meant any assumption which is made in the course of constructing an explanation. Even in this more limited context, there is no necessary implication that hypotheses are uncertain or unreliable. However, the considerations already discussed about the ultimate explanatory principles (in Rohault's sense) of nature, especially the fact that they are invisible, implies that whatever one assumes about these minute particles cannot be known directly either by experience or by reason. The principles which are eventually endorsed can be known only indirectly, by their success in providing the kinds of explanations which Cartesians were willing to recognize as legitimate. This gives a fair amount of flexibility in constructing hypotheses, in line with Descartes's claim that we are justified in assuming anything we wish on condition that the consequences agree with experience.

3. The apparent licence of 'anything goes' is qualified by various restrictions of a metaphysical and methodological nature which excluded certain kinds of assumptions. These exclusionary clauses represented the first part of the Cartesians' attempt to distinguish arbitrary from plausible hypotheses. Arbitrary hypotheses were used in the saving-the-phenomena tradition in astronomy, and they had a useful predictive role there; but they had no place in Cartesian science. Cartesian hypotheses must be framed within a coherent system which is controlled by a limited range of approved concepts, and by the basic laws of nature which were derived from Descartes's metaphysics. This ideal of systematic unity was often expressed in

[95] See e.g. Rohault, *Traité de physique*, ii. 224.

terms of deducing hypotheses from a metaphysical basis, but there is little evidence that the Cartesians ever deduced anything from their first principles in the modern, logical sense of the term 'deduce'. However, they did claim to use the laws of nature and the basic concepts discussed in Chapters 3 and 4 above as a negative criterion for excluding 'arbitrary' hypotheses.

Within the modest restrictions imposed by the laws of nature, then, and without any of the demands for mathematical rigour which one might anticipate from the rhetoric of 'mathematical deductions', Cartesians exploited their flair for model construction by imagining hypothetical explanations of a wide range of natural phenomena and, in many cases, of merely alleged phenomena. This approach to explanation was described, in a modified version of scholastic terminology, as a demonstration. The system of particles in motion was believed, with unwavering conviction, to be sufficiently resourceful to generate a complete system of scientific explanations. It was almost as if they welcomed the challenge to explain anything: 'mention a phenomenon and I can construct an explanation within our system. As a Cartesian, *hypotheses fingo*.'

The zeal for constructing hypotheses about particular phenomena coincided with a corresponding degree of conviction about the general outline of the Cartesian research programme in natural philosophy. It was, paradoxically, because they were so confident about the new laws of nature that they showed little reluctance about framing hypotheses.

The confidence about the eventual success of Cartesian theories was also a result of the perceived contrast between the type of explanation being offered by the new, mechanical philosophers and that proposed in the schools. This was a separate issue, over and above questions about the most plausible hypothesis available to explain a particular phenomenon: it concerned the concept of explanation itself, and the dramatic change, during the seventeenth century, from scholastic explanations in terms of qualities and forms to mechanical explanations which attempt to identify the efficient cause of any given effect. In expressing opinions about the plausibility of their theories in natural philosophy, therefore, Cartesians were defending not just their own preferred hypotheses; they were also contrasting the viability of their whole enterprise with that of their principal opponents. This issue is discussed in the next chapter, before returning to the question of the degree of certainty claimed by Cartesians for their scientific theories.

6

Mechanical Explanation

Mind, Measure, Rest and Motion,
With Figure, and Position,
To Matter Join'd, the Causes be
of all what here below we see.

Antoine Le Grand

THIS quatrain from Le Grand's *Institution of Philosophy*[1] provides an accurate summary of the programme of scientific explanation which Cartesians adopted as their ideal. It implies that, apart from the role of mind, only two kinds of cause are relevant to scientific explanation, and that these causes can be described adequately in terms of the fundamental qualities of small parts of matter in motion which were discussed in previous chapters. The apparent simplicity of the scientific enterprise, when it is conceived in this way, conceals a number of issues which deserve more detailed discussion.

As already indicated, the polemical articulation of the Cartesian ideal of explanation in natural philosophy was motivated by the need to distinguish it from the scholastic concept of explanation which was standardly accepted in the schools. The relative sharpness of the debate in France between defenders of the two competing concepts of explanation must be understood, at least in part, as a result of the consistent attempts by both Church and university authorities to suppress the newly emerging natural philosophy, because it was perceived as a threat to religious and political equanimity. As one might expect, those who were censored expressed their opposition to the authorities in a style which was often blunt, bitter, and even angry. Thus Malebranche, in reference to those whose reason was submerged by their allegiance to some ancient authority:

---

[1] *Entire Body of Philosophy*, p. 106.

I cannot remain calm at the thought that certain universities that were founded for no other purpose than to pursue and defend the truth have become cliques that boast of studying and defending the views of certain men. Only with indignation can I read the books that issue daily from philosophers and physicians, in which quotations are so frequent that I would take them more as the writings of theologians or canon lawyers than as philosophical or medical treatises. For I cannot allow reason and experience to be abandoned in favour of blind submission to the fictions of Aristotle, Plato, Epicurus, or any other philosopher. Yet I would perhaps remain calm and silent before such extreme behaviour if I were not harmed by it, i.e. if these gentlemen did not war against the truth, which alone I feel obliged to espouse.[2]

The vehement rejection of Aristotelianism by the Cartesians was evident in their evaluation of Aristotle's logic, physics, medicine, or metaphysics as worthless; the philosophy of the schools was also classified as positively harmful in so far as it inhibited the search for truth. Malebranche says of Aristotle that 'he talks a lot and says nothing';[3] that scholastic logic is useless 'because it occupies the mind too much and diverts attention that it should have brought to bear upon the subjects it is examining';[4] that 'substantial forms never existed in nature';[5] and finally, that 'real ideas produce real science, but general or logical ideas never produce anything but a science that is vague, superficial, and sterile'.[6] In a similarly unambiguous vein, Gadroys describes the 'common philosophy' as follows: 'It is truly a science of words; . . . it fills the mouth and leaves the mind empty.'[7] As an example of merely verbal explanation he cites the schools' theory of intentional species which, he claims, are the 'horror of the reasonable world today'.[8] Poisson had a similar reaction to Aristotle's logic, and he even invokes Bacon as a supporter of his view: 'as Bacon, the Chancellor of England, remarked: the vulgar logic, instead of giving us olives, only leaves us with thistles and thorns after a dispute.'[9]

The verbal sophistry of school philosophy appeared in many guises; it was more apparent than usual in explanations. In this

---

[2] *Search After Truth*, p. 383.   [3] Ibid. 440. See also pp. 281–2.

[4] Ibid. 437.   [5] Ibid. 75.   [6] Ibid. 247.

[7] *Influences des astres*, preface (unpaginated).

[8] *Système du monde*, p. 251. See also *Influences des astres*, p. 121, for the same point.

[9] *Remarques*, p. 7. He had an equally low opinion of Raymond Lully, ibid. 9. As a cure for this problem he recommends Clauberg's *Logic* or preferably *L'Art de penser* of Port-Royal (ibid. 12).

context, the principal argument against school philosophy was that it proposed pseudo-explanations of natural phenomena under the cloak of apparently sophisticated metaphysical terms.

Pseudo-explanations

La Forge broached this question in his commentary on Descartes's *L'Homme*, in which he contrasts two proposed explanations of the heart's beating motion. One explanation consisted of saying that the heart beats because it has a *faculté* for beating in a particular way; the alternative was to explain the motion of the heart along the lines suggested by Descartes. This latter theory assumed (incorrectly) that the diastolic motion of the heart is caused by the expansion of droplets of blood as they fall into the left ventricle of the heart. La Forge claimed that most physicians of his day attributed the beating of the heart 'to a faculty of the soul which they call pulsific'.[10] The Saumur physician was willing to retain this way of talking in deference to his medical professors; evidently if the heart beats, it must have a faculty for beating![11] However, this way of talking hardly provides any explanation of why the heart beats in its characteristic way:

But as they will find no difficulty, I imagine, in conceding that here, and in many other places, this word is useless and does nothing to explain how something happens, I hope that they will allow me to ask what this faculty is. . . . To say that it is a quality of the body or a property of the soul does nothing to explain what it is, no more than if, when asking what an elephant is, I were told that it is an animal from Africa.[12]

In a similar vein, La Forge argues that natural likes and dislikes should be explained by the disposition of various parts of the brain and that such an approach is preferable to those who talk about 'sympathy or antipathy, which are obscure terms which mean nothing, and which are only good for disguising our ignorance under the mask of a few fancy words, according to the usual style of Peripatetic philosophy'.[13]

---

[10] *L'Homme*, p. 183.   [11] Ibid. 183.   [12] Ibid. 183–4.

[13] *Traité de l'esprit*, p. 313. As an example of what La Forge was complaining about, see Jean-Baptiste de la Grange, *Les principes de la philosophie*, ch. 24: 'De l'Antipathie & Simpathie qu'il y a entre les Plantes & entre les Animaux'. The use by La Grange of attractive powers to explain the motion of falling bodies is discussed in Ch. 5 above.

The objection against scholastic explanations is often expressed by claiming that the explanatory terms used by the schools are obscure or meaningless. Malebranche adopts this formulation in the *Search After Truth*: 'The clear and distinct ideas of extension, figure, and locomotion must not be exchanged for the general and confused ideas of principle or subject of extension, form, quiddities, real qualities, or motion other than locomotion such as generation, corruption, alteration and the like.'[14] The same point is made more fully in Elucidation XII:

But it is especially in matters of physics that we take advantage of vague and general terms that do not call up distinct ideas of being or modes. For example, when we say that bodies tend toward their *center*, that they fall by their *gravity*, that they rise by their *levity*, that they move by their *nature*, that they are hard or fluid by themselves, that they successively change their *forms*, that they act by their *virtues, qualities, faculties*, and so on, we use terms signifying nothing, and all these propositions are absolutely false in the sense philosophers give them. There is no *center* in the sense ordinarily understood. The terms *gravity, form, nature* and the like call up the idea of neither a being nor a mode. They are terms devoid of sense, which wise people ought to avoid. . . . These terms are suited only for hiding the ignorance of counterfeit scholars, and for making the stupid and the skeptical believe that God is not the true cause of all things.[15]

This type of objection to scholastic explanations presupposes that the Cartesian metaphysics of substances and modes is correct. It argues that anything which is named in a theory must be recognizable as either a substance or a mode and, if not, that it is a meaningless term because it purports to denote something whereas in fact it fails to denote any of the types of entity which are acceptable in a Cartesian world-view. It was apparent to scholastic

---

[14] *Search After Truth*, pp. 246-7.

[15] Ibid. 642-3. Cf. Le Grand, *History of Nature*, p. 56: '*Occult qualities*, are by the *Peripateticks* called hidden powers, by which natural things do act or suffer any thing, and whereof no prior reason can be assigned, as immediately proceeding from the substantial forms of things. But our modern philosophers are at a loss about what the Aristoteleans mean by all this Gibberish, who denying all substantial forms, despair of ever knowing what these occult qualities are, which are the immediate products of them. Wherefore the abstruseness of some qualities doth seem only to depend on the different hypotheses of natural principles; so as to those who follow the Peripatetick hypothesis, the ebbing and flowing of the sea, and the conjunction of the iron with the load-stone, appear to be abstruse and hidden qualities; whereas, according to the principles of corpuscular philosophy they are most clear and evident effects.'

objectors, and should have been clear even to Cartesian proponents, that such a criterion of meaningfulness is completely relative to the framework in which it is expressed. Scholastic opponents might as easily have formulated the reciprocal objection to Cartesian explanations: 'since your explanations only talk of parts of extension, etc. and fail to mention the forms and qualities which define our metaphysical framework, it follows that your explanations are not only unsuccessful, but they are meaningless.' This kind of objection is doomed to fail in either direction. From within any theoretical or philosophical language it is easy to categorize an alternative language as incomprehensible or meaningless. The Cartesians' objection would fail, therefore, if they had nothing else in mind; fortunately, they could express their objection in a different way. The fundamental source of their disquiet with the language of faculties and forms was that such a language failed to *explain* anything. The dispute with the scholastics essentially hinged on a dispute about the concept of explanation.

Arnauld confronted this question directly in his *Vraies et fausses idées,* by asking why the Cartesians have such an aversion for the general terms 'nature' and 'faculty', even though the Peripatetics use them. 'Why do they find it objectionable if one says that the fire burns because that is its nature, and that it changes certain bodies into glass by a natural faculty?'[16] He replied that these general terms may be used properly or improperly. They are used improperly if they purport to denote something which is distinct from the object to which they are attributed.

One uses them badly when, by the term *faculty*, one means an entity which is distinct from the thing to which one attributes this faculty; for example, when one takes the understanding and the will as faculties which are distinct from our souls. One also uses them badly when one pretends to have explained some unknown effect, or an effect which is very poorly understood, by describing its cause with the general term 'faculty'; for example, when one says that a magnet attracts iron because it has a particular faculty, or that fire changes certain bodies into glass by a natural faculty. The principal abuse involved in using these terms is that, before one knows what being attracted to a magnet is in iron or, in respect of sand, being changed into glass by fire, one dodges by saying that the magnet and the fire each have this faculty.[17]

---

[16] *Vraies et fausses idées, Œuvres,* xxxviii. 291.
[17] Ibid. 291.

The objectionable use of faculty language is clear. It conceals our ignorance of the real causes of natural phenomena when it appears to name something which is distinct from the phenomenon being explained and at the same time implies that we know something about this distinct entity. The background assumption in the Cartesian contention is that explanation involves identifying the efficient and material causes of a given phenomenon. To redescribe the phenomenon in question in the language of the schools is unobjectionable as long as the faculties attributed to something are understood as nothing more than specifications of what needs to be explained. However, the faculty terms often carry connotations of independent entities and thereby masquerade as genuine descriptions of causes. But as such we know nothing about them, and this stratagem merely conceals our ignorance. In Le Grand's words: 'what is this else, but a profession of their ignorance, and that in plain terms they do not know the thing they pretend to explicate?'[18] This is the fundamental point about explanation which was borrowed from Rohault and caricatured in Molière's *Petit gentil-homme*.

To explain a phenomenon, therefore, is to give an account of its causes or, more specifically, of its efficient and material causes. Descartes had excluded the discussion of final causality from physical science because, he claimed, we are not in a position to discover by reason alone why God chose to arrange natural phenomena as he did. Whatever we might say on this question is the merest speculation; at the same time, we may be informed by divine revelation of some of God's motives in acting as he does. Hence Malebranche argued that there is a legitimate place for final causes in religious beliefs, but none in physics.[19] And on this question at least, there is no dispute among the Cartesians.

Likewise, even the most consistent proponents of occasionalism insisted that explanation involves two kinds of efficient cause: a general cause of all phenomena and the particular causes of specific phenomena. God is the general cause of everything, but 'it would be ridiculous to explain particular effects by recourse to the general cause'.[20] To explain any particular effect, we need to identify a cause

---

[18] *Entire Body of Philosophy*, p. 204.

[19] *Conversations chrétiennes*, in *Œuvres complètes*, iv. 60.

[20] Malebranche, *Dialogues on Metaphysics*, p. 87. See also *Conversations chrétiennes*, *Œuvres complètes*, iv. 77; *Traité de la nature et de la grace*, *Œuvres complètes*, v. 66–7.

from which the effect in question follows necessarily.[21] There is no support for short-circuiting the explanatory project by saying, simply: whatever happens is caused ultimately by God, and that is all we need to know. We also need to know the occasional or natural causes of particular phenomena.

A priori rational explanations

Any account of a phenomenon which follows the order of cause to effect was described, following Descartes's usage, as an a priori account.[22] This terminology does not have the Kantian connotations of a priori knowledge, or knowledge which is independent of experience. Rather, it contrasts the complementary operations of arguing from cause to effect as a priori, and from effects to cause as a posteriori. Whether or not either of these operations, or 'proofs' as they were generally called, depended on experience remains to be seen.

The use of the term 'a priori' by Cartesians to describe causal explanations helped foster the interpretation of their natural philosophy as an unduly rationalist enterprise. The same conclusion seemed to follow from the central role given to *raison* in science. However, the term 'reason' is just as innocent as 'a priori' in Cartesian usage, because it is normally used in a sense which is neutral with respect to the relative importance of experience or reason in natural science. The reason of a fact is its (hypothetical) cause.

The distinction between reporting alleged facts and explaining them was a standard one in the intellectual climate in which Cartesianism developed in seventeenth-century France. Claude Perrault was no Cartesian, and yet we find him suggesting the following division of labour in *La Mechanique des animaux*: 'There are two ways of knowing and explaining natural things. One is historical, to describe and enumerate what can be known by sense;

---

[21] *Conversations chrétiennes, Œuvres complètes*, iv. 77: 'For one can recognize that an effect is general, or that it is necessary to have recourse to the general cause, whenever the effect has no necessary connection with whatever seems to be its cause . . .'; this implies that particular causes and effects are linked by an appropriate *liaison nécessaire* which precludes the need to introduce God.

[22] Malebranche, *Traité de la nature et de la grace, Œuvres complètes*, v. 32–3; Régis, *Système*, ii. 111.

the other is philosophical, which tries to discover by reasoning the causes and the hidden *raisons* of all these particular phenomena.'[23] This suggests that the identification of something as a cause is achieved by reasoning of some kind, even if the cause in question could be known independently by sense. This understanding of causal connection coincides with the theory of causes articulated by Malebranche and shared by other Cartesians with greater or less explicitness. Causal connections, as such, cannot be perceived. Therefore even observable physical objects or events cannot be perceived, as causes, through sensation. One needs to engage in some form of reasoning in order to claim that one phenomenon or event is the cause of another.

The 'rational' dimension of causal explanation is clear in the very language used to describe it. Gadroys, for example, gives a summary of the Ptolemaic theory in his *Système du monde*, and then adds: 'Having supposed that, it is easy to explain (*rendre raison de*) all the observations which we have made on the motion of the sun.'[24] In fact, the kind of distinction made by Perrault had become almost standard in Rohault's scientific language, in the contrast between observation and *raison*. There are observed facts or phenomena, and there are the *raisons* of these facts, as in the following examples: 'In order to understand the reason of this experiment, it is to be observed that . . .'; 'Hence we see the reason of a fact, which we should not know but by experience; which is, that white bodies weary the sight, and black ones refresh it'; 'now the reason of this experiment is, that the strings which are concords, are capable of the same vibrations'; 'now in order to see the reason of these two effects'.[25] In all these cases, the reason of a fact or experiment is simply its explanation.

Of course this leaves open the possibility that all explanations are purely rational for Rohault; but that interpretation fails to match the texts, and is more likely to originate from an over-simple reading of the standard sense–reason dichotomy. There is a clear example of 'reason' which presupposes empirical evidence in Part II, chapter 25, of the *Traité de physique*. Rohault discusses an account of the moon which is partly based on his acceptance of the

---

[23] *Essais de physique* (1680), iii. 8. Cf. Pascal, *Fragment de préface sur le traité du vide* (1647), in *Œuvres*, ii. 131–2.
[24] *Système du monde*, p. 72.
[25] *Traité de physique*, i. 78; i. 223; i. 195; ii. 273.

Copernican theory and partly based on telescopic observations. In concluding the chapter he wonders about the possibility of life on the moon:

All these things being so; we cannot but think that the planets are very like our earth; which would not appear otherwise to a man that should look at it from the moon than the moon does to a man who beholds it from the earth. Not that I would venture to affirm, that there are living creatures in the moon, or that they generate in the same manner as upon the earth, because though this be a thing possible, yet it is also possible that it may not be so. For in things which cannot be certainly *determined by reason*, I think it very rash to stand in an opinion contrary to the common notions [emphasis added].[26]

It is clear in this context that what is determined 'by reason' is not by any means the result of pure speculation. The point is that we know a lot about the moon, partly as a result of using telescopes to observe it; yet we cannot argue from our available information to any reliable conclusion about life on the moon. This kind of incomplete, hypothetical theory construction which relies in part on empirical evidence is what Rohault means by determination by reason.

The same understanding of *raison* is supported by La Forge's discussion of the plausibility of his hypothesis about the human brain and its operations. He explains that the mere fact that various parts of the brain, on his account, are imperceptible is no objection to their plausibility. To think otherwise would be to deny many things which most anatomists of his own time were willing to accept. He continues: 'There are two ways to discover the existence of something, one is by sense, and the other by reason. We frankly agree that the senses are lacking in this context, but reason is so much in our favour that, not only does it show that the matter is very plausible . . . but that it is true . . .'[27] By 'reason', in this discussion, he means an argument in favour of a hypothetical cause which is ultimately based on anatomical observations.

One other example of a similar use of reason should be sufficient to cast doubt on the standard interpretation of Cartesian science as a

[26] *Traité de physique*, ii. 77–9.

[27] *L'Homme*, p. 308. Cf. Régis, *Système*, ii. 508, 509: 'The knowledge we can have of these parts [of animals] is of two kinds; one can be acquired by means of the senses and the other can only be acquired by reasoning. . . . There are certain things which cannot be learned at all from illustrations or lectures, whatever their quality; these can only be discovered by an *inspection du sujet*.'

rationalist enterprise which ultimately relies almost exclusively on pure speculation. Régis has already been seen, in Chapter 2 above, to have rejected a theory of innate actual ideas in the human mind. He argued instead that all knowledge is based on what he calls *la conscience* and *la raison*, which correspond roughly to *intuitus* and deduction in Descartes's *Regulae*. The scope of *la conscience* extends to everything we know directly without recourse to reasoning, that is, everything of which we are directly and immediately aware in our minds. The immediate content of consciousness had already been subdivided, by Régis, into sensation (the basis of our knowledge of physical phenomena), and ideas (the foundation of our knowledge of immaterial entities). Thus, anything of which we are directly aware through sensation or reflection falls within the scope of *la conscience*. Apart from the content of immediate awareness, all other knowledge must be acquired by reasoning. The two kinds of immediate experiences provide a basis for two kinds of knowledge, both equally the result of reasoning: these were called 'knowledge by experience' and 'knowledge by reason'.[28] It is this last choice of terminology which exemplifies the ambiguity in the use of the term 'reason', because the so-called knowledge by experience is just as much a result of reasoning as 'knowledge by reason'. Knowledge by experience includes the kind of spontaneous inferences by which we reason from our sensory experiences to the existence of external physical phenomena; it also includes the reasoning by which we argue from the perception of certain effects to the causes which are likely to explain their occurrence.

Régis was aware of this ambiguity in the term 'reason', and he adverts to it in *L'Usage de la raison et de la foy*:

As regards physical and metaphysical demonstration, although they are rather different, we still attribute both of them to the same principle. The same reason which shows us that two and two make four also assures us that the rainbow exists when it appears on our horizon. This makes the word *reason* very equivocal; for it is sometimes taken to refer to the faculty or power of the soul to judge necessary or abstract truths, and sometimes to designate the power or faculty we have to judge about contingent and individual truths.[29]

This is as clear a statement as we are likely to find on the meaning of

---

[28] *Système*, i. 191.   [29] *L'Usage de la raison*, p. 49.

the term 'reason' in Cartesian explanations. It has no necessary implications of metaphysical or purely speculative reasoning. It means, simply, that we discover the causes of physical phenomena by reasoning in some way from the available empirical evidence. In this sense, to speak about a rational explanation is to utter a pleonasm.

In the Cartesian tradition, therefore, scientific explanations are both a priori and rational, by definition. That means that a viable explanation must be an explanation in terms of causes, and that the causes in question can only be identified or discovered by reasoning retroactively from the empirical knowledge of effects to the kinds of causes which are likely to have caused them.

What is the logical structure of this reasoning, how does one get started, and what criteria guide one's progress? The most obvious feature of the logic of Cartesian explanations is that the scientist 'knows' the beginning and the end of an account which should provide, on completion, a comprehensive description of the causal origins of some natural phenomenon. In the first place, he knows the facts to be explained, from observation, experiment, or, for many Cartesians, from reports of others. This is the conclusion of his account. He also claims to know the first principles or basic laws from which any scientific account must begin, and he knows the material cause of every natural phenomenon, that is, the small parts of matter and their properties which have been discussed above. The challenge in explanation is to provide the link between the two, to fill in the story of how those kinds of particles operating under the laws of nature could have resulted in the natural phenomena which we observe. What needs to be supplied is a model of the mechanism by which the three kinds of matter, in motions which are determined by the laws of nature, may have given rise to a particular phenomenon. 'The world therefore is to be consider'd as a wonderful, and most artificially contriv'd machine . . .'[30]

Mechanical Models

Bernard Lamy accurately reflects the mood of Cartesianism when he describes the role of the philosopher, in his *Entretiens sur les*

[30] Le Grand, *Entire Body of Philosophy*, p. 107.

sciences, in terms of constructing mechanical models of natural phenomena.

> To have the right to imagine that one understands things, one must be able to explain them as one would explain a watch which one opens so that one sees the movement and shape of its parts. . . . [Descartes] tries to explain the whole world and its effects like a watchmaker who wishes to understand the way in which a watch shows the hours. . . . Just as one discovers with the help of the telescope those objects whose distance hides them from our eyes, so likewise one sees things whose small size makes them unobservable without the aid of a microscope. That is what needs to be done in order to philosophize. Because everything which appears in the body is just like the case of the watch which hides the mechanism. It is therefore necessary to open this case; however, in nature the springs are so small that our eyes cannot observe their subtlety without assistance. . . . One must recognize however that in a great many things, even with the aid of the microscope, pneumatic machines and chemistry, we still cannot penetrate what Nature had decided to conceal from us. We do not see what is inside. What can a physician do, therefore, except conjecture?[31]

This quotation summarizes a number of points about the role of mechanical models in science. It assumes the analogy between all physical bodies, including living things, and a watch, and it identifies the scientist's task as the description of the inner workings of such natural machines. Lamy readily agrees that the best way to begin this process, in the case of a living body for example, is actually to look inside. 'As it is necessary to open the case to see inside the watch, so likewise one must open natural bodies, one must dissect them and practise anatomy.'[32] It is also clear that our observations are limited even when aided by the microscope. Therefore, in attempting to construct a mechanical model, it often happens that one can do no better than conjecture. Many scientific explanations of natural phenomena are nothing more than hypothetical, mechanical models.

There is a significant difference between showing how things may have been mechanically produced, and demonstrating that they are in fact as we assume them to be. 'It is a completely different thing to demonstrate that things may be as one says, and that they are in fact as one shows they may be. Almost everything which the new philosophy can teach us is reducible to this, that things may be as it

---

[31] Lamy, *Entretiens sur les sciences*, pp. 256, 257–8, 259.
[32] Ibid. 258.

says they are. Nevertheless, that is a lot.'[33] In other words, a Cartesian explanation is a mechanical model of how natural phenomena may be produced according to the laws of nature, as long as the proposed model is described within the conceptual restrictions already discussed above.

The ideal of constructing mechanical models was not peculiar to Cartesian science; it was an ideal which was generally accepted by proponents of the new philosophy in the seventeenth century and which found expression in a wide diversity of authors, most notably in Robert Boyle's *The Origin of Forms and Qualities according to the Corpuscular Philosophy* (1666). However, the rigour of the Cartesian ideal and at the same time its uncompromising opposition to scholastic explanation reflects the dogmatic assurance which marks the Cartesians off from many of their sympathetic contemporaries. This is forcefully illustrated in the discussion of animal machines.

There was opposition from all sides on this question, from natural philosophers, physicians, and inevitably from theologians and scholastic philosophers. For example, Jean-Baptiste Denis (d. 1704) was a Cartesian on most other issues, but he supported the traditional theory of vegetative souls in plants because, he claimed, it was difficult to reject the ordinary language of the Bible and of so many theologians, philosophers, and common folk.[34] Claude Perrault also argued against the Cartesians, without explicitly naming them, in *La Mechanique des animaux*. Contrary to those who think of animals as mere machines, he defines an animal as follows: 'a being which has feeling and which is capable of exercising the functions of life by means of a principle which is called a soul.'[35] The defence of animal souls and the corresponding criticism of animal machines was most vocal, as one might expect, among scholastic philosophers. The Jesuit, Ignace Pardies, published a critique of the Cartesian position in his *Discours de la connoissance des bestes* (1672).[36] Another Jesuit apologist, Père Gabriel Daniel

---

[33] Lamy, *Entretiens*, p. 257.

[34] *Recoeuil des mémoires et conférences sur les arts & les scienses [sic], présentees à Monseigneur Le Dauphin pendant l'année MDCLXXII. Par Jean Baptiste Denis, conseiller & medecin ordinaire du roy*, in *Journal des sçavans*, 3 (1673–4), 202–3.

[35] *Essais de physique*, iii. 1. The body may be constructed like a machine, but just as an organ produces no music without an organ player, so likewise the machine of the body only functions when informed by a 'soul'.

[36] For a discussion of Pardies's objections, see Ziggelaar (1971), 86–112.

(1649–1728), joined the debate in two books: *Voiage du monde de Descartes* (1691) and, two years later, his *Nouvelles difficultez . . . touchant la connoissance des bestes* (1693). When challenged to say if the soul of an animal is spiritual or material (in the Cartesian sense), Daniel replied 'that it is neither one nor the other, that it is a kind of being to which one gives the name "material", not because it is material but because it is not a spirit. It is a being which is half way between the two . . .'[37] This may look like an untenable compromise which is logically excluded by the categories offered to Daniel; however, when the full force of the Cartesian position is seen, Daniel's compromise may have been his only way of saying that he rejected the mutually exclusive options which he was offered. At the same time, the fundamental problem of explanation remains an issue both for the Cartesians and their opponents. The Peripatetic 'soul' was exactly the kind of entity which was suspiciously like a causal account and yet seemed to be something about which nothing was known, except that it had the ability to cause the effects to be explained. The alternative proposed by Cartesians was to construct a completely mechanical explanation of all animal functions.

Besides the two reasons already considered against soul-based explanations—namely, that they are meaningless, and that they are pseudo-causal explanations—Cartesians also objected to animal souls on the grounds of simplicity. In this argument, they relied on a metaphysical assumption that God acts in the simplest ways possible; if he constructed nature as a vast machine he must be assumed to have done so as simply as possible.[38] Therefore, one should keep Occam's razor in mind as a guiding principle of method in all scientific explanations. Arnauld formulated this principle as Rule 7 in *Vraies et fausses idées*: 'The seventh [rule]: not to multiply beings without necessity, as is so often done in the common philosophy . . .'[39] In a similar way, Poisson and Cordemoy both appealed to considerations of simplicity in their rejection of animal souls. Poisson, for example, argued that the term *âme* is equivocal between a spiritual soul and a mere principle of motion. If some philosophers defend a non-thinking, spiritual soul in animals, then 'M. Descartes would not oppose that, unless he were to say

---

[37] *Nouvelles difficultez proposées par un peripateticien a l'autheur du voyage du monde de Descartes* (1693), 117.
[38] See Malebranche, *Traité de la nature et de la grace*, in *Œuvres complètes*, v. 31.
[39] *Œuvres*, xxxviii. 182.

frankly that he could not understand such a principle, and that it is very gratuitous to assume it because all the functions which one attributes to it can be supplied by a physical principle'.[40] The Cartesian objection to animal souls is summarized in the Preface to Le Grand's textbook: 'I make no scruple in this discourse . . . to render them [i.e. beasts] meer machins, which by the furniture of organs they are provided with, exert their several actions . . . they are neither more nor less than meer engins or machins.'[41]

The rejection of animal souls may no longer seem implausible to us. It should be remembered, however, that the Cartesians identified feeling as a form of thought or consciousness, so that the lack of a soul necessarily implied the lack of feeling. This was the most obvious way in which the theory seemed to fly in the face of the evidence. 'Brute animals are not only incapable of cogitation, but are also void of every simple perception.'[42] Père Daniel commented sarcastically that he had been afraid to see even a chicken killed before he had encountered Cartesianism but that, once he was convinced that animals have no feeling, there was hardly a dog in his town safe from the threat of anatomical experiment. 'But since I was once persuaded that beasts were destitute both of knowledge and sense, scarce a dog in all the town, wherein I was, could escape me, for the making of anatomical dissections.'[43]

---

[40] *Remarques*, p. 148. Cordemoy argued, in his Third Discourse, that the time-keeping of a watch should be explained by the arrangement of its parts; if someone believed that the watch also had a soul, we could hardly prove that it does not. All we could do is to appeal to the principle: 'one ought not to multiply entities without necessity.' *Discernement*, p. 123. See also his *Discourse written to a Learned Frier*, p. 264.

[41] *Entire Body of Philosophy*, unpaginated preface. Also, on p. 253: 'For all animals (man only excepted) are a kind of watches or clocks, which by a fit adaptation of their parts, have a bodily principle of motion in themselves, as long as they are well disposed, and have whatsoever is required to perform and exert the several actions to which they are design'd. For all the effects we perceived in animals (man excepted) have no other cause or principles but the body, neither is their sensitive souls any thing, but the constitution and affection of their bodily organs, and the spirits or the purest parts of the blood, fitted to the animals life, and the exercise of the senses.'

[42] Ibid. 229. This conclusion was based on a radical distinction between spirit and matter. In his *Tract on Beasts*, Le Grand argued fallaciously that, since no individual particle of matter senses or perceives, then neither can 5 or 10 or a whole cluster of them perceive. Therefore a purely material body such as that of a beast cannot perceive anything.

[43] *Voiage*, Eng. trans., p. 241.

The machine model of animals raised more problems than it solved. Even in those cases where an outline explanation was suggested by the Cartesians, the patent defects of such explanation sketches only helped to underline the essentially philosophical nature of the option in favour of mechanical explanations. This need not blind us to the wisdom, which can only be appreciated retrospectively, of endorsing a research programme which was initially a failure. Nor should the eventual acceptance of mechanical models camouflage the extent to which seventeenth-century models of animal machines promised much more explanatory resourcefulness than they provided up to that time. When Pardies or Daniel disputed the concept of a *bête machine*, there had been minimal progress made in explaining animal functions and there was little evidence to suggest that the Cartesian project was likely to succeed. The commitment to mechanism can only be understood, therefore, in terms of other factors which determined the outcome of the controversy.

Apart from its manifest lack of success, the concept of an animal machine also represented a frontal attack on the scholastic concept of explanation. If the forms which explain animal functions are redundant, then *a fortiori* forms are likely to be equally redundant in explaining non-living natural phenomena. Finally, the challenge to forms as viable explanatory concepts had obvious implications for the concept of a human soul and, as suggested above in Chapter 1, for theological doctrines which assumed any version of the soul theory, such as the doctrine of personal immortality or of reward and punishment for individuals in the afterlife. The impact of these extraneous issues exacerbated the disagreement between those who promoted an unsuccessful explanatory model for metaphysical reasons, and those who objected with equal vigour for theological reasons.

The major difficulties inherent in Cartesian mechanism became most explicit in biology. One of them derived from Descartes's mechanical explanation of the transition from non-living to living matter. The Cartesian explanation of the origin of living matter was high on theory and very poor on specifics. It included the usual acknowledgement that God is the general cause of living things, but that he operates through purely mechanical means when the laws of nature are applied to various parts of matter in motion. An ideal explanation would involve showing how very fine, moving, and branched particles could develop, on their own, into living matter.

This seemed too much to ask of science in the seventeenth century, and it struck many as being almost ridiculous even to suggest that kind of explanation. The apparent irreducibility of living bodies to complex machines is forcefully expressed by Fontenelle as follows: 'You say that animals are machines just as much as watches? However if you put a dog-machine and a bitch-machine beside each other, a third little machine may result; whereas two watches may be next to each other all their lives, without ever producing a third watch.'[44] Fontenelle's challenge can only be met by one or other of the following responses. One could provide a satisfactory mechanical account of the genesis of living matter; or one could admit that we do not understand how reproduction takes place, although we still have reason to believe that a mechanical embryology is possible. Descartes's approach was a combination of both options; it assumed rather dogmatically that only mechanical explanations are acceptable, and it also purported to provide a successful explanation within the constraints of the adopted method. However, the proposed epigenetic theory was so obviously defective that some other approach was required.

Malebranche took up the challenge of defending a more limited version of mechanism. His reforming zeal was stimulated by a number of factors. One of these was the failure of the Cartesian account, already mentioned. Two other complementary reasons were peculiar to Malebranche: one was the theory about the inertness of matter, and the second was the inefficacy of secondary causes and the dominance of God's causality in explaining any significant change in matter. All these reasons were indirectly supported by the observations of Malpighi, reported in *De Formatione Pulli in Ovo* (1673) and those of Jan Swammerdam (1637–80), which are described in his *Miraculum Naturae* (1672); Malebranche appealed to both treatises for experimental support for a preformation theory.[45]

The rejection of a mechanical embryology is found in the *Dialogues on Metaphysics*. Malebranche's spokesman, Theodore, says that it is inconceivable how purely mechanical interactions can give rise to a living being:

[44] Letters of Fontenelle, letter XI, in *Œuvres*, i. 323, quoted by Roger (1963), 346.
[45] Rodis-Lewis (1974) discusses Malebranche's use of others' scientific work, including that of Malpighi and Swammerdam; the latter's work is also summarized in Lindeboom (1982).

But we will never comprehend how laws of motion can construct bodies composed of an infinity of organs. We have enough trouble conceiving that these laws can little by little make them grow. . . . We do not comprehend how the union of two sexes can be a cause of fertility, but we do comprehend that this is not impossible on the hypothesis that bodies are already formed. But that that union should be the cause of the organization of the parts of an animal . . . is certainly something we shall never comprehend. . . . That Philosopher's [i.e. Descartes] unfinished work can help us comprehend how the laws of motion suffice to make the parts of an animal grow little by little. But that these laws can form them and bind them all together is what no one will ever prove.[46]

At face value, this is an argument against the very conceivability of a mechanical explanation of living matter; it is also a reflection on the failure of Cartesian science to provide an account which comes close to making such an ideal conceivable.

In an effort to bridge the gap between the mechanical application of laws of nature and the mysteries of conception, Malebranche developed a theory of preformation. This theory of pre-existent germs was introduced in Book I, chapter 6, of the *Search After Truth*, in which the Oratorian author was primarily concerned with the limitations of human vision. He points out that the microscope has allowed us to see 'animals much smaller than an almost invisible grain of sand'.[47] It follows that the limited powers of human vision cannot be accepted as a criterion of what may or may not exist. God's power alone, rather than human vision or imagination, sets the lower limits for the infinitely small living creatures which God may have created. At this point, some observational evidence is introduced to support the theory:

When one examines the seed of a tulip bulb in the dead of winter with a simple *magnifying lens* or convex glass, or even merely with the naked eye, one easily discovers in this seed the leaves that are to become green, those that are to make up the flower or tulip, that tiny triangular part which contains the seed, and the six little columns that surround it at the base of the flower. Thus it cannot be doubted that the seed of a tulip bulb contains an entire tulip. It is reasonable to believe the same thing of a mustard seed, an apple seed, and generally of the seeds of every sort of tree or plant . . . Nor does it seem unreasonable to believe even that there is an infinite number of trees in a single seed, since it contains not only the tree of

---

[46] *Dialogues on Metaphysics*, pp. 263, 265.   [47] *Search After Truth*, p. 25.

which it is the seed but also a great number of other seeds that might contain other trees and other seeds . . . and so on to infinity.[48]

The advantage of this hypothesis is that 'nature's role is only to unfold these tiny trees',[49] which pre-exist in miniature from the very beginning of creation, and which require no further explanation apart from saying that they were created by God.

Once this is accepted for plants, the same theory may be applied in explaining procreation among animals and human beings:

What we have just said about plants and their seeds can be said also of animals and the seeds from which they are produced. . . . We ought to accept . . . that the body of every man and beast born till the end of time was perhaps produced at the creation of the world. My thought is that the females of the original animals may have been created along with all those of the same species that they have begotten and that are to be begotten in the future.[50]

This compromise respects the Cartesian restrictions on scientific explanation, as an account which is exclusively mechanical; at the same time, it recognizes the obvious weakness of Descartes's embryology and incorporates Malebranche's strong version of occasionalism by attributing the cause of all living beings uniquely to God's original creative act. This represents a very significant modification of Descartes's claims for the resourcefulness of mechanical explanation. Despite that, it should not be understood as a rejection of mechanism in biology; it may be more sympathetically understood as merely a limitation of the fertility of mechanical explanations.[51] Malebranche is not proposing any other type of explanation as an appropriate substitute for mechanism in biology, because God's creative intervention is not part of any scientific account.

At the same time, Malebranche's reservations about mechanics implied, for his critics like Arnauld or Régis, too radical a separation between God's actions and the specific effects of his creative concurrence. It suggested that God is directly responsible for creating seeds, and that the laws of mechanics are exclusively the

---

[48] *Search After Truth*, pp. 26–7.   [49] Ibid. 27.   [50] Ibid.
[51] Cf. Rohault, *Entretiens*, p. 111, where he contrasts explaining how God may have created matter at the beginning, which is not part of science, and explaining how natural phenomena have evolved from this initial creation just as plants develop from seeds, which is the proper role of scientific explanation.

cause of the subsequent development of these seeds into either healthy well-formed members of some species, or into 'monsters' of nature. The separation of the two phases of God's activity implies that God cannot be held responsible for monsters. Régis argued, against this theory, that there is no real distinction between the will of God and the laws of nature:

It is easy to reply that there is nothing in the world, apart from moral evil, of which God is not the author . . . It would serve no purpose to say that God does indeed produce monsters, but that he is forced to produce them to satisfy the laws of nature although he would prefer if there were none. For we reply that the laws of nature are not different from the will of God, and if one says that God produces things according to the laws of nature which he would prefer not to produce, we reply again that this is to claim that the will of God is contrary to itself, which is repugnant.[52]

For those who were conscious of Jansenist claims about the immediacy of God's action in nature, there was no merit in trying to distance God's creativity from the laws of nature by separating the initial creation of seeds (by God) from the natural development of these seeds (according to mechanical laws). God is equally at work in both. Once this is accepted it is difficult to argue that God could not achieve the transition from non-living to living matter by an appropriate application of the laws of nature. One is reminded, in this context, of Locke's superadded properties in the *Essay*; just as it implies a restriction on God's power to say that he could not add the property of thinking to a material substance, it involves a similar concept of an impotent God to claim that it is impossible in principle for non-living matter to evolve into living matter according to the laws which God has imposed on nature.

The explanation of memory provides another example of mechanical models being exploited in a context in which they failed miserably to live up to Cartesian expectations. It illustrates both the commitment to mechanical explanation and the eventual fruitfulness of a theory in search of a detailed, experimentally confirmed description of animal learning. At the time of its initial proposal, it was a patently weak attempt to explain the facts available; yet it provided an almost prescient discussion of Pavlovian conditioning, and thereby pointed researchers in a new direction for explaining animal behaviour.

---

[52] *Système*, iii. 29–30.

La Forge defines *la mémoire corporelle* as follows: 'a certain facility to reopen which remains in those ventricles of the brain which have already been opened by the (animal) spirits, and in the fibres through which they have passed, whatever the cause which made the original opening.'[53] The word 'facility' should introduce a sceptical query in the reader. Is this not exactly the kind of explanation which the Cartesians were dedicated to exorcizing from science? The subsequent explanation does little to alleviate one's fears. La Forge gives a completely mechanical account of how the image on one's retina causes a flow of animal spirits through the brain, so that the central processing unit of the brain is eventually stimulated by an effect which is physically isomorphic with the retinal image. Memory is explained in terms of the disposition of the various parts of the brain to reproduce the same image with greater facility in proportion to the number of times that the animal spirits have passed through the brain with exactly the same configuration. In the case of man, those conscious ideas which are associated with various brain events are likely to be recalled on each occasion on which the brain undergoes the same physical events.

There is no indication in this account of any physical traces being left in the brain. The only effect which survives from earlier perceptions is the relative ease with which the same type of image can be communicated through nerve fibres by the flow of animal spirits. The dispositional character of the explanation is made more obvious by the analogy with piercing a taut canvas with the needles of a comb. Once pierced, the canvas has a large number of apertures; even if they close when the needles are withdrawn, the canvas retains a 'capacity' for being pierced more easily in those places which had been opened previously. This part of the explanation relies on various assumptions about the flexibility of matter which have been discussed above in Chapter 3. The crucial new element in the explanation of memory is that, by opening some of the apertures caused by the needles, one will also cause the other apertures to reopen. La Forge explains it as follows:

In the same way as when one passes a number of needles through the canvas A, the holes which they make in it will remain open after they are withdrawn; or, if they close, they leave in the places through which they passed a great facility to be opened by a similar action. And you will notice

[53] *Traité de l'esprit*, pp. 280–2.

that if one opened only a few of them, such as *a* and *b*, that would be enough to make the others, such as *c* and *d*, open at the same time, especially if all these apertures have been opened together a number of times, and if they were not accustomed to having some of them opened without the others. The same thing happens even more easily in the pores of the inner surface of the ventricles of the brain than in the canvas. When the spirits open some of the pores a second time, those which surround them also take the same path to some extent (as we find the air taking the path of rivers), and in this way they open the pores which are near them because of the facility which they find in those pores.[54]

This type of explanation is only partly mechanical; the centre of the brain is physically affected by the flow of animal spirits. But in order for the explanation to work, the brain must retain a 'facility' for being similarly affected in the future. This facility is not explained, nor is there any plausible way in which it might be described within the Cartesian account of matter. La Forge says simply: 'All the parts where they [i.e. animal spirits] have left some trace of their passage, which is capable of retracing the same species and of giving us the same thought, should be accepted as the organ of memory.'[55]

The incompleteness of the explanation does not prevent La Forge from introducing a novel discussion of animal conditioning.

Thus it usually happens that the first time one encounters a guard dog, he approaches in order to bite. However, if one takes a stick and hits him, he is forced to run; then on subsequent oçasions when one meets the dog, even without the stick, he still flees. Because by means of the strikes he got, one has joined together the passage of the spirits which our presence excited with the passage which was caused by the strikes of the stick. Since these two passages meet somewhere in the centre of the brain and become joined together, either one of them is enough at later times to reopen the ventricles of the brain, and to bring the spirits to the same muscles and cause the same actions which originally resulted from both. I am certain that if you understand this well, you will have no difficulty in explaining most animal behaviour, the most interesting examples of which come from these traces which remain in the brain; nor is there any difficulty in understanding how they are capable of discipline, and why they remember so well the paths by which they have travelled without having to attribute any knowledge to them.[56]

[54] Ibid. 282–3.
[55] Ibid. 283.
[56] Ibid. 284. See also p. 123, on the use of natural signs by dogs.

In a sense, La Forge is perfectly correct. If we could understand the internal mechanism by which the brain works, we would understand animal behaviour. He is committed to constructing a purely mechanical explanation; but the proposed explanation leaves much to be desired, and would hardly convince any perceptive opponent.

This is exactly the response one finds in Daniel's criticism of the theory of animal spirits. In his *Nouvelles difficultez*, he chides the Cartesians for promising mechanical explanations but omitting all the relevant detail.

What, I ask you, does your whole doctrine amount to? To nothing more than telling us that the animal spirits are determined by the impression of objects to flow into different muscles, from which different movements ought to follow. That's all. But I would not have to do anything more than consult the great Descartes to learn only that much. . . . I had recourse to the book of Monsieur Régis who, with such a reputation, replaces the Rohaults, the Cordemoys in our day . . . I find in his book a lot of clarity and of method, and a great understanding of the dogmas of the sect which he has embraced. But on the issues which I am questioning here, and also on all the other issues concerning the spontaneous motion of animals, it all reduces to saying that different motions come from the different objects which differently move the organs, and which open different passages to the spirits which flow into different muscles.[57]

This raises a question about the appropriateness of Daniel's objection to many other mechanical explanations which were espoused by the Cartesians. It is clear that the incredulity of opponents about the viability of mechanical explanations is much higher in biology than in astronomy or physics; it is still worth while to consider the validity of the same type of objection even in those areas where it could not easily rely on the rhetorical force of Fontenelle's challenge.

The proposed explanation of the tides is a good example of a Cartesian explanation accounting for the relevant phenomena without any reference to disbarred theoretical concepts. Rohault broaches the question in the final chapter of Part II of the *Traité de physique*.[58] He recognizes the coincidence between the relative motions of the earth and the moon, and the occurrence of tides. He

---

[57] *Nouvelles difficultez*, pp. 55, 56–67.
[58] *Traité de physique*, ii. 114. Samuel Clarke explains in a footnote to Rohault's account how 'the famous Sir Isaac Newton' gives an alternative explanation in terms of universal gravitation. See ibid. ii. 120–1 n. 1.

carefully sets out the facts available from observation, and then suggests a typical Cartesian explanation. The moon travels around the earth, carried by an elliptical vortex of heavenly matter. As the heavenly matter is forced to squeeze between the earth and the moon in its vortical motion, it presses down on the earth and thereby tends to push the earth away from the moon. This pressure is counteracted by a corresponding pressure of the heavenly matter on the obverse side of the earth. The result is that the earth is squeezed, on both sides, along a line which joins the centres of the moon and the earth. This causes the oceans to flow away from the main pressure points towards the poles, and this explains the tides. The same type of explanation is repeated by Gadroys in *Système du monde*, by Régis in his *Système de philosophie*, and by Le Grand in the *Entire Body of Philosophy*.[59] It is also adopted by Père Daniel as the standard Cartesian account, in his *Voiage du monde*.[60] However, Daniel objects that the pressure of the air which is assumed in this account would be sufficient to be detectable by a Torricelli tube: 'yet this difference has never been observ'd, though it must be very great.'[61]

The most obvious Cartesian features of this explanation are that it relies on the vortex theory of planetary motion, and that it substitutes contact action for attractive force as the mechanism by which the water on the earth's surface is affected by the moon.[62] Two other features also deserve mention: the fact that the explanation of a wide range of phenomena became quickly entrenched as orthodox 'Cartesian' explanations; and, secondly, that the explanation is a rough, qualitative model rather than a specific, detailed, or quantitative account which has disconfirmable implications. In fact, the two features are interdependent.

The ease with which Descartes's explanations became entrenched within a school raises a number of queries about what exactly his followers were hoping to achieve. This is even more evident in the explanation of blood circulation. Descartes had joined the avant-

---

[59] Gadroys, *Système du monde*, pp. 376–92; Régis, *Système*, ii. 412–23; Le Grand, *Entire Body of Philosophy*, pp. 97–8, 204–5.

[60] *Voyage*, Eng. trans., p. 234.

[61] Ibid. 290–1.

[62] Régis comments in another context that those who reject contact action 'are forced to introduce other purely chimerical principles, such as attraction, sympathy . . . and the fear of a vacuum', *Système*, i. 328. Cf. Malebranche, *Search After Truth*, p. 30.

garde on this question by endorsing Harvey's description of the relevant facts, although he disagreed with the English physician about the cause of blood circulation.[63] A half-century later, Le Grand repeats Descartes's theory for non-human animals without even mentioning Harvey, although he does refer to the 'works of Dr. Harvey' in his discussion of blood circulation in humans. Even this recognition, however, had no impact on his theory; he introduced Descartes's theory of why the blood circulates as if there were no problems and no alternatives available. 'We conclude Heat to be the bodily principle of all our motions.'[64] One finds the same uncritical repetition of Descartes's account in Rohault's *Traité de physique*, without any mention of the disputed character of the claim.[65] It is not surprising, therefore, if Leibniz reacted to the relative homogeneity of Cartesian science by suggesting that Cartesians were mere commentators rather than innovators in science. He wrote to Malebranche, in 1679: 'Most of the Cartesians are nothing but commentators, and I would wish that one of them were capable of adding as much to physics as you have contributed to metaphysics.'[66]

The lack of innovation in scientific explanation is partly explained by the poverty of the fundamental explanatory concepts which were available within this tradition. Of course, this suggestion could be understood in a way which trivializes the point, as if it were simply a question of definition. In that case, those who were innovative were by definition those who broke with a strict understanding of Cartesianism, such as Mariotte or Huygens, in order to introduce significant new developments into science. The real question is: why did eminent devotees of the Cartesian tradition refuse to change or to incorporate new theories, despite their professed abhorrence of any uncritical acceptance of tradition? The answer to this question must include some recognition of their low expectations of a scientific explanation. For the French Cartesians, it was enough to provide readers with a sketch of an explanation, a rough model of what a mechanical account might look like, without demanding a fully elaborated, quantified description which could be less ambiguously tested against the data of experience.

[63] See Clarke (1982), 149–54.
[64] Le Grand, *Entire Body of Philosophy*, pp. 253 ff., and pp. 275–6 for human beings. The quotation is from p. 275.
[65] *Traité de Physique*, ii. 266–7.
[66] Leibniz to Malebranche, May 1679, in Robinet (1955), 110.

This tolerance of crude mechanical models is partly explained by the Cartesians' perception of their objective, which was to challenge systematically the philosophy of the schools and to substitute an alternative, mechanical model of science in its place. The rhetoric of this challenge emphasized the inefficacy of Peripatetic philosophy and the merits, by contrast, of mechanical explanation. Thus the most pressing demand on Cartesianism was to indicate what a mechanical explanation of various phenomena would look like, rather than actually to construct detailed accounts which would stand up to scrutiny.

Secondly, there seemed to be a residual dilemma in combining a mechanical explanation of the origins of the universe with the Genesis account of creation. This issue was usually avoided, as it had been by Descartes in the *Discourse*, by saying that God created the world in the beginning as we see it, and therefore no detailed evolutionary account was required. However, in order for us to understand nature, we must be able to imagine how it might have evolved according to the laws of nature from the pristine chaos of swirling matter.[67] Any explanation of the origin of the world along these lines was avowedly counterfactual. Its counterfactual character diminished the demands for specificity and, more importantly, spilled over into other models by making acceptable, as an explanation, a description which was independently believed to be false.

Finally, Descartes had argued that the number of variables involved in most physical or biological phenomena are so numerous that we could not realistically hope to identify and quantify each of them so as to provide the reader with the kind of scientific account to which the modern scientist has become accustomed. The acceptability of crude models was therefore a result of recognizing the intractable complexity of reality. This amounted to endorsing Descartes's third rule of method, to the effect that one should begin with the simple and easy things before proceeding to examine the more difficult; it also implied, evidently, that one normally makes little progress beyond the simple and evident. Thus Malebranche suggests that his own first rule of method implies that 'we should always begin with the simplest and easiest things, and pause there for a considerable time before undertaking the search after the most

---

[67] See e.g. Le Grand, *Entire Body of Philosophy*, pp. 100–1.

complex and difficult ones'.[68] Poisson expresses it more pessimistically: 'There are still too many mysteries for a mind which is limited to its own natural powers and the aid of its senses.'[69]

In summary, the Cartesian concept of explanation was forged in an ongoing confrontation with a systematically and ably defended tradition of scholastic explanation. The bitterness of the controversies which separated these two traditions in the seventeenth century tended to oversimplify the issues on which they disagreed, and to narrow the Cartesians' focus to the obvious demerits of their opponents. The difference between the two sides was reduced to an apparently simple option between the pseudo-explanations of scholastic forms and qualities, and an ideal of mechanical explanation which was shared to a greater or less extent by almost all the proponents of the new sciences in the same period. The choice between these options was so obvious to proponents of the new philosophy that the limitations of their own position were almost completely ignored.

Many of the central issues about which the new scientists disagreed were decided by the type of conceptual or metaphysical arguments which have already been discussed in earlier chapters. These arguments were concerned with the number and type of explanatory concepts which are admissible in a scientific explanation. On the more limited issue of the concept of explanation itself, the Cartesians recognized the necessarily hypothetical character of most mechanical models, for two reasons: (a) the imperceptibility of the causes of most natural phenomena. If we explain observable phenomena in terms of unobservable entities, we can do no better than to postulate the existence and properties of the latter. (b) the causal relationship between hypothesized causes and observed effects cannot be observed, but must be identified by 'reasoning'. Thus even if the alleged cause of some natural phenomenon is observable, the fact that it is the true cause cannot be observed; one can only assume its causal efficacy and subsequently determine the likely consequences of such an hypothesis.

[68] *Search After Truth*, pp. 437–8. Cf. Clerselier's account of the weekly conferences which were given by Rohault: 'La méthode que Monsieur Rohault gardoit dans ses conferences, estoit d'y expliquer l'une apres l'autre toutes les question de Physique, en commençant par l'establissement des ses Principes & descendant ensuite à la preuve de ses effets les plus particuliers & les plus rares.' Unpaginated preface, *Œuvres posthumes*.

[69] *Remarques*, p. 57.

Besides, as was already indicated, there was a certain amount of pessimism evident even in Descartes about the capacity of the human mind to identify and quantify all the variables which are relevant to the explanation of any complex phenomenon. These considerations implied that the most one could often hope to achieve in natural philosophy was to construct a mechanical model which shows how the laws of nature, acting on the kinds of particle already accepted into the Cartesian framework, may have given rise to the effects we observe. This implied abandoning the strong Aristotelian demand that an explanation should help us understand how something cannot be other than it is; we can only expect to understand how it may have developed into its present condition according to the laws of nature.

In Cartesian terms, this type of explanation is 'a priori' without being independent of experience, and is 'rational' without necessarily being rationalist. In fact, it is so different from our usual anticipation of Cartesian science that it immediately raises two further questions: (*a*) how can such hypothetical models ever be 'demonstrated'?; (*b*) what kind of certainty could the Cartesians have claimed for what looks, in retrospect, like nothing more than unsophisticated models in which the disanalogies with the *explananda* considerably outweigh whatever merits they might otherwise seem to have? Both these issues are taken up in the next chapter, under the rubric of confirmation.

7

Confirmation: Experience and Reason

THE central role of hypotheses and mechanical models in Cartesian explanation raises questions about the sense in which these models were supposed to represent reality, and also about the degree of certainty which was claimed for typical scientific explanations. On the issue of realism, there were two options available: one was to concede that scientific hypotheses are nothing more than models which save the appearances more or less adequately, and in that limited sense provide an explanation or systematic redescription of natural phenomena. Alternatively, one could claim that scientific models describe the way the world is. The second question, about the relative certainty of hypotheses, is more or less crucial depending on the position one adopts about scientific realism. Mathematical models which are assumed not to correspond with reality might be employed with impunity as long as they are useful for making predictions, without raising serious questions about their certainty or otherwise; but for those who defend the claim that scientific theories describe the way the world is, there is an added dimension of urgency in assessing the degree of certainty which can be claimed for hypotheses which must be measured against the absolute demands of objective reality. Cartesians almost unanimously opted for a realist view of scientific theories; and, in their more enthusiastic reflections on Descartes's scientific bequest, they also claimed to be able to realize a degree of probability in their theories which is indistinguishable from certainty.

The development of Cartesian methodology in the seventeenth century coincided with the historical emergence of a theory of probability.[1] One might expect that the language of probability

---

[1] See Hacking (1975) and, for the dissemination of the concept of probability in England, Shapiro (1983).

would have provided the Cartesian school with an ideal instrument for describing the relative certainty of their hypotheses without conceding victory to alternative scientific theories. However, this was not as simple a task as might otherwise appear. The very language in which disputes about theories were conducted tended to undermine the flexibility promised by a theory of probability. As already indicated in Chapter 5 above, the orthodox language of the schools distinguished between science and mere opinion. This distinction was expressed in terms of the difference between 'demonstrated' and 'probable' beliefs. It implied that probable opinions had no greater support than the mere fact of not being known to be false. Given the fact that Cartesians were in open conflict with their Peripatetic opponents, they were unable to describe their hypotheses as probable without exposing themselves to the charge of defending 'merely probable' opinions in the scholastic sense. At the same time, there were many reasons—some of which have already been discussed—for admitting that at least some Cartesian explanations were only probable in the newly coined sense of the term. The two senses of 'probable' resulted in a confusion of two distinct languages. When forced to express themselves in this period of semantic ambiguity, the Cartesians avoided the connotations of patent uncertainty associated with Aristotelian probability by claiming that their well-confirmed theories were 'demonstrated'.

The new language of probability was already common in describing scientific hypotheses in the second half of the seventeenth century. For example, Fontenelle tried to identify a position which was somewhere between absolute certainty and the 'mere probability' of scholastics. We do not have a mathematical proof, he argued, for the existence of Alexander the Great; nor do we say that his existence was a mere probability. In the same way, Fontenelle's theory about inhabitants on other planets may not be as certain as our claims about Alexander the Great, but, he claimed, it was much more probable than many other historical claims which are generally accepted as facts.[2] A similar attempt at introducing a scale of probability for describing scientific hypotheses was made by Huygens. For example, he wrote to Oldenburg in 1672 concerning Newton's theory of colour: 'What you have published of

---

[2] *Œuvres*, iii. 236–8.

M. Newton in one of your last numbers confirms still more his doctrine of colours. Yet the matter could well be quite otherwise, and it seems to me that he should be content that what he has put forward should pass for a very plausible hypothesis.'[3] Six years later, Huygens presented his own theory of light to members of the Académie royale des sciences in 1678. This was published in 1690 as his *Treatise on Light*, in the Preface of which he gave a very clear expression of the type of hypothetical reasoning which is characteristic of scientific explanation, and of the level of certainty or probability which one may justifiably claim for one's results:

There will be seen in it demonstrations of those kinds which do not produce as great a certitude as those of Geometry, and which even differ much therefrom, since whereas the Geometers prove their Propositions by fixed and incontestable Principles, here the Principles are verified by the conclusions to be drawn from them; the nature of these things not allowing of this being done otherwise. It is always possible to attain thereby to a degree of probability which very often is scarcely less than complete proof. To wit, when things which have been demonstrated by the principles that have been assumed correspond perfectly to the phenomena which experiment has brought under observation; especially when there are a great number of them, and further, principally, when one can imagine and foresee new phenomena which ought to follow from the hypotheses which one employs, and when one finds that therein the fact corresponds to our prevision. But if all these proofs of probability are met with in that which I propose to discuss . . . this ought to be very strong confirmation of the success of my inquiry . . .[4]

One finds equally clear signs of accommodation to the new language of probability in Edme Mariotte and Claude Perrault. In the *Essai de logique* (1678), Mariotte lists the various criteria by which the probability of competing explanations should be decided: 'An hypothesis of one system is more probable (*vrai-semblable*) than that of another if, by assuming it, one explains all the phenomena or a greater number of phenomena more exactly, more clearly and with a stronger link with other known things; but if there is one phenomenon which cannot be reconciled with an hypothesis, then that hypothesis is false or inadequate.'[5] The

[3] Oldenberg, *Correspondence*, ix. 247–8; Huygens, *Œuvres complètes*, vii. 228–9.
[4] *Treatise on Light*, Eng. trans., pp. vi–vii.
[5] *Essai de logique* (1678), in *Œuvres*, ii. 624. This is the concluding paragraph of Mariotte's extensive discussion of probability, under the title 'Principes des propositions vrai-semblables', in the *Essai de logique*, pp. 620–4.

Popperian contrast between difficult confirmation and easy refutation is also found in a similar passage in the Introduction to Perrault's *Essais de physique* (1680):

Since physics has two parts, namely the philosophical and the historical, it is certain that one can acquire only knowledge which is obscure and uncertain in the first part which explains the elements, the primary qualities and the other causes of natural bodies by means of hypotheses that, for the most part, have no other foundation except probability. One must also admit that the other part, although it is filled with well-established facts, also contains many doubtful things; for the conclusions which one draws in this part from extraordinary phenomena and new experiences are not very certain, because we do not have all the information which is necessary to establish these conclusions properly. It also happens that the more observations one makes, the more one realizes that one is in danger of being mistaken. These new observations often serve much less to confirm than to destroy the conclusions which one had previously reached.[6]

Both Mariotte and Perrault assign a clear role to new experiments or observations in disconfirming hypotheses; neither one of them is confident about the possibility of confirmation, since any hypothesis is constantly open to the danger of being overturned by new evidence.

In contrast with these efforts to discriminate between more or less plausible claims and to identify the various factors which are relevant to determining degrees of probability in a particular case, Cartesian philosophers appeared, at least to their critics, to be claiming much more certainty than was warranted by the supporting evidence. Thus Père Daniel argued that Aristotelians were 'not for rejecting *M. Descartes's* Doctrin concerning the Seat of the Soul in the Pineal Gland, were it proposed only as a pure *Hypothesis* . . . but it was insufferable that System should be urged as a settled and demonstrated Truth'.[7] Unfortunately, Daniel's comment presupposes the standard dichotomy between demonstration and mere hypothesis which obscured the novelty of the new concept of probability. There was a third option available, the one suggested by Huygens, Mariotte, and Perrault. Cartesians could not avoid this issue; they were forced to confront the question of clarifying the

---

[6] Unpaginated preface to the *Essais de physique*, i (first 2 pages). See also i. 129, where Perrault speaks of 'confirming the probability of the principles' by showing how they explain many natural phenomena.

[7] *Voyage*, Eng. trans., p. 148.

sense in which scientific hypotheses may be certain, proved, demonstrated, or probable.

Demonstration and Probability

The Aristotelian distinction between dialectical and demonstrative syllogisms is endorsed by Régis in his *Discours sur la philosophie*. In contrast with merely dialectical arguments which rely on uncertain premisses, 'the demonstrative [syllogism] . . . contains certain and evident propositions, and its conclusion is completely convincing'.[8] This concept of demonstrated knowledge is also assumed in the *Logique*, in which the author gives the following as the third rule of synthesis: 'to prove demonstratively all the propositions which one advances by relying only on the definitions which one has proposed, on principles which have been accepted as very evident, or on propositions which have been already derived by reasoning and which subsequently serve as so many principles to prove other truths which are more remote.'[9] This is typical of school philosophy of the time; one first establishes definitions and principles, and then derives all other claims from these by a process of logical deduction.

Le Grand gives an equally uncompromising account of scientific knowledge in the Preface to the *Entire Body of Philosophy*:

For seeing that the Truth of the Principles of any Science is made manifest by the evidence of its deductions, and that their certainty is look'd upon as indubitable, if those things that are inferr'd from them, do wholly depend upon the knowledge of them; I was desirous to try, whether the several appearances of nature, or all those things which our senses perceive to be bodies, did comport with the principles laid in my *Institution of Philosophy*, and whether there be such a connection between them, as that tho' the latter may be apprehended without the former, yet the former can never be understood without the latter.[10]

The analogy between logical deduction and scientific explanation is supported by a contrast between disciplines in which we might tolerate probability, such as law and ethics, and genuine scientific knowledge of the truth which excludes all doubt and therefore

---

[8] Unpaginated *Discours sur la philosophie*, in vol. iii of *Système*.
[9] Part IV of the *Logique*, in *Système*, i. 56.
[10] *Entire Body of Philosophy*, unpaginated preface.

cannot be content with probability: 'But in the search of truth, whatsoever hath the least doubt in it, is to be rejected . . .'[11]

Both of these texts, together with many similar claims by other Cartesian authors, illustrate the extent to which the debate about the certainty of competing explanations was held captive by the scholastic distinction between genuine scientific knowledge which is absolutely certain and demonstrative, and mere probable opinions which do not deserve to be classified as scientific. At the same time, there were indications that Descartes and his followers recognized a need to transcend the scholastic dichotomy in those cases where it is not possible to have absolute certainty. Thus Descartes wrote to Mersenne, concerning the status of hypotheses used in the *Meteorology* and *Dioptrics*:

You ask if I believe that what I wrote about refraction is a demonstration. I think it is, at least in so far as it is possible to give a demonstration in this kind of study . . . and also in as much as any question of mechanics, optics or astronomy, or any other question which is not purely geometrical or arithmetical, has ever been demonstrated. To demand geometrical demonstrations from me in something which presupposes physics is to ask that I do the impossible. If one wishes to call 'demonstrations' only the proofs of geometers, then one must say that Archimedes never demonstrated anything in mechanics, nor Witelo in optics, nor Ptolemy in astronomy . . . but this is not what is said. For in these matters one is content if the authors presuppose certain things which are not manifestly contrary to experience, and if the rest of the discussion is coherent and free from logical errors, even if their assumptions are not exactly true. . . . If people say that they do not accept what I have written because I have deduced it from assumptions which are not proved, then they do not understand what they are asking for, for what they ought to ask for.[12]

This shows a beginning of awareness that mechanical explanations cannot hope to emulate the certainty of mathematical demonstrations. More to the point, one ought not to demand mathematical certainty of physical explanations under the illusion that nothing less than this degree of certainty will suffice.

In subsequent discussion of this issue in the Cartesian tradition, there was more agreement about our inability to achieve certainty than on the suggestion that we should settle for less.

The futility of attempting to achieve mathematical certainty in physical questions was explained by a contrast between the ways in

---

[11] Ibid. 5.   [12] Descartes to Mersenne, *Œuvres*, ii. 141–2, 143–4.

which we know external physical phenomena and pure ideas. For Malebranche or Régis, for example, we can provide reliable evidence to support our claims about physical phenomena, but we cannot give an 'exact demonstration' of the existence of external objects.[13] In fact, 'we cannot have an exact demonstration of other than a necessary being's existence'.[14] Since the world only exists contingently, any claims we make about it cannot be more than probably true. Thus our knowledge of natural phenomena is located by Malebranche on a three-point scale of certainty:

There are three kinds of relations or truths. There are those between ideas, between things and their ideas, and between things only. It is true that twice two is four—here is a truth between ideas. It is true that the sun exists—this is a truth between a thing and its idea. It is true that the earth is larger than the moon—here is a truth that is only between things. Of these three sorts of truths, those between ideas are eternal and immutable . . . this is why only these sorts of truths are considered in arithmetic, algebra, and geometry . . . we use the mind alone to try to discover only truths between ideas, for we almost always employ the senses to discover the other sorts of truths. . . . Relations of ideas are the only ones the mind can know infallibly and by itself without the use of the senses.[15]

Not surprisingly, physics falls short of geometrical demonstration,[16] for 'what we think [must be] in perfect agreement with experience, because in physics we try to discover the order and connection of effects with their causes'.[17] God might have arranged causal connections in nature in an infinite number of alternative ways; 'it is experience which can inform us of the way in which the author of nature acts.'[18] Therefore, all our knowledge of natural phenomena ultimately rests on empirical evidence, and must fall short of the certainty associated with relations of ideas.

These texts are not unusual in the Cartesian tradition. They rely on a distinction between relations of ideas and matters of fact. Demonstration belongs properly to relations of ideas, whereas matters of fact can only be known by means of sensory experience. As already mentioned in the discussion of innate ideas above, there

---

[13] *Dialogues on Metaphysics*, p. 133. Cf. the definition of 'demonstration' in the glossary of terms at the conclusion of Régis, *L'Usage de la raison*.

[14] *Search After Truth*, Elucidation VI, p. 574.

[15] Ibid. 433–4.   [16] Ibid. 244.   [17] Ibid. 484.

[18] Malebranche to the Abbé C.D. (de Catalan), Apr. 1687; *Œuvres*, xvii. part 1, 45–6. Cf. ibid. 55: 'Certainement on ne peut en ce cas découvrir la vérité que par l'expérience.'

are no necessary relations between the ideas which arise in our minds and the physical stimuli which occasion them. The obvious conclusion to draw from this, if logic were the only relevant factor, is that it is impossible for the hypotheses of natural philosophers to be classified as absolutely certain. One might expect that Cartesians would acknowledge the logic of their own argument and admit to some degree of uncertainty in physical science. Unfortunately, that would be equivalent to conceding too much to Peripatetic opponents whose dichotomy between demonstrated and probable opinions put the latter in the category of pure speculation. Thus the tension in Cartesian descriptions of the status of physical hypotheses arises from the attempt to satisfy these two demands, to classify scientific hypotheses as less certain than demonstrated truth, but much more probable than mere guesswork.

This tension can be seen in those cases where the two components come together. For example, Malebranche proposed a theory about the relationship between the brain (and mind) of a foetus and the body of the mother. Then he added: 'I propose all this *only as a hypothesis* that, if I am correct, will be sufficiently *demonstrated* by the following, for any hypothesis that satisfies the test of resolving whatever difficulties can be raised in opposition to it should be accepted as *an indubitable principle*.'[19] This text illustrates the vain hope that what begins as a hypothesis may be confirmed subsequently as almost equivalent to a demonstrated truth. Régis discussed a similar hypothesis in Book VIII of his *Physique*, in which he speculated that the foetus in the womb is probably fed through the mouth. In contrast with Malebranche, however, Régis underlined the point about probability: 'I have said *probably* to let it be understood that although we have no convincing reasons which assure us that the nutritive juice enters through the mouth of the foetus, there are nevertheless many reasons available for assuming it . . .'[20]

The linguistic demands of scholastic terminology, of course, were not the only explanation for exaggerated claims by Cartesians that all their theories, no matter how speculative and unwarranted, were demonstrated. Régis acknowledged a temptation to overstate the probability of hypotheses and he asked to be excused for writing with too much conviction 'about even those matters which are

---

[19] Emphasis added. *Search After Truth*, p. 113.
[20] *Système*, iii. 16.

completely problematic, such as all physical questions. I declare that it was not my intention to propose as clear everything which I described as evident, nor as demonstrated everything which I concluded to be necessary. These are ways of talking which philosophers should allow themselves, without prejudice to modesty and much less to the truth.'[21]

These considerations suggest that Cartesians were operating self-consciously within a hypothetico-deductive model of science and at the same time claiming that their theories were demonstrated. While one might understand the historical reasons which explain, in the context of a major debate between alternative paradigms of scientific explanation, why proponents of competing theories overstated the warrant for their conclusions, it is also necessary to consider the possibility that the source of the exaggerated claims was an inadequate appreciation of the role of experimental evidence in natural philosophy.

Experience and Reason

Many critics of the Cartesian tradition identified its devotion to rational argument at the expense of empirical evidence as one of the key factors which explain both its apparent dogmatism and its failure to make progress in scientific theory. For example, Edme Mariotte suggested that there were three reasons for the many disputes among his scientific contemporaries, the second of which was 'that in the natural sciences they depend too much on reasoning and too little on experiments'.[22] There is a sense in which this objection accurately identifies a basic problem in Cartesian science in the seventeenth century; however, this is true only if we understand the term 'reason' in an unusual way, and if we understand why various kinds of empirical evidence were distrusted. In order to assess the appropriateness of Mariotte's criticism, the relevant evidence needs to be presented in some detail.

Jacques Roger summarizes the attitude to empirical evidence of seventeenth-century biologists in France as follows:

Following Descartes and Gassendi and the example of English *savants*, there is no philosopher, man of science, professor or writer who does not

[21] Unpaginated preface, *Système*, i (first 2 pages).
[22] *Essai de logique*, in *Œuvres*, ii. 610.

proclaim the necessity of consulting experience or being guided by experiments. The only argument which counts is an argument of fact. As Jean-Baptiste Denis wrote in 1672, 'in physical matters, experiments (even when they are new) always win over the false conjectures of antiquity'.[23]

The historical evidence also suggests that this attitude towards the role of *expérience* did not originate with the new sciences.

It would be childish to imagine that those naturalists and biologists of the seventeenth century who were most attached to traditional forms of knowledge had deliberately turned their backs on nature and on facts, and considered that their science was like a purely logical gymnastic. On the contrary, they were all persuaded that experience is the only guide, that submission to facts is the principal virtue of a *savant*, and that the authority of the ancients should never be a decisive argument.[24]

In other words, neither the most stubborn scholastics nor their critics in the newly emerging scientific academies disputed the central role of *expérience* in choosing between competing theories; what they failed to agree on was what counts as a relevant experience. Thus many of the experiences which were invoked to support traditional claims were rejected by the new science as worthless common sense. Even within the ranks of those who broadly supported the new sciences against the claims of traditional learning, the source of unresolved disagreements was less likely to be concerned with the general principle that experience should count, and more likely to centre on which experiments should be accepted and how they should be understood.

There are no Cartesians who rejected experience as a decisive argument in scientific disputes; and where they seem to prefer 'reason' over 'experience' we can easily interpret many such texts as drawing attention to the implications of the distinction between primary and secondary qualities. As long as our perceptions are not guaranteed to resemble the phenomena which trigger them, there is a danger that we may project our perceptions on to the world around us and assume naïvely that the world is exactly as it appears to us. Apart from these general reservations about the use of sensory experience, there is no suggestion that natural philosophers could ever simply ignore empirical data. The relevant questions for the use of empirical evidence in confirming theories are: how did the Cartesians understand 'experience' in this context, to what

[23] Roger (1963), 184–5.   [24] Ibid. 31.

extent was experience decisive, and how should empirical evidence be related to other types of argument in favour of a scientific hypothesis?

That Cartesians deferred to the authority of experience, just like other scientists of the seventeenth century, is beyond dispute. Le Grand, who conspicuously lauded the ideal of a demonstrated science, summarized his policy about experiments as follows: 'There is no question, but that experiments are the best proofs of philosophical truth, and that those principles are most likely to be true, which are built and founded upon natural phaenomena, and have them to be the witnesses of their evidence.'[25] Régis expresses a similar sentiment in the Preface to the *Système de philosophie*;[26] and even Malebranche, who is less enthusiastic than other members of the French Cartesian school about the validity of experience, unambiguously endorses the same view in a number of places:

Reason demonstrates these things: but if reason can be withstood, experience cannot. . . . People who study Physics never reason counter to experience. But they also never conclude from experience what is counter to reason . . . Experience in conjunction with reason suffices for acquiring knowledge in all parts of Physics. . . . What we have proved by abstract arguments must be demonstrated through sensible experiments to see if our ideas are in agreement with the sensations we receive from objects, for it often happens that such arguments deceive us . . . There are still some persons . . . so opinionated that they do not want to see things that they could no longer contradict if they would only open their eyes.[27]

In short, 'it is ridiculous to philosophize against experience'.[28] The same expression of confidence in the irreplaceable role of experience is found in Gadroys, Poisson, or Rohault.[29]

In an effort to articulate a more precise theory of the value of empiricial evidence, Rohault distinguishes three kinds of experience.

The first is, to speak properly, only the mere simple using our senses; as when accidentally and without design, casting our eyes upon the things around us, we cannot help taking notice of them . . . The second sort is,

---

[25] *Entire Body of Philosophy*, p. 4; Latin edn., p. 9.
[26] Preface of *Système*, p. 2.
[27] *Search After Truth*, p. 257; *Dialogues on Metaphysics*, p. 343; ibid. 207; *Search After Truth*, p. 517; ibid. 91.   [28] Ibid. 342.
[29] See Gadroys, *Système du monde*, p. 205: 'Je ne dit rien icy que l'expérience ne confirme'; Poisson, *Remarques*, pp. 68–71; Rohault, *Traité de physique*, i. 58, 61, and unpaginated preface: 'experiments therefore are necessary to establish natural philosophy.'

when we deliberately and designedly make tryal of any thing, without knowing or foreseeing what will come to pass; as when, after the manner of chymists, we make choice of first one subject and then another, and make all the tryals we think of upon each of them . . . We also make experiments in this second way, when we go amongst different sorts of workmen in order to find out the mysteries of their arts, as glassmakers, enamellers, dyers, goldsmiths, and such as work different sorts of metals . . . Lastly, the third sort of experiments are those which are made in consequence of some *reasoning* in order to discover whether *it* was just or not. As when after having considered the ordinary effects of any particular subject, and formed a true idea of the nature of it, that is, *of that in it which makes it capable of producing those effects*; we come to know by our reasoning, that if what we believe concerning the *nature* of it be true, it must necessarily be, that by disposing it after a certain manner, a new effect will be produced, which we did not before think of, and in order to see if this reasoning holds good, we dispose the subject in such a manner as we believe it ought to be disposed in order to produce such an effect. Now it is very evident that this third sort of experiments is of peculiar use to philosophers, because it discovers to them the truth or falsity of the opinions which they have conceived.[30]

Rohault's preference for what we would now distinguish as scientific experiments does not imply that the first two kinds of experience ought 'to be wholly rejected as of no use to natural philosophers'. The characteristic of good experimental technique is that tests are designed on the basis of prior theory, in contrast to observing simply what naturally occurs; and, secondly, that we can arrange an experiment to test implications of our hypotheses which will help either to confirm or disconfirm their plausibility.

Rohault's discussion of experiments is less typical of the Cartesian tradition than the critical comments of Malebranche in Book I of the *Search After Truth*. Malebranche begins his assessment of 'those who perform experiments' by conceding: 'It is doubtless better to study nature than to study books; visible and sensible experiments certainly prove much more than the reasonings of men.'[31] However, there are some difficulties which are especially associated with drawing conclusions from experimental results. Among the mistakes made by experimental scientists, the Oratorian lists the following: that they often perform experiments without

---

[30] Unpaginated preface to the *Traité de physique*. The discussion of learning from the skill of artisans is corroborated by Clerselier's account, in the Preface to the *Œuvres posthumes*, of Rohault frequenting the work-places of artisans and of using their skills to design new experiments.

[31] *Search After Truth*, p. 159.

adequate theory, so that the results which are discovered by chance are difficult to interpret; that they do difficult or unusual experiments in preference to more common or simple ones; that they ignore many of the factors which affect the result of an experiment; they tend to draw too many conclusions from a single experiment; and, finally, they tend to divorce experimental work from the Cartesian idea of explanation in terms of fundamental particles and their properties.[32]

These comments reflect a fundamental bias in Descartes's own work against complex experimental work, and in favour of simple observations which leave less scope for a diversity of interpretations.[33] Secondly, they also underline the importance of engaging in philosophical discussions about the nature of matter and its properties, which is what Malebranche understands by theoretical physics. 'It is indubitable that we cannot clearly and distinctly know the particular things of physics without the more general, and without ascending even to the level of metaphysics.'[34] Thirdly, when understood as an expression of personal values and of the relative importance of experimental results *vis-à-vis* metaphysical foundations, Malebranche's comments on experiments betray his deep distrust of the ultimate significance of any work in natural science. The conflation of theology and philosophy in his work was not the result of confusion on his part; he genuinely believed that theological insights and metaphysical 'science' were much more important than anything that might be discovered by scientific research.

Men were not born to become astronomers or chemists, spending their whole life hanging onto a telescope or attached to a burner, and then drawing useless conclusions from their painstaking observations. . . . Astronomy, chemistry, and practically all the other sciences might be regarded as pastimes of an upright man; but men should not let themselves be deceived by their glamour, nor should they prefer them to the science of man.[35]

The fundamental insight of Cartesian philosophy about the significance of experiments cannot be refuted; experiments need to be interpreted, and any interpretation one makes depends on some theory or other. Therefore the theory is as important as the

---

[32] *Search After Truth*, pp. 159–60.
[34] *Search After Truth*, p. 160.
[33] See Clarke (1982), 37–40.
[35] Ibid., author's preface, p. xxvi.

experiments in evaluating the conclusions to be drawn from them. However, once that point is made and accepted generally, there is a noticeable difference between the attitude of Rohault and Régis on the one hand and, on the other, of Malebranche and other Cartesian philosophers.

Rohault's conclusion is that one should dedicate oneself in science to carefully constructed, tentatively interpreted, quantitative experiments. He argues just like other members of the school that doing experiments with no underlying theory is useless. For this reason, Rohault contends that the alchemists' attempts at trans-mutation of metals is a waste of time, in so far as 'we do not know particularly what the figure and bigness of the small component parts of metals and other ingredients which go to make such a transmutation, are'.[36] If we have failed to do the preparatory work in scientific theory, we cannot expect to compensate for it by doing random experiments and hoping that we will thereby hit upon a correct explanation of some phenomenon. Hence it is a 'great folly to attempt to find out so great a secret by reason or art; and there is scarce any thing more certain than that the person, who would try to hit upon it by chance, in making a great number of experiments, will be ruined first.'[37] In fact, Rohault's claim to a special place in the Cartesian tradition is based on the care with which he designed experiments to test accurately and confirm what, in most cases, were hypotheses directly borrowed from Descartes.[38]

Malebranche represented a quite distinct response to the unreliable character of empirical evidence. He had expounded at great length on the standard Cartesian thesis, that we may never make inferences directly from the quality of our experiences or observations to the objective properties of external objects. The extra criticism of experiments—especially the point about their complexity, and the multiplicity of factors which can affect results—resonates with Descartes's emphasis, in Rule III of his method, on the importance of simple and easily understood principles. In Descartes's case, Rule

---

[36] *Traité de physique*, ii. 154.   [37] Ibid.

[38] Cf. Clerselier, Preface to the *Œuvres posthumes*: 'Although he said nothing in this context [i.e. about magnetism] apart from what he had learned from Mr. Descartes, nevertheless since he made things observable by means of his experiments . . . one could say that he was their discoverer.' Clerselier goes on to explain that Rohault's special contribution was to explain a few general principles first, and then to deduce descriptions of particular phenomena from them and to demonstrate the whole theory experimentally.

III implied that one should prefer ordinary experience about which many observers could be certain, and in the interpretation of which there is less scope for differences of interpretation, rather than the complex experiments of scientists. In a similar way, Malebranche opted for the certainty and simplicity of less complex observations rather than results gleaned from experimental investigations.

It is in this sense that Mariotte's criticism should be understood. Cartesians displayed a strong penchant for theoretical speculation, at the expense of experimental testing. It was not that they believed that reason could successfully explain natural phenomena without recourse to observation or experiments. There are too many texts available to show that they thought this was absurd. It was rather that many Cartesians were content to develop speculative explanations, i.e. *raisons*, without a sufficiently close connection with experimental results. This tendency was fostered by their attitude towards explanation discussed above, and by their prodigal use of hypotheses. Thus, to say that Cartesians preferred reason over sense is to claim the following: that they dedicated their energies to the construction of speculative *raisons* or explanations, within the general framework of the Cartesian system, rather than to the accurate testing of hypotheses by experiment.

This kind of general comment on Cartesian methodology must be understood as a reflection of its dominant orientation, rather than as an exclusive description of its contribution to the natural philosophy of the seventeenth century. There were notable exceptions in those who specialized in experimental work, and some of their contributions are discussed below.

Confirmation and Disconfirmation

The most explicit recognition of the hypothetico-deductive structure of scientific explanations is found in those, such as Rohault and Régis, who devoted their talents to experimental work. For example, Rohault suggests an hypothesis to explain light in Part I, chapter 26, of the *Traité de physique*, which is not significantly different from the standard Cartesian theory. He then adds: 'I doubt not but that this opinion will be esteemed a conjecture only. But if it shall afterwards be made appear to have in it all the marks of truth, and that all the properties of light can be deduced from it: I hope that that which at first looks like conjecture will be then received for a very certain and manifest truth.'[39] It is not clear at this point what the first criterion means, namely that a hypothesis has 'in it all the marks of truth'; but at least the second test is straightforward. If one can deduce the observable properties of some phenomenon from a hypothetical account of its causes, then it is likely to be a 'true' hypothesis.

The same approach is just as evident in many other examples of Rohault's work. In explaining magnetism in Part III, chapter 8, of the *Traité de physique*, he writes:

I shall do here as if I were the first that had made any observation about the load-stone. And in the first place I shall reckon up some of its properties, which I shall content my self, with only assigning a *probable* reason for; and after that, I shall endeavour to establish the truth of my conjecture, by showing that all the consequences that can be drawn from it, agree with experience.[40]

When he had done the promised work of explaining a wide variety of properties by reference to a few hypotheses, he concluded: 'Thus we have seen how all the *properties* of the load-stone, hitherto mentioned, have been deduced from the *nature* ascribed to it.'[41]

Of course natural philosophers were often in the situation of having more than one hypothesis available to explain the same range of phenomena, and this dilemma was most frequently discussed in astronomy. Rohault addressed the issue as follows, when forced to choose between the theories of Ptolemy, Copernicus, and Brahe: 'Because we have here proposed three notions of the same thing, one of which only can be the true one, we must necessarily reject two of them as false, and retain the other as the only true one.'[42] The choice between them was to be decided on two criteria: 'if we find any one of them to contain any thing contrary to experience or reason, we ought not to make any difficulty in rejecting it, in order to our embracing that only, in which there are no such repugnancies.'[43] Conformity to 'reason' is similar to having 'all the marks of truth' in

[39] *Traité de physique*, i. 203.
[40] Ibid. ii. 163. Cf. ibid. 169: 'The few suppositions which I have made in order to explain the nature of iron and of the load-stone, are nothing compared with the great number of properties, which I am going to deduce from them, and which are exactly confirmed by experience.'
[41] Ibid. ii. 181.   [42] Ibid. i. 59.
[43] Ibid. Cf. also p. 123, for a hypothetico-deductive approach to explaining the nature of hard and soft bodies.

the previous paragraph. Both are taken up again below in the discussion of systems and simplicity. The other criterion, as usual, was the test of conforming to experience.

It is clear, then, that in scientific explanation one often begins with nothing more than a conjecture or guess about the causes of some phenomenon. Rohault assumed that such hypotheses or mere conjectures could be converted into reliable truths by empirical confirmation, or at least by agreement with our experience. He also assumed that plausible conjectures could be as easily disconfirmed by failing to agree with experience.

For example, Rohault claims that his explanation of the winds is 'confirmed by experience', as were his accounts of why heavy and light bodies fall at the same speed, his 'conjectures concerning *hard* and *liquid* bodies', and the 'suppositions which we have made about vision'.[44] In this last example he argues that if 'all those things, which upon these suppositions ought to come to pass, when we look through different sorts of perspective-glasses or upon looking-glasses, be agreeable to experience; . . . this will be a great proof of the truth of those suppositions.'[45] Rohault is not alone in making this type of claim. Gadroys also says that his theory of vortices is confirmed by experience;[46] and Régis almost adopts the phrase *expérience confirme* as a refrain that is interpolated at the conclusion of each explanatory hypothesis which he proposes.[47]

There was an equal respect for the finality with which experiential evidence could disconfirm hypotheses, on the assumption that our reasoning from hypothesis to expected results is above reproach. As Malebranche puts is, 'as we are always sure that our reasoning is true, if experience fails to agree with them, we see that our assumed premises are false'.[48] For example, experience disconfirms Aristotle's suggestion that 'the saltness of the sea depends upon its waters being heated by the rays of the sun, for we do not find by experience, that the heat of the sun or even that of flame, will convert fresh water into salt water.'[49] Likewise experiment shows that 'air cannot be changed into water',[50] and that comets are not in the space between the earth and the moon because the lack of

---

[44] *Traité de physique*, ii. 206; ii. 113; i. 150; i. 258.   [45] Ibid. i. 258.
[46] *Système du monde*, p. 205.
[47] Cf. *Système*, i. 449; ii. 440; iii. 192.
[48] *Search After Truth*, p. 429.
[49] *Traité de physique*, ii. 146.   [50] Ibid. ii. 134.

any measurable parallax indicates that they are much further from us than we usually imagine.[51]

Evidently, French Cartesians had joined in the formal tribute to experience which was characteristic of all the new scientists of the seventeenth century, both to confirm some hypotheses and to disconfirm others (usually those of opponents). This raises a new question about the implementation of empirical controls in science, and about what was meant by *expérience* in these cases. There are some features of Cartesian *expérience* which make it distinctive in scientific work. The first is that in many cases where *expérience confirme* a particular conjecture, nothing more is involved except that a hypothetical account does not clash with our observations of natural phenomena. This is a very weak, negative criterion; a more accurate description of the situation would be that some hypothesis is consistent with our observations.

Secondly, there is a significant number of cases where the *expérience* invoked to confirm some hypothesis is quite different from what was being initially explained. For example, when Gadroys says that one can confirm his vortex theory *par une expérience assez facile*, he was not thinking of checking the theory against astronomical observations.[52] What he had in mind was to make a bucket-shaped vessel, fill it with water, and put a paddle in the centre to turn the liquid; then drop in various bodies of different sizes and see how their relative size affects their motion in the swirling water. Likewise, when Rohault argues that his explanation of the winds is 'confirmed by experience', the evidence produced had nothing to do with winds. The hypothesis about winds being caused by vapours is corroborated by an 'experience in an aeolipile, which is a vessel made of copper or any other metal of the shape described in' the accompanying illustration.[53] The aeolipile in question is a spherical vessel with one small aperture; when it is partly filled with water and then heated so that the opening faces horizontally, the steam comes out with so much force that it seems like a wind!

These two features of theory confirmation are partly explained by the rather speculative character of the original explanations, and partly by the Cartesian understanding of explanation as model construction. There were few explanations available in which the

[51] Ibid. ii. 83.   [52] *Système du monde*, p. 207.
[53] *Traité de physique*, ii. 206.

relevant variables had been identified accurately and quantified; as a result such theories tended to be rather loose, qualitative models which were hardly specific enough to fail to agree with experience. This was also part of the implication of Mariotte's complaint about the abuse of *raison*; as the academician explained in his *Essai de logique*, 'the Cartesians explain many effects by what they call subtle matter', even though the meaning of the term is indeterminate.[54] The vagueness and qualitative character of hypotheses precluded the possibility of rigorous testing. Secondly, Cartesians assumed that if an explanation is fundamentally a mechanical model and if the properties of small parts of matter do not differ significantly from large, observable parts, then there can be no objection in principle to confirming theories about one phenomenon by doing an experiment on something quite different which serves as a mechanical model of the original.

The almost casual attitude to confirmation which characterizes most Cartesian explanation only helps to throw into stronger relief those few cases where something resembling experimental testing was undertaken with a view to theory confirmation. Even here, however, one tends to find a reliable experimental technique primarily in those cases where Descartes (or someone else) had already given a lead in quantitative techniques, such as the explanation of the rainbow which is found in the *Météors* of 1637.[55] The impression one gets is that most Cartesians could at least appreciate the significance of a well-constructed experiment, even if they shared Malebranche's reluctance about devoting their own energies to the experimental enterprise or if they were concerned about the difficulty of drawing inferences from experimental results. There is a good example of this ambivalent attitude in Rohault's work on vacua.

Rohault argued in Part I of the *Traité de physique* that the 'fear of a vacuum' is empirically a poor explanation of why mercury rises in an inverted closed glass tube, and why it rises to the extent that it does. He suggested, following Descartes and Pascal, that it was the weight of the air which forced the mercury to a given height. It follows that if one ascends a sufficiently high mountain where the weight of the air is considerably less, as Pascal had arranged at Puy-de-Dôme, then the height of the mercury should decrease pro-

---

[54] Mariotte, *Œuvres*, ii. 669.
[55] See e.g. Rohault, *Traité de physique*, ii. 224–37.

portionately. The same test could be made without mountain-climbing if a specially constructed glass tube is constructed in such a way that there is a Torricelli tube within the vacuum of a larger tube of similar design.[56] Rohault claims that he specially commissioned this type of tube from a local glass-blower, and he certainly gives the impression of someone who understood the importance of a technically well-designed test. The inner Torricelli tube functioned according to expectations. As long as it was deprived of air, the mercury failed to rise; as soon as air was allowed into the inner chamber, the mercury rose as usual.

There is another surprising example of Cartesian experimenting in the efforts of Jean-Baptiste Denis to perfect a method of blood transfusion which would be therapeutically effective for human illnesses.[57] Denis and his associate, the surgeon Paul Emerez, were working on the assumption of blood circulation, and they had little else to support their efforts except reports of earlier transfusions done on dogs by Richard Lower in 1665. Denis performed a series of tests which were reported in the *Journal des sçavans* and in translations of letters to Oldenburg in the *Philosophical Transactions of the Royal Society*.[58] There is a keen recognition of the experimental nature of the operations, as when Denis wonders about the cause of black urine in one of his patients after a blood transfusion: 'I shall here suspend my judgment, resolved not to declare my thoughts, till I have made many experiments more.'[59] Denis's pioneering work was brought to an abrupt conclusion by his involvement with a patient called Antoine Mauroy, who died under his care. Mauroy had been given two transfusions and they seemed to help his condition; but while being prepared for a third transfusion, he died suddenly before the procedure began. It was later discovered that

[56] Ibid. i. 73–5. Samuel Clarke added a footnote: 'You may find the description of an instrument not much unlike this in the experiments of the *Academy del Cimento*. But the Air Pump of the famous *Mr. Boyle* exceeds them all, and is so well known, that I need not describe it', p. 75.

[57] A. R. Hall and M. B. Hall, in discussing priority disputes about the first human blood transfusion in Hall and Hall (1980), 465, suggest that Denis was rash to experiment when so little was understood about blood. 'There can therefore be no doubt that in animal transfusion the English were right to claim priority. Equally there is no doubt that the French were the first rashly to venture on human transfusion, which the English did not attempt until late November 1667.'

[58] For a full discussion, see Brown (1948).

[59] *Philosophical Transactions of the Royal Society* (10 Feb. 1668), 623. On p. 620 he indicates that he may not be able to cure the patient in question since he had not done enough experiments to be able to explain the cause of his 'phrensy'.

his wife had also been applying her therapeutic skills by administering a 'powder' to her demented husband which probably contained arsenic. Despite that, she claimed that Denis was responsible for the patient's death, and the unfortunate physician had to appeal to the Lieutenant in Criminal Causes to clear his name. In a judgement given on 17 April 1668 Denis was exonerated of any responsibility for the death of Mauroy. At the same time, blood transfusions on human beings were restricted for the future and were not allowed 'upon any human body but by the approbation of the physicians of the Parisian Faculty'.[60] Since the esteemed members of the Paris Faculty were hardly disposed even to believe in blood circulation, there was little hope of their giving consent to further experiments and Denis's work on blood transfusions was thus brought to a premature conclusion.

In summary, Cartesians acknowledged the irreplaceable role of experience in both confirming and disconfirming scientific hypotheses. But the formal recognition of this fact was qualified by a variety of considerations which highlighted the extent to which observations and even scientific experiments may deceive the unwary. This distrust of uncritical experience was complemented by an almost unchallengeable faith in the fundamental categories and basic laws of Descartes's natural philosophy. In this sense the Cartesian tradition, with a few notable exceptions, favoured scientific theory (or *raison*) over the tedious demands of accurate scientific experimentation.

System and Simplicity

The text quoted above from Perrault's *Essais de physique* implied that we are forced to admit that our hypotheses can never be fully certified, and that future experimental evidence is just as likely to disconfirm our current theories as to confirm us in our present beliefs. Whatever way we approach the problem, we must accept the fact that we cannot know the hidden causes of most natural phenomena with certainty. This was an issue which Cartesian methodology had to address. Most of those who supported Descartes's method and who claimed to articulate its implications

---

[60] *Philosophical Transactions of the Royal Society* (15 June 1668), 714.

for the new sciences were aware of the type of claim being made by Perrault. In Cartesian terms, it would amount to this: since the causes of natural phenomena are unobservable, we must rely on hypotheses to describe them. But if we begin with hypothetical causes and then proceed by retroductive reasoning, we can never completely escape the uncertainty of our initial assumptions. In clear and distinct terms, a hypothetical science is necessarily uncertain.

There are indications that the logic of this argument had persuaded Rohault. He writes at a very early stage of the *Traité de physique*: 'Thus we must content our selves for the most part, to find out how things may be; without pretending to come to a certain knowledge and determination of what they really are; for there may possibly be different causes capable of producing the same effect, which we have no means of explaining.'[61] Had he stopped at that point, we would have at least one text in which a prominent Cartesian acknowledged the unavoidable uncertainty of scientific hypotheses. However, Rohault continued in the subsequent three paragraphs to elaborate the standard criteria by which Cartesian science claimed to be more than just plausible hypotheses:

Now as he who undertakes to decypher a letter, finds out an alphabet so much the more probable, as it answers to the words with the fewest suppositions; so we may affirm of that conjecture concerning the nature of any thing, that it is the more probable, by how much the more simple it is, by how much the fewer properties were had in view, and by how much the more properties, different from each other, can be explained by it. . . . And indeed there may be so many, and so very different properties in the same thing, that we shall find it very difficult to believe, that they can be explained two different ways. In which case, our conjecture is not only to be looked upon as highly probable, but we have reason to believe it to be *the very truth*.[62]

In this text, three new criteria are added to the empirical control already discussed. The simplicity of hypotheses, their number, and the variety of distinct phenomena which are explained by them, all contribute to the identification of one theory as 'the very truth' in preference to alternatives.

The relative importance of these new criteria is starkly underlined in a very revealing paragraph in which Rohault protects theories

---

[61] *Traité de physique*, i. 14.   [62] Ibid.

from apparently disconfirming empirical evidence. He explains that once we have good reasons to endorse a theory, we should not be too hasty in rejecting it just because there are relevant phenomena which it fails to explain:

Lastly, to prevent any scruples that may afterwards arise, we must consider, that, if our conjecture be otherwise well grounded, it does not lose its probability, because we cannot upon the spot explain by it a property, which appears from some new experiment, or which we did not before think of: For it is one thing to know certainly, that a conjecture is contrary to experience; and another thing, not to see how it agrees to it; for though we do not at all see the agreement, it does not from thence follow, that it is repugnant. And it may be, though we don't see it today, we see it to-morrow; or others who can see further than we, may at one time or other discover it.[63]

Rohault's point is well taken, although he has fudged it to some extent with the suspect distinction between a theory disagreeing with our observations, and our failing to see how it agrees with them. The implication is reasonably clear; even when our empirical evidence seems to be inconsistent with a theory, we may still endorse the theory as long as it is 'otherwise well grounded'.

As Rohault's disciple and successor in Paris, one might anticipate that Régis would adopt a similar attitude towards the relative significance of empirical evidence *vis-à-vis* other confirmatory criteria. He does, and he elaborates his claims by emphasizing the importance of systemic unity in scientific theories. In a lengthy Preface to *La Physique*, Régis explains that we must be content with probable hypotheses in physics, for reasons already discussed in Chapter 5 above. However, the probable hypotheses we accept should be constructed within 'one system which is based on the first truths of nature [i.e. the laws of nature]'. He continues by underlining the difference between his own understanding of physics and that of Perrault:

I say *of one system*, to make it understood that I do not follow the opinion of a modern philosopher* who believes that many probable systems, one more probable than another, are better than the one most probable system. He claims that there could never be one which is so probable that it resolves all the difficulties which we meet [i.e. which explains all our observations], and that those things which cannot be explained in one system may be

---

[63] *Traité de physique*, i. 14.

explained in another. [The starred modern philosopher is identified on the margin as Monsieur Perrault, in his introduction to the *Essais de physique*, vol. iii][64]

The concept of systemic unity was sometimes explained in terms of the metaphor of a machine, as already indicated. The other preferred way of explaining this concept was by reference to the relative *simplicity* of competing hypotheses. This is the approach adopted by Régis in the paragraph immediately following the one just quoted:

Since nature always acts in the most simple ways, we are persuaded that its actions could only be explained by one single system. By a SYSTEM we understand, not one particular hypothesis, but a cluster of many hypotheses which depend on each other, and which are so connected with the first truths that they are like their necessary consequences and dependents. This could not be the case for purely arbitrary hypotheses, such as most of those proposed by modern philosophers.[65]

There are at least three different suggestions being made here about what is meant by a system: (*a*) that the hypotheses which explain particular phenomena are closely related to the laws of nature, in some way which needs to be explained further; (*b*) that the simplicity of hypotheses is an important criterion in choosing between alternatives; and (*c*), that the systemic unity of Cartesian science explains why its hypotheses are true rather than arbitrary (like the saving-the-phenomena assumptions of astronomers); they are true because nature acts in the simplest way possible. In fact, all three claims are interrelated in Régis's understanding of scientific explanation, and they each require some further comments.

The apparent promise of a deductive relation between the laws of nature and the hypotheses which were used to explain particular phenomena is another example of the type of exaggeration for which we have already seen Régis apologize. The same recognition comes through in the text above where he says that particular hypotheses are '*comme* des suites & des dépendances nécessaires'.

---

[64] Régis, *Système*, i. 275. The same contrast between Régis's system and his understanding of Perrault is repeated in ii. 505. Perrault may be content with 'simple conjectures which are subject to later re-examination. Our plan is . . . to make a choice from those [hypotheses] which have been already proposed [by others], and to retain only those which seem to us to be most conformable to the laws of nature . . .'

[65] *Système*, i. 275–6.

There is a good example in his discussion of magnetism of what he means by hypotheses which are appropriately related to the fundamental laws of nature, in which the importance of the *comme* is explicit:

For example, when we wish to know the nature of the magnet, we assume that there are screw-shaped pores in it—an assumption which is not in any way opposed to the first truths which we have established; on the contrary, it seems to follow as a necessary consequence from them, because it is impossible to imagine that, among the almost infinite number of different bodies of which the world is composed, there are none which have pores of this shape. Now what we say of the magnet in particular will be applied with respect to all the other hypotheses which we make in order to explain the properties of physical bodies.[66]

Evidently, despite the fact that exactly the same phrase is used here as in the earlier text (*une suite & conséquence nécessaire*), Régis's explanation makes it very clear that hypotheses are not logically deduced from the laws of nature, but merely satisfy the much weaker condition of being consistent with them.

The criterion of simplicity is also found, on closer examination, to be as flexible as the ideal of 'demonstration'. Régis did not explain what he meant by simplicity, although it should probably be understood at least in part in terms of Occam's razor. As one might expect, many of the cases in which this criterion is applied cannot be compared by just counting the number of assumed entities and awarding the prize of plausibility to the theory with fewest types of assumed entity. For example, Régis argues that simplicity helps decide between alternative explanations of the muscular action involved in breathing;[67] of the beating of the heart;[68] of the causal significance of sperm in conception;[69] of the transmission of information along the nerves to the brain;[70] of apparent changes in the size of the moon;[71] of the identification of the physical organ of imagination;[72] and of many other phenomena. What is even more surprising is that in none of the cases mentioned does Régis claim that simplicity helps decide in favour of the true hypothesis. Rather, he always says that a number of hypotheses seem to be equally plausible, and that he will adopt what *seems to be* the simplest

---

[66] *Système*, i. 277.   [67] Ibid. ii. 551.   [68] Ibid. ii. 572.
[69] Ibid. iii. 21.   [70] Ibid. iii. 89.   [71] Ibid. iii. 243.
[72] Ibid. iii. 296–7. In some cases simplicity directly affects the intelligibility of an hypothesis and only indirectly determines its plausibility, as in ii. 572.

hypothesis as the one most likely to be correct. The explanation of the imagination is typical in this respect. After describing alternative theories, Régis can only conclude that 'we will provisionally adopt our own hypothesis as the one which seems to be more simple and natural, leaving the freedom to each person to use another one if he wishes, on condition that it conforms to the general laws of nature'.[73]

Thus apart from the more obvious implications of Occam's principle, the concept of simplicity operates as an intuitive criterion of choice between alternative hypotheses. There is one other indication of what it means, suggested by the combination 'more simple and natural': those hypotheses which are consistent with the laws of nature are simpler than those which require amendments to fundamental Cartesian assumptions. But as long as this type of consistency is so weakly understood, there is little more here than the intuitive and collective guesswork of a distinctive tradition.

If the two new criteria are as feeble as suggested, then how can Régis justifiably claim to have identified the true hypotheses in any given case? In his more careful reflections on Cartesian method, he only claims to have identified a very plausible theory:

If it sometimes happens (as it can) that different authors make different conjectures about the same subject which seem to be equally consistent with the laws of nature, we may use whichever one we wish without fear of being mistaken. We will be assured that the way which we use will be the true one or, if it is not, that it is at least equivalent to the one which nature has followed in producing the phenomenon which we wish to explain.[74]

So much for the power of systemic unity to identify the truth of hypotheses!

There is as little progress made in defining simplicity when other Cartesians use the same criterion. Rohault appeals to simplicity whenever competing hypotheses have satisfied the more basic criteria of conformity to the laws of nature and agreement with experience; 'we ought always to fix upon that, which is the most simple, and has the fewest suppositions; because the more phenomena are, which can be explained by it, without making any new suppositions, the more the proofs are that it is true.'[75] In this case

[73] Ibid. iii. 297. The phrase *plus simple & plus naturelle* is used elsewhere, for example in iii. 243.
[74] Ibid. ii. 505.
[75] *Traité de physique*, ii. 59.

'simplicity' is a function of the number of distinct suppositions which must be made to account for a given range of phenomena.

In contrast, La Forge distinguishes between the number of assumptions made, and the simplicity of any particular assumption. He strongly endorses Descartes's theory of human generation, in his commentary on Descartes's *L'Homme*, because the theory relies on principles which are 'so simple and so few in number'.[76] The principles in question are that 'there are bodies which are extended . . . which have different shapes, and which move in different ways'. These principles are *si simples et si intelligibles* that they could be challenged only if they proved to be insufficient for explaining all relevant phenomena. La Forge gives the following as a convincing example of what he has in mind; in order to explain how the seeds of man and woman can generate a body as complex as the human organism, Descartes 'only assumes that they [i.e. the seeds] are of such a nature that when they mix together, they function as a yeast for each other and make themselves ferment'.[77] To which he adds: 'Could there be anything more simple?' In this example, 'simplicity' looks like a synonym for 'easily intelligible'.

Gadroys made a similar use of 'simplicity' both to resolve his choice of astronomical hypotheses in favour of Copernicus, and also to decide the 'truth' of competing hypotheses. He acknowledges that as long as we are only trying to save the appearances, we can attribute motion either to the earth or to the heavens.[78] But Cartesian physics claims to identify a hypothesis which is true, and there are other considerations which help determine this question:

we are almost obliged to reject one as being false and to choose the other as true; since the truth is one and simple, we cannot have two different ideas of the same reality. And since the senses cannot decide the issue for us in this matter, the choice will depend on our reflections. We stop at the most simple and most appropriate hypothesis, not just to explain the appearances but also to discover their natural causes.[79]

The reflections in question are not mere speculative assessments of

[76] *L'Homme de René Descartes . . . avec les remarques de Louis de la Forge*, p. 407.
[77] Ibid.
[78] *Système du monde*, p. 62: 'when we only consider them as mere assumptions, they explain the phenomena equally well.' The same distinction between merely saving the phenomena and the philosopher's challenge to find the true causes of phenomena is repeated on pp. 126–7.
[79] Ibid. 63.

alternative theories. Chapter 5, 'Some Reflections on these Hypo-theses', begins: 'If one decides the truth of a hypothesis by its simplicity and its facility, then Ptolemy's hypothesis is very false. It assumes a multitude of things, it has the disadvantage of eccentrics and epicycles, and it encounters many problems in explaining the phenomena.'[80] One of the ways in which simplicity can be put to use has dynamical connotations: it would be simpler for God to make the earth revolve than to make all the heavens and the stars circulate about the earth.[81] Otherwise, simplicity is understood in terms of the number of assumptions which are made in any given theory. 'What ought to decide us completely in this choice, is that in assuming few things, I can show how all the parts which compose the world are disposed relative to each other in the way in which we have assumed them to be arranged.'[82]

This review of some Cartesian uses of the term 'simplicity' suggests that it sometimes functions as a synonym for 'easily intelligible'; however, whether or not a theory is intelligible depends on what prior assumptions have been made. For a Cartesian, any hypothesis which fits into the categorical and methodological restrictions already discussed in earlier chapters will be classified as readily intelligible. In this sense, therefore, simplicity is not an independent criterion; any hypothesis which is consistent with the laws of nature will be described as 'simple and natural'. The criterion of simplicity is also used as an indication of the relatively few, independent or extra assumptions which need to be made—apart from the laws of nature—in order to construct a hypothetical explanation of some phenomenon. In this context, simplicity is a feature of a comprehensive theory rather than of a particular hypothesis. The ideal theory is one which makes relatively few assumptions, and yet succeeds in explaining a wide variety of

---

[80] Ibid. 124.

[81] Ibid. 131. The same argument is used by Le Grand, *Entire Body of Philosophy*, p. 185: 'The same appearances happen to us, whether we suppose the earth only to be moved, or the heaven with the circumambient bodies; forasmuch as by this means the relation only of a body moving and at rest, is varied, the same effect being indifferently produc'd by either of them, as to us. Now this being supposed, it will not be easie for any one to believe, that nature, which always proceeds the most short and compendious way, should have chosen to perform that by the unconceivable motion of so many vast bodies, which she might, without all that ado, have brought about by the alone motion of the earth.'

[82] *Système du monde*, pp. 139–40.

disparate phenomena.[83] In other words, the simplicity of an explanation is equivalent to its systemic unity.

If one identifies a hypothesis which satisfies all these criteria—if it is not contrary to experience or to *raison* (i.e. to our already adopted theory), if it presupposes few new assumptions, and explains a variety of different phenomena—what conclusion may one draw? As already indicated, Perrault and Mariotte defended the view that even such an ideal hypothesis is only very probable; new evidence may be presented which will require a change in theory. Cartesians were not so diffident. If a hypothesis satisfies all these criteria, then it is the truth! La Forge expresses the conclusion as follows:

However the hypotheses are not only probable, but they are also *indubitable*, when they explain something very clearly and very easily, when our observations do not oppose them, when reason shows that the thing in question could not be caused otherwise since it is deduced from principles which are certain, and when these hypotheses serve not only to explain one effect, but many different effects. It is impossible that such hypotheses would never be discovered to be defective, unless they were true; that is what I claim to show in the hypothesis about the internal structure of the nerves and the muscles.[84]

In Clerselier's words, Rohault's success in constructing so many hypothetical explanations which satisfy the standard criteria for confirmation 'seem[s] to me to justify rather clearly the *truth* of the principles on which they depend'.[85]

In summary, Cartesians shared the common methodological convictions of their contemporaries about a variety of factors which are relevant to testing scientific theories. They agreed that it is absurd to argue against experience; we only know the way the world is from our sensory experience of the world. Any viable scientific theory must therefore satisfy two basic criteria: (*a*) it must not contradict our experience of the world; and (*b*) it must not be repugnant to *raison*. The second criterion meant that a hypothesis

[83] Cf. Clerselier, preface to the *Œuvres posthumes*; Rohault, *Traité de physique*, i. 280; and Perrault, *Essais de physique*, i. 174 ('De la circulation de la sève des plantes'), where he claims that the convergence of independent scientists on the same theory increases its probability.

[84] *L'Homme de René Descartes*, p. 218. Cf. Le Grand, *Entire Body of Philosophy*, p. 147, where he speaks of the 'truest' system, and p. 148, where Descartes's vortex theory is called 'the only true one'.

[85] Preface to *Œuvres posthumes*.

should not be inconsistent with the fundamental principles of Cartesian natural philosophy. In that sense many hypotheses were ruled out a priori, just as we implicitly appeal in modern times to our current scientific theory to characterize certain claims or hypotheses as 'unreasonable'.

In exploiting *raison* and experience to check the plausibility of hypotheses, Cartesians displayed a marked preference for theoretical model construction rather than careful experimental testing. This penchant for speculation was fostered by the qualitative character of many hypotheses, by the Cartesians' understanding of explanation, and by the various reasons which led them to distrust inferences which are uncritically based on experience.

Besides, the French Cartesians almost universally repeated Descartes's claim that the systematic unity of his science provided sufficiently strong reasons to believe that at least its basic principles are true. When a few, easily understood laws explain a wide variety of apparently disparate phenomena, then the simplicity of such a system of hypotheses corresponds to the simplicity of God's creative action. These claims were expressed in terms of the standard Peripatetic dichotomy between mere hypotheses and demonstrated truths. Cartesians repudiated the suggestion that their hypotheses were 'arbitrary', or that they merely saved appearances. Rather, their hypotheses were designed to provide realistic models of the way the natural world is; and, as such, they considered that they were much better confirmed than any alternatives available at the time. In fact the more basic assumptions of Cartesian science were considered to be so probable that they were described by their proponents as 'physically demonstrated', 'indubitable', or simply 'true'.

8

Cartesian Scholasticism

On ne peut contester cette gloire à notre siècle & à la France, que Descartes est le premier qui a ouvert le chemin d'une véritable Phisique.

B. Lamy[1]

FOR Bernard Lamy and many other seventeenth-century Cartesians in France, Descartes was distinguished in the history of French thought by his unique contribution to the development of a new concept of natural philosophy. The novelty of the Cartesian contribution was defined by contrast with the philosophy of the schools. The claim to novelty contained an implicit challenge: compare the ancients and those who continue to repeat their philosophy with what one finds in the Cartesian school, and it is obvious that Cartesian natural philosophy is very much superior to its scholastic alternative.[2] This evaluation might have been justified soon after the publication of Descartes's *Principles*, and it may even have been an accurate description of the relative merits of other French contributions to physics in the first part of the seventeenth century. However, the identification of Cartesianism as the leading school of physics in France was hardly an unbiased picture of the state of the new sciences during the reign of Louis XIV. The second half of the seventeenth century produced a variety of alternative concepts of science, of which the Cartesian concept was only one. The task for the historian of ideas therefore is to identify the Cartesian school as accurately as possible without relying on arbitrary lines of demarcation; to articulate its fundamental assumptions and the main lines of its development; and to explain its relations with its competitors in trying to establish, in France, a new

[1] Lamy, *Entretiens sur les sciences*, p. 256.
[2] Ibid. 233. 'I say once again with emphasis that it is in Descartes and his disciples that one should look for the principles of these sciences [e.g. catoptrics], of which antiquity had almost no knowledge at all.'

understanding of scientific knowledge which would replace the moribund philosophy of the schools.

The attempt to implement this Cartesian objective—of substituting a comprehensive and systematic philosophy for the established philosophy of the colleges and universities of France—was complicated by the theological and political context in which it was initiated. There can be little doubt that the period between 1660 and the end of the century was one of continuous controversy within the theology of the Roman Catholic Church in France. These controversies were concerned primarily with the challenge of Jansenism to the established theology and practices of the Church, with the fears of the Papacy about the growing Gallicanization of the French Church and with the ever present challenge of the reformed Christian Churches in competing for new members and in stimulating theological reflection. In this context of theological controversy, where the established theology of the schools was expressed in the language of scholastic philosophy, it was impossible to challenge any philosophical theory which had implications for Catholic theology without being drawn, wittingly or otherwise, into confrontation with ecclesiastical and royal authorities.

While the controversies with theologians were explicitly and directly concerned with issues such as the philosophical explanation of the appearances of bread and wine after the consecration of the liturgy, or with the extent to which human agents freely cause their own behaviour while being completely dependent on God's grace for salvation, there were other issues involved which help to explain why the theological difficulties proved to be so intractable. One of these was an epistemological problem about the role of faith and reason in deciding theological questions. While Christian theologians traditionally claimed certainty for many of their religious beliefs, philosophers in the seventeenth century defended the competence of human cognitive faculties to produce a type of knowledge which is as secure as beliefs based on religious faith. In this context, quite independently of advances in the new sciences, Cartesians had to make a stand on the capacity of the human mind to know anything with certainty, and on the kinds of things which could be known reliably. In particular, they had to adjudicate the competing claims of faith and reason as guides to the truth.

Faith, Sense, and Reason

As already indicated above, many Cartesians attempted to extricate themselves from theological controversies by claiming like Rohault that they were not competent to resolve theological disputes, and that they should be classified as mere physicists. Louis de la Ville addressed this strategy in his *Sentimens de M. Des Cartes* (1680). His scholastic response, echoed by many others who similarly opposed Cartesianism, was that we should question everything in philosophy in the light of reason but that we should believe religious truths without questioning.[3] The principle suggested by La Ville is relatively simple to understand, even if difficult to implement: it demands that one should first identify whatever the faith of the Church requires us to believe and one should unconditionally accept that as being indubitably true. It follows that, since one truth cannot contradict another and even the Cartesians agree with this, any philosophical claim which is inconsistent with the beliefs of the Church is false. In La Ville's words: 'we should reason on the principles of our philosophy in such a way that we always submit them to the faith, and never endorse any of them which is contrary to what the faith teaches us about our mysteries.'[4] The reason for adopting this method seemed obvious to La Ville: our reason can deceive us, whereas our faith is infallible.

Since we know that our reason is liable to deceive us and frequently to represent what is false with the same appearance of truth as the truth itself; and since we are assured, on the other hand, that the faith is infallible and that what it teaches cannot be false; what should the christian philosopher do when his reason seems to him to be contrary to the faith? . . . Should he not cling more to his faith and assume that his reason has only a false appearance of truth?[5]

La Ville's reaction was the standard one.[6] It failed to address the

---

[3] Louis le Valois (1639–1700), otherwise known as Louis de la Ville, *Sentimens de M. Des Cartes*, pp. 114–15.

[4] Ibid. 120–1.   [5] Ibid. 148.

[6] Cf. Rochon, *Lettre d'un philosophe* (1672), pp. 12–13; La Grange, *Les principes de la philosophie* (1675), p. 6: 'we maintain that his philosophy cannot be true because it is contrary to theology and to the faith'; Honoré Fabri, *Physica* (1669), i, unpaginated introduction; and G. Daniel's response to Pascal's *Provincial Letters*, *Entretiens de Cleandre et d'Eudoxe*, in *Recueil* (1724), i. 305–634.

Cartesians' question about the distinction between the mysteries of religion and the philosophical languages in which they might be more or less adequately expressed in different historical periods.

The refusal to make this distinction between the mysteries of faith and their theological expression is obvious in the Jesuit Père Rochon, and in the work of the Peripatetic Oratorian, Père La Grange. The author of the celebrated *Lettre d'un philosophe à un cartésien de ses amis* (1672) set out to identify those things which he found objectionable in Cartesianism. At the very top of his list of objections he claimed that there were many things 'in the philosophy of M. Descartes which seem to me to be inconsistent with religion'.[7] La Grange also identified the main objection to Cartesianism as its inconsistency with traditional theology. 'It is enough to know that his principles destroy a good part of theology, by completely undermining the common philosophy which Catholic theologians have in a sense consecrated by the use to which they have put it up to the present, both to explain many mysteries of the faith and to reply to the sophisms of heretics.'[8] In fact, La Grange makes it clear in his letter of dedication to the Dauphin that what is at stake is not religious faith, in the sense in which Cartesians would have agreed to recognize its authority, but rather the theological expression of that faith in the language which the schools had used for 'five hundred years'.

Once religious faith and its theological expression in scholastic categories were accepted as the primary criterion for testing the credibility of various claims, many representatives of the school philosophy chose the senses as our second most reliable source of knowledge. The theory that the validity of any cognitive faculty (such as sensation) is guaranteed as long as it operates within its proper domain was so prevalent in school philosophy that even the Cartesians accepted it, with obvious qualifications about the proper scope of sensory faculties.[9] Thus the zeal with which scholastic philosophers defended the claim that animals have genuine perceptions was only partly explained by their concerns about the fate of human souls if animal forms are made redundant; they were equally

---

[7] *Lettre d'un philosophe*, p. 4. In fact his theological objections continue up to p. 119.

[8] *Les principes de la philosophie*, p. 2.

[9] See ch. 27 of Régis's *Métaphysique*, 'That no faculty of the soul can be mistaken about its proper object', *Système*, i. 256–7.

motivated by the need to defend animal perception as an analogue of what takes place in human perception.

The scope for exercising human reason in pursuit of scientific knowledge was consequently wedged between the twin constraints of faith and infallible senses. The Cartesian response was to reorder the relative reliability of faith, sensation, and reason, and to establish human reason as the ultimate criterion for deciding all questions which fall within its competence, including some questions about the credibility or otherwise of religious claims which are proposed for acceptance by faith.

The priority of human reason is forcefully expressed by Clerselier, in his Preface to the posthumous works of Rohault: 'Since we are all men, that is to say, reasonable before we are Christians, whatever persuades *raison* enters more easily into the mind (*esprit*) than whatever we are taught by faith.'[10] One might suspect Clerselier of overstatement here in his strongly partisan defence of his deceased son-in-law. However, one finds equally clear statements of the same thesis even in Malebranche, who could hardly be described as unsympathetic to theology: 'Even the certainty of faith depends on the knowledge that reason gives of the existence of God; . . . It is obvious that the certitude of faith also depends on this premise: that there is a God who is not capable of deceiving us.'[11] This completely subverts what scholastic philosophers and theologians accepted as the orthodox relation between faith and reason. As far as the Cartesians were concerned religious faith depends on reason, at least in the sense that reason must be able to establish the existence of God independently (and to identify some of his properties, such as non-deceptiveness) before we can have any reason to believe what God is said to have revealed.

Likewise, in response to the claimed reliability of the senses, the heretical *Cartists* joined the ever-expanding number of those philosophers who recognized a distinction between primary and secondary qualities. Once this distinction is accepted, it follows that we can no longer assume that objective states of affairs are as we

---

[10] Unpaginated preface, *Œuvres posthumes*.

[11] *Search After Truth*, pp. 291, 482. The same view is repeated in the *Conversations chrétiennes*, in *Œuvres complètes*, iv. 14: we could not believe God's word and would have no reasonable basis for religious belief if we had not first proved that God exists.

subjectively perceive them to be. We cannot take our perceptions as reliable guides to the way the world is.

The effect of these two contentions was to identify human reason as the cognitive faculty on which we must depend to provide a basis for any knowledge which we claim to be reliable, and to establish criteria for testing the certainty of knowledge claims which rely on either faith or sensory perception. Malebranche expressed it clearly in the Preface to the *Search After Truth*: 'Be advised, then, once and for all, that only reason should stand in judgment on all human opinions not related to faith . . .'[12] As indicated above, even faith ultimately rests on metaphysical claims about the existence of a non-deceptive God who reveals the content of faith. I have argued in Chapter 2 above that this is the fundamental inspiration of the Cartesian theory of seeds of truth in the soul.

There are no indications that any of the French Cartesians believed that the human mind is created with any ideas or axioms actually present in the mind. On the contrary, the language of 'innate ideas' is used so liberally that even those ideas which are caused ('occasionally') by external stimuli are said to be innate. The innateness theory therefore responds to two quite different issues in explaining the source and the reliability of human knowledge. It implies that the existence of ideas in the human soul is irreducible to the physical stimuli which occasion their occurrence. And secondly, it underlines the autonomy of the human mind in being able to formulate basic principles or criteria on which it subsequently relies for distinguishing between valid and invalid reasoning. If the human mind could not forge some kind of foundations of knowledge from its own resources, then we would embark on an infinite regress in testing knowledge claims against criteria which, in turn, could be further challenged. The innateness theory is therefore an integral part of Descartes's foundationalism, and of his demand that any knowledge which claims to be scientific must be capable of being absolutely certain.

The autonomous resources of 'reason' are deployed in a variety of ways by the Cartesians in France. The most obvious manifestation of human reason's competence is found in the validation of knowledge against the challenge of scepticism. Once this is accomplished by reference to the mind's reflections on its own

---

[12] *Search After Truth*, p. xxviii.

powers, then the human knower is in a position to distinguish true knowledge from mere opinion, and he has at his disposal some of the most fundamental criteria in terms of which to implement this kind of distinction. Any knowledge which deserves the honorific title 'science' must be certain, and claims to certainty are tested by reference to criteria of clarity and distinctness. One cannot fail to notice, in this context, the persistent deference towards pure mathematics as a paradigm of genuine scientific knowledge and as a model of the kind of clarity and certainty which distinguishes scientific knowledge.

By focusing attention on this type of model, and by adopting the language of 'demonstration' in which the school philosophy expressed its corresponding fascination with the rigour of geometrical proof, Cartesians mislead their readers into assuming that physical science can be, or ought to be, constructed in accordance with the strict requirements of the mathematical model. There are signs of this hankering after an ideal science of natural phenomena in Malebranche's discussion of a completely scientific medicine, in which the detailed knowledge of the individual parts of a human body together with a similar knowledge of the small parts of any proposed medicine would deductively imply what we ought to anticipate when the sick patient takes the medicine. Unfortunately, we cannot in fact acquire this level of detailed knowledge; we must be content with hypothetical science.

Given that it was generally accepted that we have to settle for a second best, the relevant question is: what did the Cartesians think of this second best? Was it an interim solution which was only reluctantly accepted, and which should therefore be described in some other terms apart from the word 'science'; or were the limits one encounters in physical science so characteristic of the discipline that we ought to change our concept of science to fit the reality of human knowledge rather than decry our failure to realize a goal which is, at least in principle, within our reach?

Hypothesis and Demonstration

The recognition that the scientific method which is appropriate to the explanation of physical phenomena must be hypothetical is one of the enduring credits of the Cartesian tradition. Once Descartes crossed the threshold from describing the essential properties of matter to speculating about the size, shape, and speed of particular particles, it was clear that there was no conceivable way in which he might deduce these details from his metaphysical discussions. So he conceded quite openly that, at this stage of theory construction, one is entitled to assume whatever one wishes about the small parts of matter in motion, on condition that one does not assume anything which conflicts with the Cartesian theory of matter and, more importantly, that one's hypotheses may be used to explain all the relevant phenomena. The clarity of this recognition needs to be underlined, because it tends to be forgotten in the subsequent attempts to reconstruct scientific explanations in the logical form of demonstrations. The Cartesian insight, which was so ably articulated by Régis, was: the properties of small parts of matter cannot be observed, even with the help of microscopes; nor can they be deduced from a general theory of matter. At the same time, any satisfactory explanation of physical phenomena must begin with a description of precisely those particles of matter, the properties of which can be neither directly observed nor deduced from metaphysical axioms. There is no alternative, therefore, but to assume certain values for these properties initially, and to test the reliability of our assumptions subsequently. In other words, the explanation of natural phenomena is necessarily hypothetical. Lamy reflects this insight clearly in his comments on Descartes's method: 'It is Descartes who has shown the way; here it is his method which one ought to follow. I say his method, because most of his explanations should be regarded, not as the truth, but as *reasonable conjectures*.'[13]

If we are forced to hypothesize about the size, shape, and speed of small particles of matter, and if we can do no better than conjecture about the unobservable interactions of these theoretical entities, what should we think of the status of the resulting explanations? The traditional theory of science within which the Cartesians attempted to articulate their methodology only provided two options here: such conjectures were either *mere* hypotheses, similar to the mathematical models of astronomers, or they should be realistically understood in the way in which Aristotelian physical theory purported to describe and explain how the .world is. Cartesians rejected the first option; they were not interested in what

---

[13] *Entretiens sur les sciences*, p. 261. Emphasis added.

they generally called 'arbitrary' hypotheses. Theirs was an attempt to explain how the world is; Cartesian hypotheses should be realistically understood.

However, if scientific hypotheses purport to describe the way the world is, should we also assume that they are true, or probable, or perhaps that their truth value is indeterminable in principle? Many seventeenth-century philosophers were astute enough to realize that once one begins with an hypothesis, there is no conceivable way in which it can be conclusively confirmed by the truth of other propositions which may be deduced from it. Consequently, many scholastic philosophers who were sensitive to the fallacy of affirming the consequent would have preferred to describe the Cartesian enterprise as a system of *ad hoc* conjectures which remained *ad hoc* whatever anyone might subsequently say in their defence. However, to admit that their hypotheses were *ad hoc* in this sense was equivalent, from the Cartesian perspective, to joining the tradition of Ptolemaic astronomy. Whatever else they were, Cartesian hypotheses were not to be understood in this way as arbitrary.

In the context in which this challenge was faced, it seemed as if the only other option available was to describe physical science as true, and demonstrated to be true. With this in mind the French Cartesians appealed to all those criteria of good hypotheses which have become standard in more recent philosophy of science. They claimed that their hypotheses were simple, and were consistent with an already established metaphysical foundation; that they were able to explain many disparate phenomena by using few hypotheses; that their hypotheses agreed with the available empirical evidence; and that they helped anticipate effects which had not otherwise been observed. Cartesians went even further and claimed that, once certain assumptions were made, they were in a position to construct a comprehensive explanation of any physical phenomenon which would satisfy all the demands of a demonstrative ideal of science. In other words, they could put in place a metaphysical system from which they could 'deduce' many of the properties of matter. By adding some carefully selected assumptions, they could develop this account so that the final product looked like a long list of deductions, beginning with metaphysics and concluding with a true description of the physical phenomena to be explained.

Of course such a long series of 'deductions' is not an Aristotelian demonstration at all. So why not just admit that the explanations of physical science cannot be demonstrated in the scholastic sense of the term, that they are not absolutely certain, and that we have to settle for probable explanations in the sciences? This was a step which the seventeenth century was extremely reluctant to take.

The main reason for the reluctance about probability was the entrenched tradition, originating twenty centuries earlier in Plato, which equated scientific knowledge with knowledge which was absolutely certain. Descartes evidently endorsed this traditional account of science, so that his followers in France were constrained by the competing demands of two incompatible insights: that genuine knowledge must be absolutely certain, and that the explanation of physical phenomena cannot avoid relying on hypotheses.

The attempted reconciliation of these insights was to some extent facilitated by the relatively loose sense in which the term 'demonstration' was understood during this period. Cartesians supported the semantic development which allowed them to describe their own hypothetical explanations as demonstrations. One might suspect them of straining the language of the schools in this case, in order to accommodate their defective reasoning to an ideal which was unrealizable in principle. However, there were many other independent witnesses to the new usage, and the evidence suggests a widespread reinterpretation of the term 'demonstration' even among those who were not committed to Cartesian orthodoxy. Thus not only Samuel Sorbière, but Grotius, Pufendorf, and Locke have been seen to describe their contributions to political or legal theory as 'demonstrations'.

The most sympathetic reading of the semantic innovations of the French Cartesians and their contemporaries is to interpret their suggestions as an almost unconscious attempt to revise the language in which the methodology of physical science may be correctly described. The unpalatable implication of this move was the recognition that scientific explanations cannot be absolutely certain. The scope of the term 'demonstration' may be widened to include hypothetico-deductive reasoning; but if this is done, one could hardly maintain that such demonstrations deliver the indubitability which Descartes required in an ideal science.

It was on this point, rather than on the question of redefining the scope of 'demonstration', that the Cartesian school differed so markedly from its contemporaries. The Cartesians willingly endorsed the hypothetical method, but only on condition that it did not compromise the certainty of the resulting 'deductions'.

The ambiguity of their position is partly explained by an implicit distinction between an ideal science of nature on the one hand and, on the other, the kind of scientific knowledge which we are actually capable of acquiring. This distinction is found, for example, in Malebranche's discussion of an ideal medicine and in Régis's two versions of the impact rules. If we knew all the values of the relevant variables (perhaps through divine revelation), then we would be able to construct the kind of a priori demonstration of which Sorbière spoke. We would begin with an exact knowledge of the small parts of matter, as the hidden causes of physical phenomena, and we would move in a series of valid deductions to a description of whatever effects arise from the interactions of such particles. We are not in a position to do this, as human beings. Instead, we are constrained to argue hypothetically. However, the success of Cartesian hypotheses—in some cases, more carefully, of the more general and fundamental assumptions of Cartesianism—leads us to believe that we are so close to realizing an ideal, a priori science of nature that the difference between the ideal and the reality is lost sight of. In fact, the Cartesians assumed that once we have identified a system of successful hypotheses, we can reorder the presentation of our physics so that it has the logical structure of an a priori demonstration.

This reaction to the conflict between demonstration and uncertainty was to narrow the difference between an ideal physics and the kind of physics which is possible for human knowers. An alternative reaction, which was also adopted on occasion by the Cartesians, was to admit that any physics which we can hope to construct is so far removed from the ideal that we should just settle for plausible mechanical models which are not remotely like demonstrated truths. The ambiguity generated by adopting both solutions and by limiting the range of demonstrated truths to those which are most fundamental in physics, such as the laws of nature, camouflaged the issue to such an extent that Cartesian science in the seventeenth century failed to address adequately the challenge of Mariotte and Huygens to recognize the probabilistic character of physical science. This was a missed opportunity which continued to influence developments in the methodology of science for another two centuries.

Metaphysics and Physics: the Role of Experiments

Régis wrote at the beginning of the *Système de philosophie*, in his introductory letter to M. l'Abbé de Louvois, that the work which he was publishing depended in an essential way on experimental results. 'If the system which I present to you contained nothing but truths which could be known by common sense alone, and by the natural insight of a sharp mind, my work would be of no use to you . . . but since the discoveries which are made in philosophy depend on a long series of experiments by which savants correct their meditations from day to day',[14] then it may be instructive even for very intelligent patrons to read the books which are dedicated to them.

Régis's presentation of his work as significantly dependent on experiments raises a number of issues about the sense in which metaphysical foundations determined the main lines of Cartesian science. Do the laws of nature logically imply scientific explanations of natural phenomena? Or does metaphysics provide limits and criteria within which physical science must be constructed? In either case, to what extent can experimental work serve to challenge the metaphysical foundations of physical sciences? And depending on the answer to this last question, what is the ultimate source of warrant for a Cartesian metaphysics?

However one understands the ambiguous role of metaphysics in Cartesian systems, it seems to be relatively uncontentious that some kind of metaphysics must be established as a first step in scientific knowledge. There was nothing unusual in the context of seventeenth-century science that theoretical work in physics or physiology was inextricably joined with the discussion of questions which were peculiar to traditional metaphysics. Cartesians, just like their scientific contemporaries, did philosophy and physics together. The feature which characterized the Cartesian synthesis was the primary role given to metaphysics, and the way in which metaphysical foundations of science were justified. Both these comments require some expansion.

The first peculiarly Cartesian feature of metaphysics was the priority it enjoyed in natural philosophy. Descartes had criticized

---

[14] *Système*, Letter to M. l'Abbé de Louvois.

Galileo's contributions to mechanics because they were not sufficiently integrated into a complete system.[15] By that he meant, not that Galileo should have tried to explain everything, but that he ought to have provided the kind of general metaphysics which Descartes required as a prerequisite for doing physics. It also meant doing the metaphysics first. It would not satisfy the Cartesian requirements if one were to construct a comprehensive system of hypotheses and, at the same time, engage in philosophical reflections on the ontological implications of one's scientific theorizing. The priority of metaphysics meant that it was a distinctive discipline which was more certain than any other kind of human knowledge; that it did not rely on physics for its warrant but, conversely, that physics was based in some sense on metaphysics; and that one cannot begin to do physical science in the modern sense unless one has first articulated a metaphysical framework which is adequate to its ambitions.

I have argued above that Cartesian metaphysics should not be understood as if it logically implied a complete physics. Clearly, there was an effort to deduce the laws of nature from metaphysical axioms or principles, but these attempts were very limited in their influence on physics. Apart from its claimed role of defending the cognitive capacities of the human mind, the predominant impact of metaphysics on Cartesian physics was a negative one; it served to identify those concepts which were acceptable as explanatory concepts and it allegedly provided a clear criterion for recognizing those concepts which were unacceptable. Thus the priority of metaphysics, in the Cartesian tradition, includes the following: (*a*) the construction of a theory of knowledge. This provides a defence against scepticism, delineates the relative competence of different cognitive faculties, and establishes the possibility of a physics which is not subject to the kind of objections levelled against its Peripatetic counterpart. (*b*) the identification of a number of basic concepts by which we can claim to know physical reality, and the articulation of a small number of axioms or principles which express, in a non-trivial way, how these fundamental concepts are applicable to physical phenomena. The laws of nature and the identification of basic concepts go hand in hand. (*c*) a philosophical discussion of the

---

[15] Descartes to Mersenne, 11 Oct. 1638: 'without having considered the first causes of nature, he has merely sought the explanations of a few particular effects and he has thereby built without foundations.' *Œuvres*, ii. 380.

concept of explanation. This involved two related elements. One was a critique of the non-explanatory character of scholastic physics, and the proposal of an alternative concept of explanation which is defined in terms of mechanical models. The other, more directly negative, feature was the application of a criterion of 'clarity and distinctness' as a test for the acceptability of any concept in physical science.

If metaphysics is to exercise this guiding, critical role in the construction of physical science, then it is of the utmost importance to clarify the warrant of the metaphysics. How does metaphysics get started, what kind of evidence does it rely on, and what kind of certainty does it claim to provide about those concepts which are most relevant to physical science? The answers to these questions determine the second characteristic feature of Cartesian metaphysics mentioned above.

Chapters 3 and 4 above discuss the ontological squeamishness which was typical of the Cartesian tradition in science. This was characterized by a high level of intolerance of any so-called occult properties where 'occult' was defined, not in terms of whether or not properties were hidden from human perception, but by reference to peculiarly Cartesian criteria of what counts as a legitimate explanatory concept in natural philosophy. The obvious reluctance of Cartesians about a whole range of concepts which were proposed by their contemporaries is partly explicable as an over-reaction to the metaphysical prodigality of earlier theories. By analogy with the logical positivism of a later period, there was a strong element of methodological and ontological positivism involved in the inflexibility with which so much was excluded, uncompromisingly, from the domain of physical theory. Concepts were examined piecemeal, and if they did not satisfy the strict criteria which were applied, then their possible contributory role in a successful theory was judged to be irrelevant. Concepts had to pass the test of being meaningful (to Cartesians) before they could even be considered as part of any theory.

The criterion of meaningfulness was simply: every concept must satisfy the conditions required by Cartesian method and science. This involved satisfying the general condition which applies to any discipline, that a concept be 'clear and distinct'. Clarity and distinctness were often synonyms for a completely intuitive test of whether something seemed to be relatively obvious and unmuddled.

When not masquerading in this way for a purely psychological criterion, 'clear and distinct' was explained in terms of conditions which were directly implied by Cartesian method and metaphysics. What tests should one apply, then, to decide if a concept is clear and distinct? For example, should one accept the concepts of elasticity (*ressort*) or of force as concepts which have a legitimate place in physical science?

Two principal considerations came into play at this point. One was the assumption that the concepts which are appropriate for describing small, invisible parts of matter and their motions are the same as those which we apply correctly to macroscopic bodies; the only difference between large-scale physical bodies and theoretical entities is one of size. Secondly, we ought to decide on the acceptability of concepts for describing macroscopic bodies by reference to the methodology of mechanical models. In describing mechanical models, the only concepts we need are those of size, shape, speed, and so on; and we understand these latter concepts better by reflecting on our experience of physical bodies in motion rather than by consulting the esoteric definitions which have been proposed by philosophers.

In parallel with considerations about what is necessary for successful mechanical explanations, Cartesians also exploited their fundamental objection to all explanations which relied on forms or qualities. Thus the concept of force failed the test of acceptability in a second, complementary way; it was much too close to scholastic forms to merit inclusion in any mechanical ontology. As a substitute for such dubious, 'occult' powers, Cartesians recommended small parts of matter which were described exclusively in mechanical terms, the properties of which could only be known indirectly by hypothesis.

The simple parts of matter and their properties are known through so-called 'simple' ideas. The Cartesian interest in simple ideas may be understood as a modified version of the scholastic theory of cognitive faculties. Scholastics had argued that our cognitive faculties never deceive as long as they are used properly and applied to their proper objects. Père Pardies reflects this almost axiomatic belief as follows:

Here is something else which is even more surprising. Up to now our senses were capable of judging about sensible things; their judgment was absolute, and no one challenged their jurisdiction. When it was a question of colours

or sounds . . . no one believed that there could be any mistakes involved. . . .
But now we are being warned that we deceive ourselves in this matter; that
it is only by an illusion of our senses that we . . . imagine colours and
qualities where they do not actually exist . . . In short, that everything
which the common philosophy calls sensible qualities are not really
accidents of bodies, but that they are modes of our souls, that is to say, that
in fact they are thoughts which we have when we encounter objects which
are presented to our senses.[16]

Ironically, Cartesians argued in a similar way that 'no faculty of
knowing or willing can deceive us as long as we contain it within
its proper limits'.[17] The only source of disagreement between the
two schools involved the question where to draw the appropriate
limits for the competence of different faculties. Apart from these
differences, Cartesians accepted the scholastic theory in a new form;
since God is a non-deceiver, we can show that our cognitive
faculties are underwritten by God's veracity. Therefore if, for
example, we exercise our reason properly, whatever ideas we
identify as being clear and simple must correspond to the way
things are. Thus the realistic interpretation of scientific theories
hinges on a scholastic theory of the validity of faculties, together
with a peculiarly seventeenth-century theory of simple ideas.

The dominant role of metaphysics in the Cartesian system was
partly a result of this insistence that metaphysics must logically
precede physics, rather than accompany it as a partner of equal
standing; and that metaphysical clarity and certainty is realized by
concentrating on those simple ideas which were claimed to be clear
and distinct. The ideas which satisfied this test in the context of
physical science were limited to those which resulted from
analysing our everyday experience of macroscopic physical objects.

This also explains why this tradition of explanation was perceived
by contemporaries to be unduly dependent on 'reason' at the
expense of empirical evidence. Even the Jesuit critic, Père Daniel,
who could hardly be described as a spokesman for the new sciences,
objected to the lack of empirical input into Descartes's logic of
discovery. 'It was his custom, as we know, to try to confirm by
experience those truths which he had discovered by an exclusive use
of his mind.'[18] As already suggested above, Jacques Roger's
comment about physiology in the seventeenth century applies

---

[16] *Discours de la connoissance des bestes*, pp. 10, 12–13.
[17] Régis, *Système*, i. 258. [18] *Voyage*, Fr. edn., p. 9.

equally to the Cartesian tradition of physical explanation. No Cartesian ever suggested—indeed, no representative of any scientific school in the seventeenth century ever claimed—that one could do physical science without recognizing a central role for empirical evidence. The relevant question for Cartesians was: what experiences does one consult, and at what stage of the enterprise should they be taken into account? The answers to both questions were only implicitly given, but they were reasonably clear and consistent. One consults one's reflections on ordinary experience to provide the concepts from which metaphysics and the laws of physics are formulated. As soon as one's metaphysics is in place, one may then consult a more systematic type of experience, namely scientific experiments, in order to construct those detailed hypotheses which are required in applying our general laws of nature to complex physical phenomena.

The priority of metaphysics over physics and the preference for reflection on ordinary experience as a basis for metaphysical speculation was characteristic of the scholastic philosophy which the Cartesians so much despised.

Cartesian Scholasticism

In a letter to Malebranche in 1679, Leibniz criticized the spirit of scholastic loyalty with which Cartesians defended their favourite theories against the many new insights which had been made public since Descartes's death. The unflinching loyalty of the Cartesian school displayed some of the features which characterize a sect:

That is why the three illustrious academies of our time, the Royal Society of England, which was founded first, and also the Royal Academy of Science in Paris and the Accademia del Cimento in Florence have strongly protested that they did not wish to be either Aristotelian [or Cartesian], or Epicurean, or followers of any other sect. I have also discovered by experience that those who are completely Cartesian have little capacity for [scientific] discovery. All they do is to act as interpreters or commentators on their master just as the philosophers of the schools did with Aristotle; so that among all the exciting new discoveries which have been made since Descartes, there is none that I am aware of which comes from a Cartesian. I know these gentlemen fairly well and I defy them to name one of their number [who made an important discovery].[19]

[19] Robinet (1955), 113.

Leibniz had already reproached Descartes for spending too much time 'in reasoning about the invisible parts of our bodies before having adequately researched those which are visible'.[20] This criticism, taken in conjunction with the claimed lack of originality, implied that Cartesians were primarily concerned with repeating the metaphysical insights of Descartes's system rather than devising the kind of mechanical explanations to which the official methodology of the Cartesian school committed them. Unlike Mariotte or Huygens, Leibniz was much more of a metaphysician than an experimental natural philosopher; therefore, if he voiced objections similar to those of Mariotte or Huygens, there must be a serious question about the dedication of Cartesians to reforming the philosophy of the schools and to substituting mechanical explanations for scholastic pseudo-explanations.

To what extent, therefore, did Cartesianism constitute a type of reformed, scholastic sect which deserved the consistent criticism of Leibniz?

There is no doubt that many contemporaries perceived the followers of Descartes as a sect. In the course of examining Malebranche's theory of ideas, Simon Foucher wrote about sects which demand fidelity to a master rather than respect for rational debate. Père Daniel likewise identified Cartesianism as similar to 'all the other sects, where there is always some important point of doctrine with very wide implications, which is the true mark of members of a sect'.[21] The use of the term sect does not tell us much about the sociology of Cartesianism in the seventeenth century, because there were many philosophical 'sects' in this loose sense, including the most notorious one which was equally sensitive to the charge of being a sect, namely the Peripatetics. The relevant point for assessing the contribution of Descartes's followers to the development of science is this: to what extent did they simply repeat the master's system of thought with minor emendations to accommodate new empirical results, or to what extent did they see their role as radically revising Descartes's ideas whenever it seemed necessary to do so?

---

[20] Ibid. 119. Pascal had also classified Descartes as a scholastic for proposing an invisible, subtle matter; see Mouy (1934), 42–3.

[21] Foucher, *Critique*, p. 6; Daniel, *Voyage* (1702 edn.), p. 429. See also Rochon, *Lettre d'un philosophe*, p. 214, where he thinks there is something ridiculous about those who regard Descartes as infallible.

As already indicated above, there is a problem of definition in deciding who should be classified as a Cartesian. One might define the Cartesians as those who followed the letter of Descartes's system of ideas, and then it would be trivially true that none of them made any significant contribution to the new sciences. I have defined the Cartesians as those who considered themselves to be followers of Descartes; it is therefore an open question whether they can respond to Leibniz's challenge and claim responsibility for major contributions to scientific development. Unfortunately, the historical record shows that, in general, the French followers of Descartes in the period 1660–1700 deserved Leibniz's assessment of their creativity.

Some of the reasons for the relative stagnation of Cartesian natural philosophy have already been discussed. Cartesians understood their role as one of developing a viable alternative to the philosophy of the schools; as a result, the underlying structure of their discourse was one of contrasting the benefits of Cartesianism with the defects of Peripatetic natural philosophy. This contrast, together with the explicit objective of providing a substitute for the manuals used in schools, partly explains the scholastic format in which the new philosophy was presented. However, there is a second reason for the critique made by Leibniz, namely, that Cartesians were not as emancipated from some of the basic categories of scholastic natural philosophy as they might have assumed themselves to have been.

The ambivalence involved in the break with scholastic categories can be seen even in Descartes. There are clear indications in the *Regulae* and in various items of correspondence that Descartes wished to be rid of all those questions of traditional metaphysics about the 'nature' or 'essence' of physical things.[22] Descartes's physics depended on the possibility of substituting mechanical models for essences and natures. At the same time, Descartes continued to talk the language of forms and qualities, and he is completely at home in the language of the schools in his dualistic description of man as a combination of matter and form. The influence of this scholastic metaphysics permeated the foundations of Cartesian physics, to such an extent that one finds Descartes renege on his earlier insight and begin to discuss the 'essence' of

---

[22] See J.-L. Marion's discussion of this in Marion (1975).

matter in the *Principles of Philosophy*. Most of those who took issue with Descartes in the period under discussion based their criticisms on the *Principles*, and most of his vehement critics argued from a scholastic perspective. In other words, Cartesians were sufficiently immersed in traditional scholastic metaphysics that they provided the common ground on which their opponents could engage them in philosophical controversy. The same metaphysical foundation which triggered the hostility of orthodox theologians also limited the extent to which Cartesians could envisage a completely new type of physical science.

Père Pardies saw this problem clearly when he challenged Descartes's position on the soul of animals. If we can argue that the behaviour of human beings requires a substantial form in order to explain it, why should we not follow the same logic in the case of animals?[23] More generally, if the explanations of scholastic metaphysics have any role at all in physical science, how can one non-arbitrarily limit their function to a discussion of God and the human soul, as Descartes tried to do? The failure to emancipate scientific explanations from this tradition of speculative common sense, and the simultaneous failure to effect a coherent synthesis between the two, left unresolved the status of a philosophy of nature.

It is ironic, therefore, to notice the extent to which Cartesians were successful in persuading scholastic philosophers, including many Jesuit professors in France, to incorporate the new mechanical philosophy of Descartes into a curriculum which was still dominated by Thomistic metaphysics. Père Claude Buffier (1661–1737) was professor at the Jesuit college of Louis-le-Grand in Paris from 1698 to 1737. During his tenure at Louis-le-Grand, he published the *Éléments de métaphysique* (1704), *Examen des préjugés vulgaires* (1704), and his most well-known work, the *Traité des premières verités*.[24] Buffier's discussion of *sens commun*, of first principles, and even of the mind–body problem are obviously influenced by Descartes.[25] While he is critical of specific Cartesian theses and

---

[23] *Discours de la connoissance des bestes*, pp. 191–3.

[24] The 3 books are edited in a single volume by F. Bouillier. An Eng. edn. of the *Éléments* was published as *Conversations on the Elements of Metaphysics* (1838). For studies of Buffier, see O'Keefe (1974) and Wilkins (1969).

[25] Cf. *Remarques sur divers traités de métaphysique* (Bouillier edn.), pp. 219–34; see also the *Traité des premières vérités* (Bouiller edn.), esp. pp. 6–7, 165–9. Buffier defines *sens commun* as follows (p. 15): 'la disposition que la nature a mise dans tous les hommes ou manifestement dans la plupart d'entre eux, pour leur faire porter,

reproaches Descartes for confusing abstractions such as 'extension' with the realities of which they are predicated, he is generally sympathetic to the Cartesian critique of ancient philosophy, and he unequivocally installs common sense as the foundation of metaphysics and natural philosophy: 'Let us not imagine that, in order to become a Philosopher, it is necessary to renounce Common Sense;—rather let us make Common Sense the foundation of all our Philosophy, admitting such principles as it would be downright absurdity not to admit.'[26] For Buffier at least, there was no significant difference between scholastic philosophy and Descartes concerning the source of metaphysical insight; it was based on 'common sense' or on reflection on ordinary experience.

The *rapprochement* between the two apparently irreconcilable schools is even more evident among those Jesuit professors who tried to show, in the early eighteenth century, that Cartesianism was a natural development of principles which were implicit in traditional philosophy. The scholastic integration of Descartes's contribution to physics was evident even during the seventeenth century, for example in the work of Père René Rapin (1621–87); his *Reflexions sur la philosophie ancienne et moderne* (1684) was sympathetic to Descartes's innovations, even though it was critical of the enthusiasm of most of his followers.[27] Père Noel Regnault (1683–1762), for a long time professor of mathematics and physics at Louis-le-Grand, published a three-volume work on *L'Origine ancienne de la physique nouvelle* (1734), in which Descartes is said to perfect what is already found less explicitly in the ancients.[28] Not only is Descartes credited with fulfilling the implicit promise of ancient philosophy, but Jesuit professors also hastened to explain how Descartes and Newton each made valuable contributions which could be integrated into a revised scholastic metaphysics. For example, Père Louis Castel published his reconciliation of Newton and Descartes in 1743, entitled *Le vrai systême de physique generale de M. Isaac Newton, exposé et analysé en parallele avec celui de*

quand ils ont atteint l'usage de la raison, un jugement commun et uniforme sur les objets différents du sentiment intime de leur propre perception; jugement qui n'est point la conséquence d'aucune principe antérieur.'

[26] *Éléments de métaphysique*, Eng. edn., p. 110; Bouillier edn., p. 308.

[27] Cf. Sortais (1929), 5. Sortais quotes Rapin as follows: 'On ne peut pas toutefois approuver toujours la fierté de la plûpart de ses disciples, qui traittent tous les autres Philosophes d'ignorans.'

[28] Cf. Sortais (1929), 7–8.

Descartes; à la porté du commun des physiciens.[29] Despite the date of final publication, the author explains that he had completed the work twenty-one years earlier, i.e. about 1722.[30] Castel adopts a Cartesian position *vis-à-vis* the 'occult properties' used by Newton: 'Attraction, gravitation, action at a distance, which compose the basis of the Newtonian system, are only jargon; Newton protests in many places that he only uses those terms for the convenience of his exposition.'[31] By contrast, Descartes avoided these problematic terms and 'wished to explain everything physically, by means of physical causes; that is, according to him, by means of mechanical and corporeal causes, which depend on the matter and form of bodies.'[32] Evidently, the kinds of causes which Descartes preferred were compatible with a scholastic metaphysics of matter and form.

The adoption of Cartesian categories and their establishment as a natural development of traditional metaphysics in the philosophy of common sense in Buffier, and the integration of Cartesian natural philosophy into the physics of the schools by Regnault, Castel, and Paulian—following an earlier attempt at synthesis by Pardies—is a tribute to the Cartesians' success in reforming the physics curriculum in French colleges. The smoothness of the transition from scholastic natural philosophy to Cartesian physics underlines the essential continuity between the two traditions.[33] This continuity is most evident, as already indicated, in their common allegiance to a

[29] Castel was not the only Jesuit professor in this period who attempted to integrate Newton and Descartes into scholastic metaphysics. Père Aimé-Henri Paulian (1722–1801), who taught physics at Aix and Avignon, published his *Traité de paix entre Descartes et Newton, précédé des vies littéraires de ces deux chefs de la physique moderne* in 1763.

[30] *Le Vrai Systême,* p. 1. His religious superior, Jean Lavaud, gave permission to publish on 29 Apr. 1742 and Castel claims to have had the manuscript ready for publication 20 years before that.

[31] Ibid. 7.   [32] Ibid. 42.

[33] This coincides with the conclusion in Brockliss (1987) that philosophy teaching in France changed very little even during the 18th cent., whereas the curriculum in physics and medicine was able to adapt to new experimental discoveries. 'The most striking feature of courses in the moral and metaphysical sciences in seventeenth- and eighteenth-century France was the way in which both their structure and content remained virtually unchanged. . . . In the teaching of physics and medicine, professors managed to do what was singularly not being done in the teaching of the ethical and metaphysical sciences. . . . At least from the mid-seventeenth century professors of physics and medicine were busy telling their students what was the latest news from the world of the virtuosi and the scientific academies, regardless of the fact that this meant initially they were doomed to tie themselves up in explanatory knots, trying to save the fundamental principles of the physical doctrine they espoused', pp. 332, 441–2.

(revised) version of scholastic metaphysics which is logically and pedagogically prior to physics, and in their recognition of *sens commun* rather than scientific experiments as the decisive source of evidence in constructing a foundational metaphysics. In this sense, Cartesians in the reign of Louis XIV represent an alternative form of scholasticism.

However, their distinctive contribution to philosophy of science in the seventeenth and eighteenth centuries remains. The acclaim from Bernard Lamy which was quoted at the beginning of this chapter was echoed by the Jesuit, Père Castel, in the first decades of the eighteenth century: 'The hypotheses which they [i.e. Cartesians] adopt are intelligible and they adopt them . . . as hypotheses. They weigh and measure all their degrees of probability and improbability; they make all the applications of the hypotheses and construct from them the whole edifice [of science].'[34] In persuading a whole generation of natural philosophers in France to look for mechanical causes of physical phenomena in place of the pseudo-explanations of the schools, Cartesians acknowledged that they could not avoid constructing hypotheses about the imperceptible causes of natural phenomena. Therefore, despite the fact that their theory construction continued to be limited by the categories of a metaphysics based on ordinary experience, Cartesians deserved to share the credit with Descartes for, in Lamy's words, 'opening the path for a genuine physics', that is, a physics of more or less probable hypotheses about the imperceptible physical causes of natural phenomena.

[34] *Le Vrai Systême*, pp. 12–13.

BIBLIOGRAPHY

Primary Sources

ARNAULD, ANTOINE, *Œuvres de Messire Antoine Arnauld Docteur de la maison et société de Sorbonne*, 43 vols. (Paris: S. D'Arnay, 1775–83).

—— and NICOLE, PIERRE, *La Logique ou l'art de penser* (1662), critical edn. by P. Clair and F. Girbal, 2nd edn. (Paris: Vrin, 1981).

—— —— *The Art of Thinking: Port-Royal Logic*, trans. with an introd. by J. Dickoff and P. James (Indianapolis: Bobbs-Merrill, 1964).

BERKELEY, GEORGE, *The Works of George Berkely, Bishop of Cloyne*, ed. A. A. Luce and T. E. Jessop (Edinburgh and London: Thomas Nelson, 1951).

BUFFIER, CLAUDE, *Conversations on the Elements of Metaphysics*, trans. from the French with notes by the Revd Richard Pennell (Bath and London: Simms and Collins, 1838).

—— *Œuvres philosophiques du Père Buffier de la compagnie de Jésus*, with notes and introd. by F. Bouillier (Paris: Charpentier, 1843).

CASTEL, LOUIS, *Le Vrai Systême de physique generale de M. Isaac Newton, exposé et analysé en parallele avec celui de Descartes; à la porté du commun des physiciens* (Paris: Claude-François Simon fils, 1743).

CORDEMOY, GERAULD DE, *Œuvres philosophiques avec une étude bio-bibliographique*, ed. P. Clair and F. Girbal (Paris: Presses universitaires de France, 1968).

—— *Discours physique de la parole*, facsimile repr. of 1677 edn., with commentary by H. E. Brekle (Stuttgart: Verlag, 1970).

—— *A Philosophical Discourse Concerning Speech* (1688), and *A Discourse written to a Learned Frier* (1670), ed. Karl Uitti (New York: AMS Press, 1974).

[DANIEL, GABRIEL], *Voiage du monde de Descartes. Suivant la copie* (Paris: Veuve de Simon Benard, 1691). [Author's name omitted]

—— *A Voyage to the World of Cartesius: Written Originally in French, and now Translated into English*, trans. with introd. by T. Taylor (London: Thomas Bennet, 1692).

—— *Nouvelles difficultez proposées par un peripateticien a l'autheur de voyage du monde de Descartes. Touchant la connoissance des bestes. Avec la réfutation de deux défenses du systême général du monde de Descartes* (Paris: Veuve de Simon Benard, 1693). [Author's name omitted]

[DANIEL, GABRIEL], *Suite du voyage du monde de Descartes, ou nouvelles difficultez proposées a l'autheur du voyage du monde de Descartes, avec réfutation de deux défenses du systéme générale du monde de Descartes* (Amsterdam: Pierre Mortier Libraire, 1696). [Author's name omitted]

—— *Voyage du monde de Descartes. Nouvelle ed., revûë & augmentée d'une cinquiéme partie, ajoûtée aux quatre precedentes* (Paris: Nicolas Pepie, 1702).

—— *Voiage du monde de Descartes* (Paris: Chez les Freres Barbou, 1720). [Incorrect title; this is in fact the *Suite du voyage*]

—— *Recueil de divers ouvrages, philosophiques, théologiques, historiques, apologétiques et de critique*, 3 vols. (Paris: D. Mariette and J. B. Coignard fils, 1724).

DENIS, JEAN-BAPTISTE, 'An Extract of a Letter of M. Denis, Prof. of Philosophy and Mathematicks to M. *** touching the Transfusion of Blood, of April 2, 1667', *Philosophical Transactions of the Royal Society* (6 May 1667), 453.

—— 'A Letter Concerning a new way of curing secondary diseases by Transfusion of Blood, Written to Monsieur de Montmor, Counsellor to the French King, and Master of Requests', *Philosophical Transactions of the Royal Society* (22 July 1667), 489–504.

— 'An Extract of a Letter, written by J. Denis, Doctor of Physick, and Professor of Philosophy and the Mathematicks at Paris, touching a late Cure of an Inveterate Phrensy by the Transfusion of Blood', *Philosophical Transactions of the Royal Society* (10 February 1668), 617–23.

—— 'An Extract of a Printed Letter, addressed to the Publisher, by M. Jean Denis, D. of Physik, and Prof. of the Mathematicks at Paris, touching the differences risen about the Transfusion of Bloud', *Philosophical Transactions of the Royal Society* (15 June 1668), 710–15.

DENZINGER, HENRICUS, *Enchiridion Symbolorum, Definitionum et Declarationum de rebus fidei et morum*, 31st edn., ed. Karl Rahner (Rome: Herder, 1960).

DESCARTES, RENÉ, *Œuvres*, ed. C. Adam and P. Tannery, new edn. (Paris: Vrin, 1974).

—— *The World*, trans. and introd. by M. S. Mahoney (New York: Abaris Books, 1979).

—— *Principles of Philosophy*, trans. with notes by F. R. Miller and R. P. Miller (Dordrecht: Reidel, 1983).

—— *The Philosophical Writings of Descartes*, trans. by J. Cottingham, R. Stoothoff, and D. Murdoch, 2 vols. (Cambridge: Cambridge University Press, 1985).

DESGABETS, ROBERT, *Réponse d'un cartésien à la lettre d'un philosophe de ses amis*, in Paul Lemaire, *Le Cartésianisme chez les bénédictins* (Paris: Felix Alcan, 1902).

Du Roure, Jacques, *Philosophie divisée en toutes ses parties, établie sur des principes évidents & expliquée en tables et par discours, ou particuliers, ou tirez des anciens, des nouveaux auteurs; & principalement des Peripateticiens, et de Descartes* (Paris: Thomas Jolly, 1654).

Fabri, Honoré, *Philosophiae Tomus primus: qui complectitur scientiarum methodum sex Libris explicatum: Logicam analyticam, duodecim libris demonstratum, & aliquot controversias logicas, breviter disputatas. Auctore Petro Mosner Doctore medico. Cuncta exerpta ex praelectionibus R. P. Hon. Fabry, Soc. Jes.* (Lyons: Joannis Champion, 1646).

—— *Tractatus Physicus de motu locali in quo effectus omnes, qui ad impetum, motum naturalem, violentum & mixtum pertinent, explicantur, & ex principiis Physicis demonstrantur. Auctore Petro Mousnerio, Doctore medico cuncta excerpta ex praelectionibus R. P. Honorati Fabry, Societatis Jesu* (Lyons: Joannes Champion, 1666).

—— *Physica, id est, scientia rerum corporearum, in decem tractatus distributa. Auctore Hororato Fabri Soc. Jesu* (Lyons: L. Anisson, 1669).

Fontenelle, Bernard le Bovier de, *Entretiens sur la pluralité des mondes* (Paris: Chez la veuve C. Biageart, 1686).

—— *A Discourse of the Plurality of Worlds*, trans. by Sir W. D. Knight (Dublin: Crook and Helsham, 1687).

—— *Histoire de l'académie royale des sciences. Tome 1: depuis son établissement en 1666 jusqu'à 1686* (Paris: Martin, Coignard, and Guerin, 1733).

—— *Conversations on the Plurality of Worlds*, trans. from the last edn. of the French (Dublin: Wilson, 1761).

—— *Œuvres de Fontenelle*, 5 vols. (Paris: Salmon, Peytieux, 1825).

Foucher, Simon, *Critique de la recherche de la vérité* (Paris: Martin Coustelier, 1675), repr. with an introd. by R. A. Watson (New York: Johnson Reprint Corporation, 1969).

Gadroys, Claude, *Discours sur les influences des astres, selon les principes de M. Descartes* (Paris: Jean-Baptiste Coignaret, 1671). [Author's name omitted; identified as 'C.G.' in the *privilège du roi*]

—— *Le Système du monde, selon les trois hypotheses, où conformement aux loix de la mechanique l'on exlique dans la supposition du mouvement de la terre, les apparences des astres, la fabrique du monde, la formation des planetes, la lumière, la pesanteur, &c. Et cela par de nouvelles demonstrations* (Paris: G. Desprez, 1675). [Author's name omitted]

Grotius, Hugo, *De Jure Belli ac Pacis*, Carnegie Institution of Washington edn., 2 vols., i: Text of 1646; ii: trans. by F. W. Kelsey (Oxford: Clarendon Press, 1925).

—— *De Jure Praedae Commentarius*, i: trans. of the text of 1604 by G. L. Williams (Oxford: Clarendon Press, 1950).

HUET, PETER DANIEL, *Censura Philosophiae Cartesianae* (Helmstedt: G. W. Hammius, 1690).

HUYGENS, CHRISTIAAN, *Œuvres complètes, publiées par la société hollondaise des sciences*, 22 vols. (The Hague, 1888–1950).

—— *Traité de la lumière. Où sont expliquées les causes de ce qui luy arrive dans la reflexion, & dans la refraction. Avec un discours de la cause de la pesanteur* (Leiden: P. Vander, 1690).

—— *Treatise on Light* (1690), Eng. trans. by S. P. Thompson, repr. (New York: Dover, 1952).

LA FORGE, LOUIS DE, *L'Homme de René Descartes et un traité de la formation du foetus du mesme autheur, avec les remarques de Louis de la Forge, docteur en medecine, demeurant à la Fleche, sur le traitté de l'homme de René Descartes, & sur les figures par luy inventées* (Paris: Jacques le Gras, 1664).

—— *Traitté de l'esprit de l'homme et de ses facultez et fonctions, et de son union avec le corps. Suivant les principes de René Descartes* (Paris: T. Girard, 1666).

—— *L'Homme de René Descartes et la formation du foetus, avec les remarques de Louis de la Forge, a quoy l'on a ajouté le monde ou traité de la lumiere du mesme autheur*, 2nd edn. (Paris: C. Angot, 1667).

—— *Renati Des-Cartes, Tractatus de Homine, et de Formatione Foetus. Quorum prior Notis perpetuis Ludovici de la Forge, M. D. illustratur* (Amsterdam: D. Elsevier, 1667).

—— *L'Homme de René Descartes, et la formation du foetus, avec les remarques de Louis de la Forge*, new edn. (Paris: Compagnie de Libraires, 1729).

—— *Œuvres philosophiques avec une étude bio-bibliographique*, ed. P. Clair (Paris: Presses universitaires de France, 1974).

LA GRANGE, JEAN-BAPTISTE DE, *Les principes de la philosophie, contre les nouveaux philosophes Descartes, Rohault, Regius, Gassendi, le P. Maignon, &c.* (Paris: G. Josse, 1675).

LAMY, BERNARD, *Entretiens sur les sciences* (1683), critical edn. by F. Girbal and P. Clair (Paris: Presses universitaires de France, 1966).

LA VILLE, LOUIS DE, *Sentimens de M. Des Cartes touchant l'essence & les proprietez du corps, opposez a la doctrine de l'Eglise, et conformes aux erreurs de Calvin, sur le sujet de l'eucharistie. Avec une dissertation sur la pretendue possibilité des choses impossibles* (Paris: E. Michallet, 1680).

[LE BOSSU, RENÉ], *Parallèle des principes de la physique d'Aristote & de celle de René Des Cartes* (Paris: Michel le Petit, 1674). [Author's name omitted]

LE GRAND, ANTOINE, *Institutio Philosophiae, secundum Principia Domini Renati Descartes: Novo Methodo Adornata & Explicata In Usum Juventuti Academicae* (London: F. Martyn, 1672).

—— *Historia Naturae, variis Experimentis & Rationiis elucidata secundum Principia Stabilita in Institutione Philosophiae Edita ab eodem Authore* (London: F. Martyn, 1673).

—— *An Entire Body of Philosophy According to the Principles of the Famous Renate Des Cartes, in three Books. Written Originally in Latin by the Learned Anthony Le Grand*, ed. and trans. by Richard Blome (London: S. Roycroft, 1694).

LEIBNIZ, G. W., 'Remarque de Monsieur de Leibnits sur un endroit des Memoires de Trevoux du mois de Mars 1704', *Mémoires pour l'histoire des sciences & des beaux arts* (i.e. *Mémoires de Trévoux*) (March 1708), 488–91.

—— *New Essays Concerning Human Understanding. Together with An Appendix consisting of some of his shorter pieces*, trans. by A. G. Langley (New York: Macmillan, 1896).

—— *Philosophical Papers and Letters*, trans. and ed. by L. E. Loemker, 2nd edn. (Dordrecht: Reidel, 1969).

—— *New Essays on Human Understanding*, trans. and ed. by R. Remnant and J. Bennett (Cambridge: Cambridge University Press, 1981).

LOCKE, JOHN, *An Essay Concerning Human Understanding* (1690) (Oxford: Clarendon Press, 1975).

MALEBRANCHE, NICOLAS, *Œuvres complètes*, 20 vols. (Paris: Vrin, et le Centre nationale de la recherche scientifique, 1962–9).

—— *The Search After Truth, and Elucidations of the Search After Truth*, trans. by T. M. Lennon and P. J. Olscamp, together with a philosophical commentary by T. Lennon (Columbus, Ohio: Ohio State University Press, 1980).

—— *Dialogues on Metaphysics*, trans. and introd. by W. Doney (New York: Abaris Books, 1980).

MARIOTTE, EDME, *Œuvres de Mr Mariotte, de l'académie royale des sciences*, 2 vols. (Leiden: Pierre Vander, 1717).

—— *The Motion of Water, and other Fluids, Being a Treatise of Hydrostaticks. Written originally in French, by the late Monsieur Mariotte, Member of the Royal Academy of Sciences at Paris* (London: Senex and Taylor, 1718).

—— *Discours de la nature de l'Air, de la végétation des plantes, nouvelle découverte touchant la vue* (Paris: Gauthier-Villars, 1923).

Mémoires pour l'histoire des sciences & des beaux arts [i.e. the *Mémoires de Trévoux*], January 1701–

NEWTON, ISAAC, *Mathematical Principles of Natural Philosophy and his System of the World*, trans. into Eng. by A. Motte in 1729, trans. rev. and suppl. with an historical and explanatory appendix by Florian Cajori (Cambridge: Cambridge University Press, 1934).

—— *Opticks, or A Treatise of the Reflections, Refractions, Inflections &*

Colours of Light, 4th edn. (London: 1730), repr. (New York: Dover Publications, 1952).

OLDENBURG, HENRY, *The Correspondence of Henry Oldenburg*, ed. and trans. by A. R. Hall and M. B. Hall, 9 vols. (Madison, Wis., and London: University of Wisconsin Press, 1965–73).

PARDIES, IGNACE-GASTON, *Discours de la connoissance des bestes* (Paris: S. Mabre-Cramoisy, 1672).

—— *Œuvres du R. P. Ignace-Gaston Pardies, de la compagnie de Jésus* (Lyons: Freres Bruyset, 1725).

PASCAL, BLAISE, *Œuvres de Blaise Pascal*, ed. L. Brunschvicg and P. Boutroux, 11 vols. (Paris: Hachette, 1908–14), repr. (New York: Kraus Reprint Ltd., 1965).

—— *Thoughts, Letters and Minor Works*, trans. by W. F. Trotter, M. L. Booth, and O. W. Wight, Harvard Classics, 48 (New York: Collier, 1910).

—— *The Provincial Letters*, trans. with an introd. by A. J. Krailsheimer (Harmondsworth: Penguin, 1967).

PERRAULT, CLAUDE, *Essais de physique ou recueil de plusieurs traitez touchant les choses naturelles*, 4 vols. (Paris: Jean-Baptiste Coignard, 1680–8).

PETERMAN, D. A., *Philosophiae Cartesianae adversus Censuram Petri Danielis Huetii Vindicatio, in qua pleraque intricatoria Cartesii loca clare explanantur* (Leipzig: J. Caspar Meyer, 1690).

[POISSON, NICOLAS-JOSEPH], *Discours de la methode pour bien conduire sa raison, & chercher la verité dans les sciences. Plus la dioptrique, les meteors, la mechanique, et la musique, qui sont essais de cette methode. Par René Descartes. Avec des remarques & des éclaircissemens necessaires* (Paris: Charles Angot, 1668). [Author's name omitted]

—— *Traité de la mechanique, composé par Monsieur Descartes. De plus l'abregé de musique du mesme autheur mis en françois. Avec les éclaircissemens necessaires* (Paris: Charles Angot, 1668). [Editor's name given as N.P.P.D.L.]

—— *Commentaire ou remarques sur le méthode de Mr Descartes. Où on établit plusieurs principes generaux, necessaires pour entendre toutes ses œuvres* (Paris: Veuve de Claude Thiboust & Pierre Esclassan, 1671).

PUFENDORF, SAMUEL, *De Jure Naturae et Gentium*, 2 vols., i: text of 1688; ii: Eng. trans. by C. H. Oldfather and W. A. Oldfather (Oxford: Clarendon Press, 1934).

RÉGIS, PIERRE-SYLVAIN, *Système de philosophie, contenant la logique, la métaphysique, la physique et la morale*, 3 vols. (Paris: Denys Thierry, 1690).

—— *Réponse au livre qui a pour titre P. Danielis Huetii, Episcopi*

Suessionensis designati, Censura Philosophiae Cartesianae (Paris: Jean Cusson, 1691).

—— *L'Usage de la raison et de la foy, ou l'accord de la foy et de la raison* (Paris: Jean Cusson, 1704).

[ROCHON, A.], *Lettre d'un philosophe à un cartesien de ses amis* (Paris: T. Jolly, 1672). [Author's name omitted; sometimes attributed to I.-G. Pardies]

—— *Œuvres posthumes de M^r· Rohault*, ed. Claude Clerselier (Paris: G. Deprez, 1682).

—— *A System of Natural Philosophy*, illus. with Dr Samuel Clarke's notes, trans. by John Clarke (London: Knapton, 1723), repr. with a new introd. by L. L. Laudan (New York: Johnson Reprint Co., 1969).

—— 'Discours sur la fièvre', in R. Descartes, *Les Passions de l'ame, le monde, ou traité de la lumière et la géometrie* (Paris: Compagnie des libraires, 1726).

—— *Jacques Rohault, 1618–1672: bio-bibliographie, avec l'édition critique des entretiens sur la philosophie*, ed. P. Clair (Paris: Centre nationale de la recherche scientifique, 1978).

SORBIÈRE, SAMUEL-JOSEPH, *Lettres et discours de M. de Soribière sur diverses matières curieuses* (Paris: F. Clousier, 1660).

Secondary Sources

AITON, E. J. (1972), *The Vortex Theory of Planetary Motions* (London: Macdonald).

ALQUIÉ, FERDINAND (1972), 'Science et métaphysique chez Malebranche et chez Kant', *Revue philosophique de Louvain*, 70: 5–42.

ARMOGATHE, JEAN-ROBERTS (1977), *Theologia Cartesiana: L'explication physique de l'eucharistie chez Descartes et Dom Desgabets* (The Hague: M. Nijhoff).

BALZ, ALBERT G. A. (1951), *Cartesian Studies* (New York: Columbia University Press).

BARBER, W. H. (1955), *Leibniz in France from Arnauld to Voltaire: A Study in French Reactions to Leibnizianism 1670–1760* (Oxford: Clarendon Press).

BATTAIL, JEAN-FRANÇOIS (1973), *L'Avocat philosophe Géraud de Cordemoy (1626–1684)* (The Hague: Nijhoff).

BELAVAL, YVON (1960), *Leibniz critique de Descartes* (Paris: Gallimard).

BETTENSON, HENRY (1963), ed., *Documents of the Christian Church*, 2nd edn. (London: Oxford University Press).

BETTS, C. J. (1984), *Early Deism in France* (The Hague: Nijhoff).

BODEMER, CHARLES W. (1972), 'Developmental Phenomena in 17th-century Mechanistic Psychophysiology, with Special Reference to the Psychological Theory of Nicolas Malebranche', *Epistéme*, 6: 233–46.

BOS, H. J. M. *et al.* (1980), eds., *Studies on Christiaan Huygens* (Lisse: Swets & Zeitlinger).

BOUILLIER, FRANCISQUE (1868), *Histoire de la philosophie cartésienne*, 2 vols. (Paris: Delagrave).

BOULENGER, JACQUES (1920), *The Seventeenth Century* (New York: G. P. Putnam's Sons).

BRACKEN, HARRY M. (1963), 'Berkeley and Malebranche on Ideas', *The Modern Schoolman*, 41: 1–15.

—— (1974), *Berkeley* (London: Macmillan).

BROCKLISS, L. W. B. (1981*a*), 'Aristotle, Descartes and the New Science: Natural Philosophy at the University of Paris, 1600–1740', *Annals of Science*, 38: 33–69.

—— (1981*b*), 'Philosophy Teaching in France, 1600–1740', *History of Universities*, 1: 131–68.

—— (1987), *French Higher Education in the Seventeenth and Eighteenth Centuries* (Oxford: Clarendon Press).

BROWN, HARCOURT (1948), 'Jean Denis and the Transfusion of Blood, Paris, 1667–1668', *Isis*, 39: 15–29.

—— (1967), *Scientific Organizations in Seventeenth-Century France (1620–1680)* (1934) (New York: Russell & Russell).

BRUNET, PIERRE (1931), *L'Introduction des théories de Newton en France au xviiie siècle, i: Avant 1738* (Paris: Blanchard).

—— (1947), 'La Méthodologie de Mariotte', *Archives internationales d'histoire des sciences*, 1: 26–59.

BUGLER, G. (1950), 'Un précurseur de la biologie expérimentale: Edme Mariotte', *Revue d'histoire des sciences et de leurs applications*, 3: 242–50.

CANTOR, G. N. and HODGE, M. J. S. (1981), *Conceptions of Ether: Studies in the History of Ether Theories 1740–1900* (Cambridge: Cambridge University Press).

CHARTIER, R., COMPÈRE, M.-M., and JULIA, D. (1976), *L'Éducation en France du xvie au xviiie siècle* (Paris: CDU).

CHURCH, RALPH WITTINGTON (1931), *A Study in the Philosophy of Malebranche* (London: Allen & Unwin).

CLAIR, PIERRE (1976), 'Louis de la Forge et les origines de l'occasionalisme', *Recherches sur le xviie siècle*, 1: 63–72.

CLARKE, DESMOND M. (1982), *Descartes' Philosophy of Science* (Manchester: Manchester University Press).

COHEN, I. BERNARD (1964*a*), ' "Quantum in se est": Newton's concept of Inertia in relation to Descartes and Lucretius', *Notes and Records of the Royal Society of London*, 19: 131–55.

—— (1964*b*), 'Isaac Newton, Hans Sloane and the Académie Royale des

Sciences', in *L'Aventure de la science: Mélanges Alexandre Koyré* (Paris: Herman), i. 61–116.

——(1968), 'The French Translation of Isaac Newton's Philosophiae Naturalis Principia Mathematica (1756, 1759, 1966)', *Archives internationales d'histoire des sciences*, 21: 261–90.

CONNELL, DESMOND (1967), *The Vision in God: Malebranche's Scholastic Sources* (Louvain: Nauwelaerts; Paris: Béatrice-Nauwelaerts).

COOK, MONTE (1974), 'Arnauld's Alleged Representationalism', *Journal of the History of Philosophy*, 12: 53–62.

COSTABEL, PIERRE (1949), 'Le Paradoxe de Mariotte', *Archives internationales d'histoire des sciences*, 2: 864–81.

——(1964), 'L'Oratoire de France et ses collèges', in R. Taton, ed., *L'Enseignement et diffusion des sciences au dix-huitième siècle* (Paris: Hermann), 66–100.

——(1966), 'Contribution à l'étude de l'offensive de Leibniz contre la philosophie cartésienne en 1691–1692', *Revue internationale de philosophie*, 20: 264–87.

——(1967), 'La Participation de Malebranche au mouvement scientifique', in *Malebranche, l'homme et l'œuvre*, ed. Centre internationale de synthèse (Paris: Vrin), 76–110.

——(1973), *Leibniz and Dynamics: The Texts of 1692*, trans. R. E. W. Maddison (Paris: Hermann; London: Methuen).

——(1974), 'Notes fugitives sur l'absolu et le relatif chez Leibniz et Newton', *Archives internationales d'histoire des sciences*, 24: 112–21.

CRAGG, GERALD R. (1970), *The Church and the Age of Reason 1648–1789*, rev. edn. (Harmondsworth: Penguin).

DAVIDSON, DONALD (1980), *Essays on Actions and Events* (Oxford: Clarendon Press).

DE DAINVILLE, FRANÇOIS (1964), 'L'Enseignement scientifique dans les collèges des jésuites', in R. Taton, ed., *L'Enseignement et diffusion des sciences au dix-huitième siècle* (Paris: Hermann) 27–65.

DIAMOND, SOLOMON (1969), 'Seventeenth-Century French "Connectionism": La Forge, Dilly, and Régis', *Journal of the History of Behavioral Science*, 5: 3–9.

DICK, STEVEN J. (1982), *Plurality of Worlds. The Origins of the Extraterrestrial Life Debate from Democritus to Kant* (New York: Cambridge University Press).

DIJKSTERHUIS, E. J., *et al.* (1950), *Descartes et le cartésianisme hollondais* (Paris: Presses universitaires de France).

DRAKE, STILLMAN (1957), ed., *Discoveries and Opinions of Galileo*. Trans. with an introd. and notes by S. Drake (New York: Doubleday Anchor Books).

DUGAS, RENÉ (1958), *Mechanics in the Seventeenth Century*, trans. by F. Jacquot (Neuchâtel, Switzerland: Éditions du Griffon).

DUHEM, PIERRE (1916), 'L'optique de Malebranche', *Revue de métaphysique et de morale*, 23: 37–91.

EASLEA, BRIAN (1980), *Witch-hunting, Magic and the New Philosophy* (Sussex: Harvester Press).

EDGLEY, R. (1970), 'Innate Ideas', in G. N. A. Vesey, ed., *Knowledge and Necessity* (London: Macmillan), 1–33.

ESCHOLIER, MARC (1968), *Port-Royal: The Drama of the Jansenists* (New York: Hawthorn Books).

FERREYROLLES, GÉRARD (1984), *Pascal et la raison du politique* (Paris: Presses universitaires de France).

FERRIER, FRANCIS (1968), *William Chalmers (1596–1678): étude bio-bibliographique avec des textes inédits* (Paris: Presses universitaires de France).

—— (1980), *Un oratorien ami de Descartes: Guillaume Gibieuf et sa philosophie de la liberté* (Paris: Vrin).

GABBEY, ALAN (1982), 'Philosophia Cartesiana Triumphata: Henry More (1646–1671)', in T. Lennon *et al.*, eds., *Problems of Cartesianism* (Kingston and Montreal: McGill-Queen's University Press), 171–250.

GARBER, DANIEL (1986), 'Learning from the Past: Reflections on the Role of History in the Philosophy of Science', *Synthèse*, 67: 91–114.

GIRBAL, FRANÇOIS (1964), *Bernard Lamy (1640–1715): étude biographique et bibliographique* (Paris: Presses universitaires de France).

GOLDEN, RICHARD M. (1981), *The Godly Rebellion: Parisian Curés and the Religious Fronde, 1652–1662* (Chapel Hill, NC: The University of North Carolina Press).

GOUHIER, HENRI (1926), *La Vocation de Malebranche* (Paris: Vrin).

—— (1978), *Cartésianisme et augustinisme au xviie siècle* (Paris: Vrin).

GRANT, EDWARD (1981), *Much Ado About Nothing: Theories of Space and Vacuum from the Middle Ages to the Scientific Revolution* (Cambridge: Cambridge University Press).

—— (1984), 'In Defence of the Earth's Centrality and Immobility: Scholastic Reaction to Copernicanism in the Seventeenth Century', *Transactions of the American Philosophical Society*, 74: 1–69.

GREENBERG, JOHN L. (1986), 'Mathematical Physics in Eighteenth-Century France', *Isis*, 77: 59–78.

GERAULT, MARTIAL (1954), 'Métaphysique et physique de la force chez Descartes et chez Malebranche', *Revue de métaphysique et de morale*, 59: 113–34.

GUERLAC, HENRY (1981), *Newton on the Continent* (Ithaca and London: Cornell University Press).

HACKING, IAN (1975), *The Emergence of Probability: A Philosophical Study of Early Ideas about Probability, Induction and Statistical Inference* (Cambridge: Cambridge University Press).

HAHN, ROGER (1971), *The Anatomy of a Scientific Institution: The Paris Academy of Sciences, 1666–1803* (Berkeley: University of California Press).

HALL, A. RUPERT (1975), 'Newton in France: A New View', *History of Science*, 13: 233–50.

—— and HALL, M. B. (1980), 'The First Human Blood Transfusion: Priority Disputes', *Medical History*, 24: 461–5.

HANKINS, THOMAS (1967), 'The Influence of Malebranche on the Science of Mechanics during the Eighteenth Century', *Journal of the History of Ideas*, 28: 193–210.

HESSE, MARY B. (1955), 'Action at a distance in Classical Physics', *Isis*, 46: 337–53.

HEYD, MICHAEL (1982), *Between Orthodoxy and the Enlightenment. Jean-Robert Chouet and the Introduction of Cartesian Science in The Academy of Geneva* (The Hague: Nijhoff).

HEYNDELS, RUDOLF (1976), 'Le Voyage du monde de Descartes du Père Gabriel Daniel', *Annales du l'institut de philosophie*, 45–66.

HIRSCHFIELD, JOHN MILTON (1981), *The Académie Royale des Sciences 1666–1683* (New York: Arno Press).

HOBART, MICHAEL E. (1982), *Science and Religion in the Thought of Nicolas Malebranche* (Chapel Hill, NC: University of North Carolina Press).

HOLLAND, ALAN J. (1985), ed., *Philosophy, its History and Historiography* (Dordrecht: Reidel).

HOSKIN, MICHAEL (1961), ' "Mining all Within": Clarke's Notes to Rohault's Traité de Physique', *Thomist*, 24: 353–63.

HUNTER, MICHAEL (1981), *Science and Society in Restoration England* (Cambridge: Cambridge University Press).

HUTCHISON, KEITH (1982), 'What Happened to Occult Qualities in the Scientific Revolution?', *Isis*, 73: 233–53.

ILTIS, CAROLYN (1971), 'Leibniz and the *Vis Viva* Controversy', *Isis*, 62: 21–35.

—— (1973), 'The Decline of Cartesianism in Mechanics', *Isis*, 64: 356–73.

JOLLEY, NICHOLAS (1984), *Leibniz and Locke: A Study of the New Essays on Human Understanding* (Oxford: Clarendon Press).

JOURDAIN, CHARLES (1888), *Histoire de l'université de Paris au xviie et au xviiie siècle*, 2 vols. (Paris: Firmin-Didot and Hachette).

JOY, LYNN SUMIDA (1982), 'Gassendi the Atomist, Advocate of History in an Age of Science', Ph.D. diss., Harvard University.

KALMAR, MARTIN (1981), 'Some Collision Theories of the Seventeenth Century: Mathematicism vs. Mathematical Physics', Ph.D. diss., Johns Hopkins University.

LALLEMAND, PAUL (1888), *Histoire de l'éducation dans l'ancien oratoire de France* (Paris: Thorin).

LAPORTE, JEAN (1951), *Études d'histoire de la philosophie française au xviie siècle* (Paris: Vrin).

LAUDAN, LARRY (1966), 'The Clock Metaphor and Probabilism: the Impact of Descartes on English Methodological Thought, 1650–65', *Annals of Science*, 22: 73–104.

—— (1977), *Progress and its Problems* (Berkeley: University of California Press).

—— (1981), *Science and Hypothesis* (Dordrecht: Reidel).

—— (1986), 'Some Problems Facing Intuitionist Meta-Methodologies', *Synthèse*, 67: 115–29.

LAYMON, RONALD (1982), 'Transubstantiation: Test Case for Descartes's Theory of Space', in T. Lennon *et al*, eds., *Problems of Cartesianism* (Kingston and Montreal: McGill-Queen's University Press), 149–70.

LEMAIRE, PAUL (1902), *Le Cartésianisme chez les bénédictins: Dom Robert Desgabets, son système, son influence et son école* (Paris: Felix Alcan).

LEMOINE, ROBERT (1964), 'L'Enseignement scientifique dans les collèges bénédictins', in R. Taton, *L'Enseignement et diffusion des sciences au dix-huitième siècle* (Paris: Hermann), 101–23.

LENNON, THOMAS (1980), 'Representationalism, Judgment and Perception of Distance: Further to Yolton and McRae', *Dialogue*, 19: 151–62.

—— NICHOLAS, JOHN M. and DAVIS, JOHN W. (1982), eds., *Problems of Cartesianism* (Kingston and Montreal: McGill-Queen's University Press).

LINDEBOOM, GERRIT A. (1982), 'Jan Swammerdam (1637–1680) and his Biblia Naturae', *Clio Medica*, 17: 113–31.

LOVEJOY, A. O. (1923), ' "Representative Ideas" in Malebranche and Arnauld', *Mind*, 32: 449–61.

MCCLAUGHLIN, T. (1974), 'Une lettre de Melchisédech Thévenot', *Revue d'histoire des sciences*, 27: 123–6.

—— (1975), 'Sur les rapports entre la compagnie de Thévenot et l'académie royale des sciences', *Revue d'histoire des sciences*, 28: 233–42.

—— (1977), 'Le Concept de science chez Jacques Rohault', *Revue d'histoire des sciences*, 30: 225–40.

—— (1976), 'Censorship and Defenders of the Cartesian Faith in Mid-Seventeenth Century France', *Journal of the History of Ideas*, 40: 563–81.

—— and PICOLET, G. (1976), 'Un exemple d'utilisation du minutier central de Paris: la bibliothèque et les instruments scientifiques du physicien Jacques Rohault selon son inventaire après décès', *Revue d'histoire des sciences*, 29: 3–20.

MCCRACKEN, CHARLES, J. (1983), *Malebranche and British Philosophy* (Oxford: Clarendon Press).

McMullin, Ernan (1970), 'The History and Philosophy of Science: A Taxonomy', in R. G. Stuewer, ed., *Historical and Philosophical Perspectives of Science*, Minnesota Studies in the Philosophy of Science (Minneapolis: University of Minnesota Press), 12–67.

—— (1978a), *Newton on Matter and Activity* (Indiana: University of Notre Dame Press).

—— (1978b), 'The Conception of Science in Galileo's Work', in R. E. Butts and J. C. Pitt, eds., *New Perspectives on Galileo* (Dordrecht: Reidel), 209–57.

Marion, Jean-Luc (1975), *Sur l'ontologie grise de Descartes* (Paris: Vrin).

Marsak, Leonard M. (1959a), 'Cartesianism in Fontenelle and French Science, 1686–1752', *Isis*, 50: 51–60.

—— (1959b), 'Bernard de Fontenelle: The Idea of Science in the French Enlightenment', *Transactions of the American Philosophical Society*, ns, 49: 3–64.

Maury, L.-F. Alfred (1864), *L'Ancienne académie des sciences* (Paris: Didier).

Mendelsohn, Everett (1964), 'The Changing Nature of Physiological Explanation in the Seventeenth Century', in *L'Aventure de la science: Mélanges A. Koyré* (Paris: Hermann), i. 367–86.

Methivier, Hubert (1983), *Le Siècle de Louis XIV* (1950) (Paris: Presses universitaires de France).

Morris, John (1969), 'Pattern Recognition in Descartes' Automota', *Isis*, 60: 451–60.

Mouy, Paul (1927), *Les Lois du choc des corps d'après Malebranche* (Paris: Vrin).

—— (1934), *Le Développement de la physique cartésienne 1646–1712* (Paris: Vrin).

—— (1983), 'Malebranche et Newton', *Revue de métaphysique et de morale*, 45: 411–35.

O'Keefe, C. B. (1974), *Contemporary Reactions to the Enlightenment (1728–1762)* (Geneva: Librairie Slatkine; Paris: Honoré Champion).

Parker, David (1981), 'Law, Society and the State in the Thought of Jean Bodin', *Journal of the History of Political Thought*, 2: 253–85.

—— (1983), *The Making of French Absolutism* (London: Edward Arnold).

Pav, Peter A. (1974), 'Louis Carré (1663–1711) and Mechanistic Optics', *Archives internationales d'histoire des sciences*, 24: 340–8.

Pleadwell, Frank Lester (1950), 'Samuel Sorbière and his Advice to a young Physician', *Bulletin of the History of Medicine*, 24: 255–87.

Potts, D. C., and Charlton, D. G. (1974), *French Thought since 1600* (London: Methuen).

Radner, Daisie (1978), *Malebranche: A Study of a Cartesian System* (Amsterdam: Van Gorcum).

REIF, PATRICIA (1969), 'The Textbook Tradition in Natural Philosophy, 1600–1650', *Journal of the History of Ideas*, 30: 17–32.

ROBINET, ANDRÉ (1955), *Malebranche et Leibniz: relations personnelles* (Paris: Vrin).

—— (1960), Le Groupe malébranchiste introducteur du calcul infinitésimal en France', *Revue d'histoire des sciences*, 13: 287–308.

—— (1964), 'Du rôle accordé à l'expérience dans la physique de Malebranche', in *L'Aventure de la science* (Paris: Hermann), 400–10.

—— (1970), *Malebranche de l'académie des sciences* (Paris: Vrin).

—— (1974), 'Dom Roberts Desgabets. Le conflit philosophique avec Malebranche et l'œuvre métaphysique', *Revue de synthèse*, 95: 65–83.

ROCHE, DANIEL (1978), *Le Siècle des lumières en province: académies et académiciens provinciaux, 1680–1785* (Paris: Mouton).

ROCHOT, B. (1953), 'Roberval, Mariotte et la Logique', *Archives internationales d'histoire des sciences*, 6: 38–43.

RODIS-LEWIS, GENEVIÈVE (1950), 'Augustinisme et cartésianisme à Port Royal', in E. J. Dijksterhuis *et al.*, eds., *Descartes et le cartésianisme hollandais* (Paris: Presses universitaires de France), 131–82.

—— (1963), *Nicolas Malebrance* (Paris: Presses universitaires de France).

—— (1974), 'Sources scientifiques du premier ouvrage de Malebranche', *Études philosophiques*, 481–93.

ROGER, JACQUES (1963), *Les Sciences de la vie dans la pensée française du xviiie siècle: la génération des animaux de Descartes à l'encylopédie* (Paris: Armand Colin).

—— (1982), 'The Cartesian Model and Its Role in Eighteenth-century "Theory of the Earth"', in T. M. Lennon *et al.*, eds., *Problems of Cartesianism* (Kingston and Montreal: McGill-Queen's University Press), 95–112.

ROME, BEATRICE K. (1963), *The Philosophy of Malebranche* (Chicago: Regnery).

RORTY, R., SCHNEEWIND, J. B., and SKINNER, Q. (1984), eds., *Philosophy in History: Essays on the Historiography of Philosophy* (Cambridge: Cambridge University Press).

ROSENFIELD, LEONORA COHEN (1957), 'Peripatetic Adversaries of Cartesianism in 17th Century France', *The Review of Religion*, 22: 14–40.

RUESTOW, EDWARDS G. (1973), *Physics at Seventeenth-Century Leiden: Philosophy and the New Science in the University* (The Hague: Nijhoff).

SALOMON-BAYET, CLAIRE (1978), *L'Institution de la science et l'expérience du vivant: méthode et expérience à l'académie royale des sciences 1666–1793* (Paris: Flammarion).

SCOTT, WILSON L. (1970), *The Conflict between Atomism and Conservation Theory 1644–1860* (London: Macdonald; New York: Elsevier).

SEDGWICK, ALEXANDER (1977), *Jansenism in Seventeenth-Century France. Voices from the Wilderness* (Charlottesville: University Press of Virginia).

SHAPIRO, BARBARA J. (1983), *Probability and Certainty in Seventeenth-Century England* (Princeton, NJ: Princeton University Press).

SHUSTER, JOHN (1975), 'Jacques Rohault', *Dictionary of Scientific Biography*, 11: 506–9.

SKINNER, QUENTIN (1978), *The Foundations of Modern Political Thought*, ii (Cambridge: Cambridge University Press).

SORTAIS, GASTON (1929), 'Le Cartésianisme chez les jésuites français au xviie et au xviiie siècle', *Archives de philosophie*, 6: 1–93.

STEWART, M. A. (1979, 1980), 'Locke's Mental Atomism and the Classification of Ideas, I and II', *The Locke Newsletter*, 10: 53–82, 11: 25–62.

—— (1979), ed., *Selected Philosophical Papers of Robert Boyle* (Manchester: Manchester University Press; New York: Barnes & Noble).

STRUIK, DIRK J. (1981), *The Land of Stevin and Huygens* (Dordrecht: Reidel).

SUTTON, GEOFFREY VINCENT (1982), 'A Science for a Polite Society: Cartesian Natural Philosophy in Paris during the Reigns of Louis XIII and XIV', Ph.D. diss., Princeton University.

TATON, RENÉ (1964), *L'Enseignement et diffusion des sciences au dix-huitième siècle* (Paris: Hermann).

—— (1969), 'Madame du Châtelet, traductrice de Newton', *Archives internationales d'histoire des sciences*, 22: 195–210.

TAVENAUX, RENÉ (1965), *Jansénisme et politique* (Paris: Armand Colin).

THEAU, JEAN (1976), 'La Critique de la causalité chez Malebranche et chez Hume', *Dialogue*, 15: 549–64.

TOCANNE, BERNARD (1978), *L'Idée de nature en France dans là seconde moitié du xviie siècle* (Strasbourg: Klincksieck).

TOURNADRE, GÉRAUD (1982), *L'Orientation de la science cartésienne* (Paris: Vrin).

TREASURE, G. R. R. (1966), *Seventeenth Century France* (New York: Barnes & Noble).

ULTREE, MAARTEN (1981), *The Abbey of S. Germain des Prés in the Seventeenth Century* (New Haven and London: Yale University Press).

VROOMAN, JACK ROCHFORD (1970), *René Descartes: A Biography* (New York: Putnam's).

WATSON, RICHARD A. (1964), 'A Note on the Probabilistic Physics of Régis', *Archives internationales d'histoire des sciences*, 17: 33–6.

—— (1966), *The Downfall of Cartesianism 1673–1712* (The Hague: Nijhoff).

—— (1981), 'Cartesianism Compounded: Louis de la Forge', *Studia Cartesiana*, 2: 165–71.

—— (1982), 'Transubstantiation among the Cartesians', in T. M. Lennon *et al.*, eds., *Problems of Cartesianism* (Kingston and Montreal: McGill-Queen's University Press), 127–48.

WEAVER, F. ELLEN (1978), *The Evolution of the Reform of Port-Royal. From the Rule of Citeaux to Jansenism* (Paris: Editions Beauchesne).

WEBSTER, CHARLES (1975), *The Great Instauration: Science, Medicine and Reform 1626–1660* (London: Duckworth).

WILKINS, KATHLEEN SONIA (1969), *A Study of the Works of Claude Buffier*, Studies on Voltaire and the Eighteenth Century, 66 (Geneva: Institut et Musée Voltaire).

WILLIAMS, BERNARD (1978), *Descartes: The Project of Pure Enquiry* (Harmondsworth: Penguin).

WOOLHOUSE, R. S. (1979), 'Berkeley and "a famous man of modern times"', *Berkeley Newsletter*, 3: 5–7.

—— (1983), *Locke* (Sussex: Harvester Press).

YOLTON, JOHN W. (1956), *John Locke and the Way of Ideas* (Oxford: Oxford University Press).

—— (1975), 'Ideas and Knowledge in Seventeenth-Century Philosophy', *Journal of the History of Philosophy*, 13: 145–65.

—— (1984*a*), *Perceptual Acquaintance from Descartes to Reid* (Oxford: Basil Blackwell).

—— (1984*b*), *Thinking Matter: Materialism in Eighteenth-Century Britain* (Oxford: Basil Blackwell).

ZIGGELAAR, AUGUST (1971), *Le Physicien Ignace Gaston Pardies s.j. (1636–1673)* (Copenhagen: Odense University Press).

INDEX

(Note: the index does not include references to Descartes or to the more prominent members of the Cartesian tradition in France whose names occur very frequently in the text)

natural signs 50
Newton, Isaac 7–8, 131, 132, 161, 193–4
Nicole, Pierre 86

occult powers 73–4, 99, 121, 167–9, 235, 243
O'Keefe, C. B. 241 n.
Oldenburg, Henry 193
Olscamp, P. J. 52 n.
Oratory 20, 36
original sin 118
Osiander, Andreas 138

Pardies, Ignace-Gaston 16 n., 176, 179, 236–7, 241
Parker, David 29 n., 33 n.
parlement of Paris 11
Pascal, Blaise 33, 83, 171 n., 210, 239 n.
Paulian, Aimé-Henri 243 n.
pavlovian conditioning 183–5
Perrault, Claude 28, 40, 94, 133, 160 n., 170–1, 176, 195, 212–13, 220
physics, practical and speculative 136–7
Poisson, Nicolas-Joseph 20, 139–42
positivism 235
Port-Royal *see under* jansenism
Port-Royal Logic *see under Art de penser*
preformation theory *see under* embryology
Prestet, Jean 20
principles
    axioms of logic 66
    axioms of physics 67
    two senses of 149
probability 192–5
Ptolemy 142 n., 156–7, 207
Pufendorf, Samuel 147 n.
Puy-de-Dôme 83, 210

qualities, primary and secondary 24–5, 48–51, 53, 71, 101, 226–7

Radner, Daisie 52 n.
rainbow, explanation of 162
Rapin, René 21 n., 242
rapport 46, 47, 50, 52
realism, scientific 192, 218
reason
    rational explanations 171–4
    scope of 173, 226–8
Regius *see under* de Roy
Regnault, Noel 242

Reif, Patricia 15 n.
Remnant, R. 70 n.
Renaudot, Théophraste 38, 40
Reyneau, Charles-René 20
Roberval, Gilles Personne de 40
Robinet, André 9 n., 52 n., 188 n., 238 n.
Roche, Daniel 38 n.
Rochon, Père 21 n., 225, 239 n.
Rochot, B. 17 n.
Rodis-Lewis, Geneviève 28 n., 52 n., 180 n.
Roger, Jacques 138 n., 180 n., 200–1, 237
Rorty, Richard 1 n., 2 n.
Royal Society 7
Ruestow, E. G. 5 n.

St Augustine 33–4, 43, 105, 117
Saint-Cyran, *L'abbé de* 15
St Francis de Sales 29
St Vincent de Paul 29
scholasticism 12, 34–7, 73, 165–9, 238–44
science, definition of 144–5, 228
scientific societies 37–41
Sedgwick, A. 28 n.
sensation
    definition of 45, 53–4, 56, 64
    reliability of 225–7, 236–7
    senses deceive 64–5
sens commun 241–2, 243, 244
Shapiro, Barbara 192 n.
simplicity of hypotheses 215–20
Skinner, Quentin 33 n.
Sloane, Hans 7
Sorbière, Samuel 39, 146, 232
Sortais, Gaston 6 n., 16 n., 242 n.
soul
    and mechanism 27–8
    in animals, plants 27–8
Stewart, M. A. 72 n., 100 n.
Struik, D. J. 5 n.
substance
    and accidents 23–4
    and modes 107–8
    concept of 82
Swammerdam, Jan 180
systems of hypotheses 214–20

Tavenaux, R. 33 n.
Taylor, Charles 2 n.
theological controversy 12–13, 22–34, 223–7